physical education and development 3–11

a guide for teachers

Jonathan Doherty and Peter Brennan

Routledge
Taylor & Francis Group

LONDON AND NEW YORK

First published 2008 by Routledge
2 Park Square, Milton Park, Abingdon, Oxon, OX14 4RN

Simultaneously published in the USA and Canada
by Routledge
270 Madison Ave, New York, NY 10016

Routledge is an imprint of the Taylor & Francis Group, an informa business

Typeset in Palatino and Helvetica by BC Typesetting Ltd, Bristol
Printed and bound in Great Britain by
TJ International Ltd, Padstow, Cornwall

British Library Cataloguing in Publication Data
A catalogue record for this book is available from the British Library

Library of Congress Cataloging in Publication Data
A catalog record for this book has been requested

ISBN 10: 1–84312–456–4
ISBN 13: 978–1–84312–456–6

Contents

Acknowledgements

We would like to express our sincere thanks to Tracey Riseborough and to Sara Porter from David Fulton for their continued support and encouragement throughout the writing of this book.

Thanks also to the UoN SofE research committee for supporting the writing process and to colleagues for their advice and guidance. We should also mention Anne-Marie Latham, Gillian Harrison, and both the Comberton and Peterborough School Sports Partnerships for providing inspiration, material and helpful suggestions on earlier drafts. Not least, we would like to thank all the teachers, students and pupils with whom we have worked over the years for their enthusiasm, constant questioning and willingness to keep pushing the boundaries in PE.

Special thanks to Ally, Joe and Alfie Brennan and to Katherine Doherty for their unfailing encouragement and continuing inspiration.

Jonathan Doherty and Peter Brennan

Introduction

The accomplished poet W.B.Yeats once wrote that 'education is not filling a pail but the lighting of a fire'. A principal aspiration in writing this book is to do precisely that: to inspire readers to light the fires of those young people in their classes in their current or future teaching so that they too will be inspired and enthralled about the unique subject that is Physical Education (PE). This aspiration tasks us as authors to go beyond informing about curriculum requirements in PE or providing an 'off the shelf' manual of activities. In order to realise this aspiration we need to go much further. We need to excite you as a reader about the depth and the scope of PE and to encourage you to want to understand it as fully as possible. We want to make you knowledgeable about children's development from birth until the end of their primary school years and we want to share with you stimulating ways to plan for, teach and assess children in PE in the areas of the statutory curriculum. We want to do this in ways that will enable you to look critically and respond creatively and skilfully in teaching the areas of learning in PE.

This book is written at an important time. The debate on a justification for PE in the primary curriculum has been fuelled recently by issues such as its status amongst core subjects, the emergence of school sport, practical resourcing and evidence of anxiety amongst many teachers about their knowledge and skill to teach the practical areas of activity. These issues are set against the Government's commitment to PE and sport in schools through the Physical Education, School Sport and Club Links (PESSCL) strategy and an aim to increase the percentage of children who spend at least two hours each week on *high quality* PE and school sport in and outside the curriculum to 85 per cent by 2008. Wider concerns about increasing levels of obesity in our nation's children have also been laid at the feet of physical educators in this country. The successful British bid to host the Olympic Games in 2012 offers a wonderful opportunity to address some of these issues *and* to raise the profile of primary school PE and sport.

The book is aimed primarily at undergraduate and post-graduate students on primary and early childhood education courses, although it is also applicable to teachers who are non-specialists in PE, HLTAs and other para-professionals who wish to update their knowledge and pedagogy through the ideas presented in this text as a school resource or as a supplement on In-service courses. The reduction in time given to PE in many teacher education courses has resulted in many students exiting their training with only a general subject knowledge and a modicum of pedagogical skills to deliver the subject. As authors we have found that a number of students approach PE with a degree of negativity, often based on their own personal experiences at school and lack confidence in their abilities to teach it effectively to children. Based on our experiences of teaching across the primary age range and of teaching specialist and non-specialist physical education courses to university students, we believe we are in prime positions to write a book that meets the needs of such a readership and redresses such negative experiences of PE.

A variety of pedagogical features are included to enhance the text. These include chapter objectives, boxed examples, tasks for reflection, chapter summaries, further reading and web links that are linked to practical teaching and education research. We believe that this book has three compelling features that make it distinctive from other texts. First, it encompasses the 3–11 age range whilst all other texts separate Foundation Stage and Key Stages 1 and 2. Second, no other text combines theoretical frameworks with practical activities and teaching strategies into *one* book. Third, its style of writing is immediately accessible to readers and provides a worthy overview of physical education and a vision for its future, as well as a 'dip in' resource bank of developmentally appropriate practical ideas to teach all activity areas in PE confidently and proficiently.

The book's structure of ten chapters is divided into three parts. Part 1 offers a clearly articulated overview of the subject, moves on to developmental aspects in relation to PE and movement skills and then highlights relevant contemporary issues. In Chapter 1 Foundations of physical education 3–11, we begin by considering personal views of and experiences in PE reported by teachers, student teachers and pupils. This leads on to a discussion on defining and characterising physical education for children 3–11 from the research literature in which the historical and contemporary aims of the subject, its underpinning values and key principles are made explicit. The chapter concludes by addressing the concept of children as physically educated learners to complement the rationale for physical education and in keeping with the philosophy of a whole child approach advocated in the chapter. The contribution that PE makes to the holistic development of children is taken up in Chapter 2 Understanding development, movement and skill, in terms of how physical education contributes to children's physical, intellectual, linguistic, social and emotional development from birth through to middle childhood. The chapter makes it clear how movement is at the heart of PE for all children in the Foundation Stage and intrinsic to the areas of activity in Key Stages 1 and 2. The chapter suggests practical ways in which movement can be integrated and progressed across the curriculum. With reference to motor learning theories, we show how movement skills progress from simple to complex and from general to specific movements relevant to the 3–11 age range. In Chapter 3 Issues in physical education today we introduce the wider picture by discussing a range of contemporary issues that include high quality PE (HQPE), sport education, physical literacy, and gifted and talented pupils and show how these issues relate to the primary PE context.

In Part 2 we focus on the 3–11 curriculum. Chapter 4 Physical education in the Foundation Stage explains the curricular requirements of the Physical Development area of learning in the Foundation Stage. It highlights the importance of play in early physical education experiences for young children. The chapter provides ideas to support skill development in both indoor and outdoor settings through free play and more structured learning experiences. We conclude by suggesting that approaches to teaching PE in the Foundation Stage have much to offer Key Stages 1 and 2. Chapter 5 Physical education in Key Stage 1 and Chapter 6 Physical education in Key Stage 2 interrogate National Curriculum PE (NCPE) and provide readers with many stimulating ideas to deliver meaningful learning experiences to pupils in both these key stages. The practical activities in Part 2 are all road-tested with nursery and primary children first-hand, through our own teaching experiences.

In Part 3, planning teaching and assessment are considered and a range of practical strategies are offered to help readers feel confident and competent in preparing, delivering, assessing and reporting children's PE experiences. Chapter 7 What happens *before* the lesson? Planning and preparation covers pre-lesson preparation needed and the lexicon of planning for short-, medium- and long-term teaching episodes. The chapter retains the focus on the pupil and links NCPE activity areas to pupils' thinking. Examples from an authentic school policy and planning grids are provided, including the STEP framework to guide differentiation, that will assist readers to construct quality schemes and individual teaching episodes for all learners. Chapter 8 What happens *during* the lesson? Teaching a lesson, outlines the characteristics of effective teaching and considers various strategies (such as observation, explaining, demonstrating and the use of questions) and teaching styles in PE to provide a toolkit of instructional ideas. The chapter returns to the movement concepts and skills described in Chapter 2 as organising centres that give cohesion to teaching the Foundation Stage and Key Stage 1and 2 curriculum in a sequential and progressive way. Chapter 9 What happens *during* and *after* the lesson? Assessment, recording and reporting demystifies the whole area of monitoring and assessing children's achievement in PE. It helps you understand the principles and purposes associated with effective assessment of pupils' achievement and progress in PE, using real examples of qualitative and quantitative data. The importance of observation and the use of technology to support this assessment tool are highlighted, and a section on assessment for learning emphasises the links between planning and assessment (AfL). Excellent examples of recording and reporting are given in this chapter to enhance your skill in judging pupil attainment in PE and providing reliable evidence for those judgements. Chapter 10 Physical education in the future, summarises the coverage in the book from our articulation of PE, the new definition offered of it and the unique contribution it makes to the education and lives of all pupils in Part 1, through to the knowledge and skills demanded from those who plan, teach, assess and report progress in Parts 2 and 3. It highlights some of the challenges facing professionals charged with the responsibility of teaching PE to children both now and in the future and concludes by proposing a series of solutions to these challenges.

This innovative text uniquely covers teaching 3–11 PE in one book. It shows the reader how to guide children's physical experiences from the Foundation Stage right through to the end of Key Stage 2 of the National Curriculum. With a theoretical underpinning in a clear and accessible style of writing, it presents a wealth of practical advice on activities to use and how to teach this exciting curriculum area in ways that will inspire confidence and have children demanding more!

Jonathan Doherty and Peter Brennan

PART

1

Overview and issues

CHAPTER

Foundations of physical education 3–11

Chapter objectives

By the end of this chapter you should be able to:

- Provide a reasoned justification for physical education based on knowledge of its purpose, scope and contributions and the new definition of it presented;

- Know the aims for the subject and appreciate how historical aims have influenced contemporary ones;

- Know and value the key principles that underpin the subject for children 3–11;

- Understand the concept of children as physically educated learners.

Perceptions of physical education

IN WRITING THE FIRST CHAPTER of this book it seems appropriate that we begin by describing how different people perceive physical education, since perceptions of what physical education is, and what it has to offer children, are in no small way coloured by our past and present experiences of it. These perceptions have obvious implications for the teaching of this subject in primary schools. There is a growing amount of research and an abundance of anecdotal evidence indicating that teachers, student teachers and pupils view PE as a unique and therefore essential area of the school curriculum. One early (1983) survey (Williams, 1989) found that primary teachers ranked PE third in importance behind the core subjects of Maths and English. Reasons given in this study support the view that PE is certainly not a marginalised subject, but one that many teachers perceive to be at the very heart of any curriculum. Such a view is reflected in the comments presented below:

> 'I think children down here wouldn't do much if they didn't have physical education – they sit around and watch TV a lot'

> 'Children who can't do certain skills in a classroom have a chance to shine in physical education'

3

'It gives those who are not very gifted in academic subjects the chance to show some potential in something'

(Williams, 1989, pp. 17–18)

These views are quite typical of teacher perceptions of PE elsewhere that endorse it as a subject that offers something very special indeed for children. In their survey, for example, Birtwistle and Brodie (1991) report that teachers and pupils rate PE amongst the most important curriculum areas. Yet it would be naive to present views that only paint a rosy picture of PE. To balance the positive experiences presented above, the less than positive view of PE expressed by a teaching colleague in a Year 3 class some years ago has remained with me to this day:

'PE is important but parents won't come to you and say, My child can't do a forward roll. They will come and say, My child can't read.'

Such a statement supports the subject's merits but also carries a clear message about its position alongside core literacy in the primary curriculum. Recent evidence (Hardman and Marshall, 2001) has shown that pupils in the UK have an entitlement to fewer hours of PE than pupils in Europe and have pointed to the risk of the subject becoming marginalised in schools. The National Association of Head Teachers (1999) identified that many schools are struggling to provide even baseline PE as a result of reduced curriculum time and the status of the subject.

Comments from student teachers who were not PE specialists in a small survey carried out by the authors in both our institutions indicated, in contrast, that their primary school experiences of PE were very positive. The quotes that follow from trainee early years and primary teachers reflect this and give an indication of the type of activities that formed their physical education experiences:

'I remember the climbing frame. It seemed huge. I used to love going on this!'

'We played a lot of rounders and netball in my final year.'

'Country dancing and we had music and movement a lot too. I think it's good to do this. It makes you think about what your body can do.'

'I loved primary – but not secondary.'

Positive again, but a less than positive view from one trainee teacher pointed to the paucity in her PE curriculum in primary school:

'Your teacher stumbled across rounders or gymnastics and that was it –you were stuck. Week in, week out, the same equipment came out of the games cupboard and the same people would smile; others cringe.'

The voices of children also present feelings of the worth of PE experiences in school and these are expressed with the clarity and sincerity of youth. Two voices from primary-aged pupils exemplified what PE means to children in Margaret Talbot's address to the World Summit on Physical Education in Berlin (1999):

'On Mondays we do ball skills; on Tuesdays we go swimming; on Thursdays we dance; on Fridays we do gymnastics – in gymnastics we do jumping, rolling and thinking.'

'It makes me feel as if I could fly away.'

These three perspectives on PE, from teachers, trainee teachers and pupils serve to say something about what PE is all about and the type of activities that appear to define it. As professionals, it is important that we are able to present our feelings and views on the subject. We also need to fully understand what PE is all about to be able to justify it as a learning experience for children and articulate this to a variety of audiences in and outside of education. It is a hope that this book will provide such knowledge and justifications to enable readers working with 3–11 children to articulate the uniqueness of the subject and the particular demands of its pedagogy.

In this next section we consider the purpose and contribution that PE makes in more detail. Before this, spend fifteen minutes recollecting your own experiences of PE in the primary years in the task that follows.

Task 1 Memories of primary school physical education

Recall what physical education meant to you as a pupil in primary school. Think about the experience and the type of activities you took part in before writing anything down. The following prompts should help you:

- Would you say PE was an enjoyable experience for you?

- Why was this?

- If the experience or some of the experiences were not so enjoyable, what were the reasons for this?

- What activities can you remember? Did these change as you progressed through primary school?

- *Where* did PE generally take place for you in primary school? Outside, or in the school hall?

- What can you remember about *how* PE was taught?

- Are these experiences different to the experiences of children in schools nowadays?

- Would you change anything about the experiences you had?

- What does the type of PE provision recollected tell you about your teachers' or your school's priorities for PE?

Defining and characterising physical education for children 3–11

By way of answering the perhaps obvious questions of 'What is the purpose of physical education?' and 'Why is it important?' this section begins by stating a point which we feel underpins any discussions on the purpose and value of PE. Capel (2000) points out that when asked about the nature of PE, many people proceed to offer a list of activities associated with it but decline to provide their own or indeed an agreed definition of the subject. You may have noted that many of the quotes in the previous section in this chapter talk of discrete activities such as 'gymnastics' 'rounders', 'country dancing' and so on. One reason, she suggests for the propensity to list activities, is that there in fact exists a lack of consensus of a definition of PE with little agreement inside and outside of the teaching profession as to what PE actually has at its core. The absence of such conceptual agreement has been highlighted by many writers in the period leading up to the establishment of the National Curriculum in the 1980s but remains so in the present day (Murdock, 1986; Parry, 1988; Alderson and Crutchley, 1990; Kirk and Tinning, 1990; Penny, 1998). By way of addressing this shortfall, we present a new definition of physical education that reflects our interpretation of the subject today and our aspirations for it for the future:

> Physical education, as part of the whole education process is a field of endeavour that is concerned with lifelong physical, intellectual, social and emotional learning that accrues through experiencing physical activities in a variety of contexts.

We also feel it important that readers of this book are presented with the key determinants of the subject in a clear form, in order to understand the nature of the subject more fully. Evidence of what amounts to a robust rationale for PE, ironically, exists readily in the literature. For more detailed philosophical discussions on the nature of the subject than are possible in this text, readers are encouraged to consult a number of other writers – Arnold, 1997; Carr, 1997; Parry, 1998; Reid, 1997; Green, 2000. Streamlining Talbot's list of the characteristics of PE (1999), however, encapsulates the breadth of the subject and portrays its core ingredients admirably.

Physical education:

- is an entitlement for all children;
- has a focus on the body and its movements;
- is associated with the overall development of young people;
- uses the physical to make demands and increases in physical capacities such as skills, speed, stamina, mobility and physical responsiveness;
- is central to the whole learning process;
- passes on knowledge, understanding and respect for the body and its achievements;

- involves the learning of physical skills, critical reflection, refinement and improvement;
- is working towards physical competence and physical literacy;
- integrates the physical self with the thinking and social person;
- has a shared language and value system that has the capacity for adaptation of practice according to children's needs;
- has activities that meet developmental and individual learning needs;
- works towards understanding and appreciation of the role of physical development and physical activities in personal development, health maintenance and social lifestyle.

(Adapted from Talbot, 1999, p. 107)

The literature reveals that many ways of describing the subject have been proffered in the past. Whitehead (2000) distinguishes between *physical education* and *sport*. PE is delivered as part of the school timetable and, in England and Wales, is governed by the National Curriculum for Physical Education. It is a compulsory school subject from Key Stage 1 to Key Stage 4. Sport, on the other hand, is referred to as a physical activity with a competitive element, it usually has a cost involved and it may be delivered by a professional player or unpaid enthusiast. Activities embrace individual, partner, team, contact and non-contact, motor-driven or perceptually dominated sports (Coalter, 2001). Earlier, Arnold (1979) referred to PE's firm associations with movement. Parry (1988) saw its status linked it to the promotion of valued cultural norms. Almond proposed it as 'an umbrella term for a wide range of purposeful physical pursuits that can enrich lives and improve the quality of living' (2000, p. 4). A most helpful categorisation is that provided by Kirk (1993) who identified the domains of psychomotor, cognitive, social and affective that comprise the subject. As we shall argue in this chapter, PE has a strong physical dimension but is also concerned with the development of the intellect, ways of working with other people and the development of attitudes and character dispositions.

Our starting point involves reference to PE in the whole process of education (Bruner, 1972). Physical education is part of this broad process and is concerned with developing children's full potential to enrich their lives and the culture in which they live. Added to this, its content areas must contain activities of intrinsic value. In their analysis of the goals of education, Dewey's idea of study being inappropriate 'unless it is worthwhile in its own immediate having' (1916, p. 109) and Peters' idea of 'worthwhile activities' (1963, p. 144) become immediately relevant. We, as authors of this book in advancing a rationale for PE that includes a new definition of it, champion its uniqueness and support this claim in two important ways. First, by evidencing its distinctiveness in the process of education with characteristics that *no* other school experience shares. It is integral to the *Physical Development* area of learning within the Foundation Stage curriculum and is identified as a foundation subject in the National Curriculum for Key Stages 1 and 2. As part of the wider school curriculum it also contributes to learning across the curriculum and to a variety of community partnerships in the extended curriculum. A more developed discussion of the curricular requirements in these age phases will be given in Chapters 3–5 later in the book. The following are some of the unique and specific contributions that PE makes to the educational process:

- Through its emphasis on the body it contributes to all aspects of children's education (including spiritual, moral, social and cultural understanding).
- It remains the only 'subject' that focuses on the body and physical development (DES, 1991) and learning in/through/about the physical (Kirk, 1997).
- It fosters the development of a range of physical skills (Sallis *et al.*, 1997).
- It educates children about health and fitness.
- Cognitive skills of problem-solving, decision-making, creative thinking, strategising and evaluating are fostered (Doherty, 2003).
- It fosters critical thinking (Bell and Penney, 2004).
- It develops personal qualities such as independence, tolerance and empathy.
- It provides real contexts for learning about fairness, competition and sportsmanship.
- It enables an appreciation of skilful performance by developing artistic and aesthetic understanding within and through movement (PEA UK, 1998).
- It uses movement as integral to the whole process of education and involves 'learning to move ' and 'moving to learn' (Sugden and Talbot, 1998).
- Academic skills can be enhanced (Shephard, 1997).
- It contributes to and reinforces learning across the curriculum (language, numeracy, ICT, safety, etc.).
- It is concerned with physical literacy.
- It can lead to positive attitudes towards school and it can aid retention (DCMS, 1999).

Our second claim is that PE makes a unique and sustainable contribution to the lives of children. Again drawing upon a variety of sources, the following statements are made in support of this claim:

- It enables the promotion of personal autonomy and decision-making to make informed choices about involvement in recreation and sport.
- It encourages healthy lifestyles and prevents certain risk behaviours (Boreham *et al.*, 1997; Freedman *et al.*, 2001).
- By advocating participation in physical activity it makes contributions to young people's mental and social health (Svoboda, 1994; Dishman, 1995).

- It lays the basis for lifelong participation in physical activity.

- It is fundamental to the expression of young people's human rights.

- It makes positive contributions to the development of self-esteem (Fox, 1988).

- It includes all children regardless of gender, ability, ethnicity.

- It helps to develop coping strategies to deal with success and failure.

- It promotes an understanding of risk and the development of survival skills.

- With links to health promotion, it encourages children to respect their own bodies and those of others.

- It promotes a sense of national identity and cultural pride.

- It provides knowledge and skills relevant to vocational opportunities in later life.

- It provides a sound preparation for children's future lives.

More recently, the importance of PE is captured and lucidly presented in the opening section to the National Curriculum for Physical Education, which states:

> Physical education develops pupils' physical competence and confidence, and their ability to use these to perform in a range of activities. It promotes physical skilfulness, physical development and a knowledge of the body in action. Physical education provides opportunities for pupils to be creative, competitive and face up to different challenges as individuals and in groups and teams. It promotes positive attitudes towards active and healthy lifestyles. Pupils learn how to think in different ways to suit a wide variety of creative, competitive and challenging activities. They learn how to plan, perform and evaluate actions, ideas and performance to improve their quality and effectiveness. Through this process pupils discover their aptitudes, abilities and preferences, and make choices about how to get involved in lifelong physical activity.
>
> (DfEE/QCA, 1999, p. 15)

In short, physical education is concerned with what children can do, what they know, and what they understand.

Task 2 What does PE offer children?

List your responses under four headings: Knowledge (e.g. rules of games); Skills (e.g. communication); Concepts (e.g. safety) and Attitudes (e.g. healthy lifestyle, using space). Try ranking your responses under each heading, in order of importance.

Historical and contemporary aims of PE

There is no doubt that the history of physical education has served to shape many of the aims and objectives of contemporary PE. It has reflected the changing economic, industrial, religious and cultural environments of people and the dominant ideas of particular times and places. In primitive societies, proficiency in physical skills, especially those needed for hunting, raised the social standing of warriors as prowess in throwing the spear and covering huge distances in search of food were deemed essential survival skills. The importance of ceremonies which involved dancing to appease tribal gods and celebrations of wedding alliances or rites of passage portray primitive societies with aims closely linked to survival. These aims would have been achieved through indoctrination into the ways of that culture and by children imitating the behaviours of adults (Van Dalen and Bennett, 1971). Physical education in Greek society varied according to the ethos of its city states. In Sparta, physical training dominated a harsh disciplined society where, as Laker (2000) points out, it was education of the physical in its extreme! In contrast, Athenian culture prized social and moral attitudes alongside physical development and may well have used physical education as a means of educating the citizenry to prepare them for life in an educated culture (ibid.). From Roman society we inherit an emphasis on health where sport was for all the population to participate in and lifelong participation in physical activity was positively encouraged. Similar aims are reflected in our programmes today.

Moving from the 'dark times' of Renaissance Europe, to nineteenth-century Britain where the public school system was born, a strong tradition of games playing and 'athleticism' emerged (Mangan, 1981). Indeed some would argue that games playing as the dominant ideology for PE has not left us. The end of that century saw a combination of Swedish gymnastics in all-girls schools through the influence of Mathias Roth. Military drill was commonplace in the belief that its adoption would lead to health and physical development and good habits of obeying orders. By the beginning of the twentieth century, schools had a responsibility to develop fair play and loyalty to one another, which was seen as a basis for loyalty in later life (McIntosh, 1976). In elementary schools free-standing exercises, playground games, swimming and some field games were introduced in a period characterised by a reduced formality in the curriculum and teaching methods. After the Second World War, movement became a principal aim of school PE. This was supported by the publication in 1952 of the Ministry of Education's *Moving and Growing* and, in 1953, *Planning the Programme* and the influential Rudolph Laban claim that moving was fundamental to all PE – which remains evident in dance and educational gymnastics programmes in many primary schools today.

The Education Reform Act (1988) and the establishment of the first national curriculum in England and Wales represented a major landmark for education. National Curriculum Physical Education (NCPE) became a compulsory subject in the 5–16 curriculum, securing its place for the first time amongst other traditionally more 'academic' subjects. This articulated the entitlement for *all* pupils to receive a curriculum that was both broad and balanced and included PE. The importance of the physical dimension was still very much in the minds of policy makers as an aim for the subject. The purpose of learning in the subject was to develop specific knowledge, skills and understanding and to promote physical development and competence (DES, 1992). Non-statutory guidance highlighted the emphasis on the physical, confirming the emphasis on learning in a mainly physical context. A further aim was to 'teach pupils, through experience, to know about and value the benefits of participation in physical activity while at school and throughout life' (NCC, 1992), signifying the importance of lifelong learning and involvement in PE. In 1995, Ofsted published their survey of PE and sport in schools which contained the following aims:

> Physical education, as a foundation subject, aims to develop control of the body, to improve physical skills, to give pupils the ability to make decisions and to apply their growing knowledge and understanding about movement and the body in a variety of activities and contexts.
>
> (Ofsted, 1995)

With the further revision of the curriculum in 1995 (DfE, 1995), the alliance between PE and sport, which had been stressed as separate in the 1992 curriculum, gathered momentum. The gauntlet was thrown down by the then Prime Minister John Major, who vowed to 'put sport back at the heart of weekly life in every school' (DNH, 1995, p. ii) and the publication of *Sport: Raising the Game* (DNH, 1995), was a direct and unequivocal statement on school sport from Government never witnessed before. Almost in parallel, was an identification of the *process* that defined PE in this new curriculum. The importance of this was to firmly establish planning, performing and evaluating as the interrelated elements to be addressed in teaching curriculum PE. The emphasis on educational processes, not sporting outcomes, reflected an increased interest in learning, its nature, how it is promoted and its place in society (Murdoch, 1997).

In relation to the curriculum for pupils aged 3 to 5, six areas of learning were established through the creation of the Foundation Stage curriculum by the end of the decade. The *Early Learning Goals* (QCA, 1999) define six areas of learning. These are personal, social and emotional development; language and literacy; mathematical development; knowledge and understanding of the world; physical development; and creative development. These goals establish the expectations for the majority of children to achieve by the end of the Foundation Stage. The aim of the Physical Development goal (which is developed in Chapter 4) is to support and promote 'opportunities for all children to develop and practise their fine and gross motor skills, increase their understanding of how their bodies work and what they need to be healthy and safe' (QCA, 1999, p. 10).

In what was a decade of enormous changes for teachers, yet another National Curriculum was established around the same time (DfEE, 1999). For PE, four aspects were established through which pupils progress within and across the key stages:

■ Acquiring and developing skills

■ Selecting and applying skills, strategies, tactics and compositional ideas

■ Evaluating and improving performance

■ Knowledge and understanding of fitness and health

(DfEE, 1999, p. 6)

These four aspects of PE are developed through a range of practical activities that form the programmes of study at each key stage. These in turn, are the contexts and experiences through which the knowledge, skills and understanding that define the subject are taught. The specific requirements relating to Key Stage 1 (for pupils aged 5 to 7 years) are discussed in Chapter 5 and for Key Stage 2 (for pupils aged 7 to 11 years) in Chapter 6. Critics highlight the mandate to follow programmes of study in multiple areas, believing that they increase teachers' feelings of inadequacy in delivering NCPE and diminish the unity of the learning experience for pupils (Almond, 1997). Others suggest that the areas of activity framework imposes a 'secondary and distinctly specialist frame' upon PE in the primary sector and encourages curricular divisions rather than linkages in teaching and learning (Penney and Evans, 1999, p. 22). These criticisms may well hold true and you, the reader, are encouraged to form your own opinion on the viability and integrity of this latest curriculum. What is clear, however, is that this curriculum does prescribe the content of PE and reflects thinking on the current aims for the subject. The next task requires you to rank some of the key aims of contemporary PE in order of their importance to you.

Task 3 Ranking aims of contemporary PE

Below are listed ten aims of physical education. You are asked to rank them 1–10 (where 1 is the most important and 10 is the least important) in order of their importance to *you*. This is a 'non versus' exercise, i.e. no one aim is better than another, they just reflect different priorities.

continued on facing page

Aim	Ranking
To promote physical literacy	
To educate children about health and fitness	
To contribute to all aspects of children's education	
To foster holistic development	
To lay the basis for lifelong participation in physical activity	
To develop personal qualities such as independence, tolerance, empathy	
To contribute to the development of self-esteem	
To develop a range of physical skills	
To contribute to and reinforce learning across the curriculum	
To meet developmental and individual learning needs	

Key underpinning principles

Earlier in this chapter it was stated that when asked what PE is, the response from many people, including many PE teachers, is often a list of activities that amounts to a PE curriculum rather than a definition of the subject (Capel, 2000). The point was made that in order to justify its unique place in the curriculum, the subject must be more than a list of activities in which pupils participate. For this to be the case, a set of principles that underpin any activities that children are engaged in is needed. The tables below summarise the principles upon which physical education is founded for children aged 3–11, with Table 1.1 presenting those most applicable to children in the Foundation Stage and Table 1.2 applicable to children in Key Stages 1 and 2.

A successful PE curriculum for all children demands but also utilises these important principles. By using them as the starting point for designing a PE curriculum, it avoids a curriculum that is little more than a hodgepodge of activities with no common bonds and irrelevant to the individual needs of every child. In doing so, it moves from an emphasis on product (e.g. specific skills and drills to be learned and performed) to a desirable *process* model that all children can enjoy, learn from and discover their full potential. Blurred aims for the subject do not allow this, nor will they provide clarity

TABLE 1.1 Principles on which physical education depends for children aged 3–5 (adapted from Manners and Carroll, 1995)

Key principle	Descriptor
It builds on what children can do already.	Many basic motor actions have already been explored by the time children reach school age, e.g. running, climbing, throwing, etc. From 3 onwards, children seek to use these skills in purposeful and progressive ways.
Children should be as physically active as possible.	Children benefit from safe, vigorous activity that increases their heart rate and helps to keep them fit. Time for changing, putting out equipment is not counted. Activity can be in indoor and outdoor environments.
Learning episodes require clearly identified and structured outcomes.	PE activities combine exploration with those of a structured nature. Teachers should be mindful of ways of maintaining challenge for every child.
A range of activities are needed and an adequate allocation of time.	The Foundation Stage and the National Curriculum provide opportunities for many different physical activities. Concern should be for holistic child development.
A balanced programme requires sufficient equipment and adequate facilities.	Children require a range of equipment appropriate to their age and capabilities. These include benches, balls, climbing frames, mats, ropes, etc.
All children are entitled to the best physical education possible.	All children are special. They are entitled to the best we can provide for them. All programmes should be inclusive.

in describing what a child going through such a programme should be able to do, know and understand. In contrast, agreed aims, and a clear view of what in essence makes a physically educated person in the subject, will. This is the topic we address in the next section.

Children as physically educated learners

What does it mean to be physically educated for children in the Foundation Stage or in Key Stages 1 and 2 of the National Curriculum? To be educated mathematically would involve competence in areas such as number, shape and space, measure, etc. We also talk about being 'literate' in subjects such as technology, and the term 'computer literate' is used in common parlance. Is there an equivalent in physical education and if so how is this defined?

TABLE 1.2 Principles on which physical education depends for children aged 5–11

Key principle	Descriptor
Access	Children need access to a programme of study appropriate to their age/ability.
Opportunity	All children have opportunities to participate in and achieve in different activities.
Inclusiveness	Every child is important. The achievements of all children are valued.
Breadth	A broad curriculum allows children to appreciate what each activity area can offer and the learning experiences in each.
Balance	Allows every child to benefit from the richness of PE. Each area of activity offers its own unique challenge and suits different needs.
Coherence	Planned as a whole experience and not as discrete unconnected units. Mapping each child's experiences and progress through this curriculum is vital.
Integrity	It is not sufficient to engage children in physical activities. What is required for them is purposeful physical education.
Differentiation	Matches tasks to ability, needs and interests. It balances challenge with achievement.
Relevance	Takes into account previous learning, readiness, interests and achievements.

Task 4 What characterises a physically educated child?

- In your opinion what are the characteristics of such a child?
- Are these characteristics constant across the Foundation Stage and KS 1 and KS 2?
- Will these characteristics change for secondary pupils in KS 3 and KS 4?
- How do these relate to the aims for the subject?
- Is it possible to be physically educated in one or more practical activity areas only (e.g. a games specialist or a swimmer)?
- Do current modes of assessment allow for such identification?

The term 'physical literacy' has in recent times been used but has never been defined properly and the characteristics of a physically literate individual have not been clearly presented. A more realistic solution to our question is to draw upon existing literature to provide guidance. There have been a number of attempts to establish standards in relation to the knowledge, skills and understanding of PE, mastery of which is assumed to correspond to a person being physically educated. Contemporary views associate it with having an understanding of the history of physical education and the cultural role of sports; having an understanding of health, nutrition and physical fitness; valuing being healthy, and possessing skills to enable participation in everyday life, as well as sport and recreation.

Of particular importance in developing our understanding of the concept and its practical application to children in schools, was the 'Outcomes Project' of the National Association for Sport and Physical Education (1990) in the USA. They identified five categories to describe a physically educated individual:

1   Possession of relevant motor skills

2   Physical fitness

3   Participation in physical activity

4   Knowledge of the benefits of involvement in physical activities

5   An appreciation of the values of physical activity and its contribution to a healthy lifestyle.

Accompanying these categories are a series of twenty benchmark statements intended to assist teachers in assessing pupil progress towards becoming physically educated. Of interest and pertinent to our discussion here are that nine of these relate to physical outcomes whilst the remaining eleven relate to non-physical ones. The complete benchmark statements are:

A physically educated pupil is one who:

Has learned skills necessary to perform a variety of physical activities:

1   Moves using concepts of body awareness, space awareness, effort and relationships

2   Demonstrates competence in a variety of manipulative, locomotor and nonlocomotor skills

3   Demonstrates competence in combinations of manipulative, locomotor and nonlocomotor skills performed individually and with others

4   Demonstrates competence in many different forms of physical activity

5   Demonstrates proficiency in a few forms of physical activity

6   Has learned how to learn new skills

Is physically fit:

7 Assesses, achieves and maintains physical fitness

8 Designs safe, personal fitness programs in accordance with principles of training and conditioning

Does participate regularly in physical activity:

9 Participates in health-enhancing physical activity at least three times a week

10 Selects and regularly participates in lifetime physical activities

Knows the implications of and the benefits from involvement in physical activities:

11 Identifies the benefits, costs and obligations associated with regular participation in physical activity

12 Recognizes the risk and safety factors associated with regular participation in physical activity

13 Applies concepts and principles to the development of motor skills

14 Understands that wellness involves more than being physically fit

15 Knows the rules, strategies and appropriate behaviours for selected physical activities

16 Recognizes that participation in physical activity can lead to multicultural and international understanding

17 Understands that physical activity provides the opportunity for enjoyment, self-expression and communication

Values physical activity and its contribution to a healthful lifestyle:

18 Appreciates the relationships with others that result from participation in physical activity

19 Respects the role that regular physical activity plays in the pursuit of lifelong health and well-being

20 Cherishes the feelings that result from regular participation in physical activity

(NASPE, 1990)

Earlier in this chapter it was argued that physical education is concerned with what children can do, know and understand. These elements define what PE is all about and are explicit in the NASPE construct. The different domains of PE through which PE is commonly understood in the UK are also clearly present. Statements 1–6 refer to the psychomotor domain (as do statements 7 –10 on physical fitness); the cognitive domain is covered by statements 11–17, and the affective domain by the final statements, 18–20. Such a framework does three important things. First, it encapsulates what a physically educated individual is. Second, it reinforces the importance of PE's physical dimension and the complementary role of the cognitive and affective dimensions. Finally, it gathers together aims, characteristics and dimensions of the subject into one coherent rationale for PE that is relevant to children of all ages. For readers who prefer a summary statement of this rather than a set of benchmark statements, the one provided by Stephen Klesius fits very well. He describes the physically educated person as,

> being able to select developmentally appropriate physical activities, participate voluntarily and regularly in these activities, and enjoy these activities as evidenced by positive verbalization patterns, and observable efforts to find opportunities to extend the repertoire of skill, increase the level of performance, or intensify the frequency of participation. This person is self-directing and self-actualizing.
>
> (Klesius, 1971, p. 47)

We conclude that becoming physically educated might well be seen as the ultimate goal of any programme of physical education, and in the chapters that follow we endeavour to provide guidance as to the content material to support 3–11 physically educated learners and teaching approaches and assessment modes to foster this goal.

Chapter summary

Physical education has a unique contribution to make to the early years and primary school curricula and to the lives of children. In this chapter a rationale for PE has been presented that embraces its purposes, characteristics and values, and a new definition that reflects the different domains that it incorporates has been presented. Although the physical dimension is paramount, both cognitive and affective domains were shown to be integral to this definition and understanding of how the subject is conceptualised. Contemporary aims have come about from a varied world history and led to aims for the subject relevant to children in the Foundation Stage and those across the primary years.

The concept of children as physically educated learners complements the rationale for physical education presented in the chapter and is in keeping with the philosophy of a whole child approach advocated by many early years and primary educators.

Questions for reflection

- Can you describe the essence of PE in terms of knowledge, concepts, skills and attitudes?
- What should learning outcomes for PE attempt to do and is there research evidence to support them?
- Do the aims of primary PE reflect areas unique to PE or do they relate to the aims of the entire Foundation Stage and/or primary school curriculum?
- What does it mean to be a physically educated learner at ages 3, 7, and 11? Does this change as children grow older or does it remain constant?

Web links and further reading

www.peprimary.co.uk

www.pea.co.uk

www.baalpe.org

Bailey, R. (2001) *Teaching Physical Education: A Handbook for Primary and Secondary Teachers*. London: Kogan Page.
The first chapter is a most readable and succinct summary of the aims of PE and its statutory requirements.

Capel, S. and Piotrowski, S. (2000) (eds) *Issues in Physical Education*. London: Routledge-Falmer.
A detailed read. Chapter 1 contains an interesting discussion on the aims of PE today.

DES (1972) *Movement: Physical Education in the Primary Years*. London: HMSO.
Although not current, this book is the bedrock for all subsequent books. The first three chapters are especially relevant here.

DfEE (1999) *Physical Education in the National Curriculum*. London: DfEE/QCA.
Provides statutory requirements for PE in relation to each key stage.

DfES (2000) *Curriculum Guidance for the Foundation Stage*. DfES/QCA.
Provides the statutory curriculum for children aged 3–5. Describes the six areas of learning and associated goals that include physical development.

Laker, A. (2000) *Beyond the Boundaries of Physical Education: Educating Young People for Citizenship and Social Responsibility*. London: Routledge-Falmer.
Chapter 2 on the history of physical education is not bettered anywhere else.

Thomas, J.R., Lee, A.M. and Thomas, K.T. (1988) *Physical Education for Children*. Champaign, Illinois: Human Kinetics.
As the title suggests, this book takes a very child-centred approach to teaching PE. Certainly worth a read.

Understanding development, movement and skill

Children's development

THE GROWING CHILD is a dynamic individual whose all-round development occurs rapidly in the years between three and eleven. Understanding how children develop is important for physical educators for many reasons, but chief amongst these is in providing information as the basis for developmentally appropriate practice in PE. To achieve the aims of the subject outlined in the previous chapter, planning, teaching and assessment must be appropriate to the needs of all children. A major impediment to this is a starting point in some PE programmes that assumes adult sports skills and games play are appropriate for this age group. Nothing could be further from the truth – children are not mini-adults and practices that treat them as such can only serve as a recipe for frustration, anxiety, boredom and possible injury. Practices that engage children below the age of 11 in adult-type games, are governed by adult rules or that use inappropriate equipment form *no* part of a quality and a developmentally appropriate programme of physical education. Quality in PE comes from lessons that are developmentally and instructionally matched to the needs of the children engaged in them.

Task 5   Identifying appropriate practice in PE

■ What do you think constitutes developmentally appropriate practice in PE?

■ What constitutes developmentally inappropriate practice?

■ List some examples of both.

To assist the reader's understanding it may be useful at this point to introduce and explain some terminology associated with development. *Development* is a lifelong process of change that is the product of the interplay between genetic inheritance and the environment. Children inherit certain characteristics from their parents which they carry with them through life. The environment determines how they use these characteristics in interaction with other people and in various situations. Development is usually categorised into physical, intellectual, linguistic, emotional and social (and remembered through the unfortunate mnemonic of PILES!). *Maturation* is the genetically programmed sequence of change towards a mature state. *Learning* is a change in behaviour due to experience.

Development is a complicated process of change. Most researchers agree that it is a result of the interaction of *both* maturation and learning (Gallahue and Ozmun, 1998) and this is certainly evident within PE. Adults frequently comment upon the increase in size or height of children as they leave one academic year group and enter another. The interaction between the two can also be seen by the difficulties experienced by a child learning to control a ball in Foundation Stage to the proficiency which the same child in Year 5 demonstrates in dribbling a basketball.

Most authorities also emphasise connections between the areas of development. Wright and Sugden's transactional model (1999) links an individual's maturation to the learning and experiences within the environment and to the particular demands of the task itself. This characterises the important role that teachers play in providing activities and contexts that best fit the needs of the *individual* child and adapting the learning environment to accommodate them. In PE, so much attention is given to the physical dimension but, because of this relationship, it is also vital to consider other aspects of development in a holistic way. Field (1990), among many writers, believes that the development of movement skills influences intellectual, social and emotional development. How children's play changes as they mature, the language they use to articulate physical actions, how they feel about themselves and the processes through which they learn to perform such actions are good examples of this interrelationship. In early infancy, children use movement skills to learn about themselves and their physical and social environment. Reaching out to grasp a bright toy prompts the co-ordinative systems responsible for the reaching–grasping action to function. Further investigation of the object provides information about its shape, weight, size and texture that fuels the growing brain. Subsequent physical achievements follow a similar pattern and provide necessary stimulation to the infant's perceptual and cognitive systems. They provide a catalyst for language development and help build self-esteem. As the child grows older, the same process continues. PE establishes itself as a wonderful vehicle to promote all-round development. Rudimentary physical skills of sitting, standing and walking remain major achievements and are soon replaced by later skills such as jumping, running, skipping, etc. but the involvement of the other aspects of development is just the same. By seeing development in this holistic way, teachers avoid identifying PE as a solely physical medium and in turn are much more empowered to deliver richer and more meaningful movement experiences for all children.

Development in the early years

For many years it was thought that the newborn baby came into this world as a helpless being, far from capable of thinking or communicating. Flailing arms and legs were assumed to be randomised insignificant movements. Untrue! We know that development proceeds at an amazing pace in all areas. In fact we are just beginning to discover how much has already taken place during the period in the womb. Through maturation the growing brain's specialist functions enable important motor, language, visual and auditory processing to take place. Rather than the 'blank slate' notion put forward by philosophers such as Locke centuries ago, newborns arrive with a repertoire of cognitive skills, abilities and dispositions that enable them to survive and to start them off on their individual developmental journey. They arrive eager to find out about the strange new world that now surrounds them, to find out more about it and to move!

The pre-school years between 2 and 5 reveal further remarkable changes taking place. Note the frustrations of the 2 year old who is yet to play co-operatively with other children, moves around with some confidence but still requires a lot of concentration to do so, and keenly observes adults and copies what they do as a way of learning. So too the 3 year old gaining hand–eye co-ordination, who feels more confident in social situations and whose intellectual progress can be seen in an activity like drawing. Four year olds have friendships that are more stable. Gender stereotypes are established that result in different expectations for boys and girls and they have some understanding of 'right' and 'wrong'. Manipulative skills have increased and they enjoy experimenting with movement in activities like hopping, running and jumping. The 5 year old has a vocabulary of several thousand words, values the friendships of other children, has an increased memory, is physically much taller and heavier and has developed hand–eye co-ordination. All these advances prepare the child for the advent of formal schooling.

Key accomplishments in development in the early childhood years from 2 to 5 are summarised in Table 2.1.

Movement mastery

This period is also characterised by massive advances in movement skills. Aided by increases in brain development and body strength, reflexive reactions are gradually phased out and replaced by conscious voluntary movement within the first two years. Acquiring rudimentary skills including rolling, sitting, creeping, standing upright and crawling are the major challenges for the under twos. From 2 to 5 years, new movement skills build upon these important foundations. Children in this age group are physically active. Gross motor skills such as running, jumping, skipping and climbing are learned in both indoor and outside environments. Fine motor skills are similarly learned through activities such as clay modelling, sand and water play, painting and basic typing on a computer.

Development in the primary years

The explosion of growth and physical ability characteristic of the early childhood phase is not sustainable in the next phase of development. This middle childhood phase is characterised by consolidation and steady progress. From 6 to 12 years sees a period where the growing child is steadily gaining in height and body mass and undergoing changes in body proportions. Allied to these changes comes a steady increase in co-ordination, body strength and physical ability. Neurological development allows for greater movement control. The years until the onset of puberty have been described as the 'skill hungry years' (Maude, 1996) and for very good reason. The earlier gross motor skills, such as running, jumping and throwing, and dribbling and striking a ball, become more refined. Parallel improvement in flexibility and power enable faster, farther and more accurate movements in a variety of PE activities. Improvements in fine motor control in activities such as drawing and writing are easily discernible. As social skills develop, school-age children become more aware of themselves and present their own individual personalities. Key accomplishments in development in the primary years are summarised in Table 2.2.

TABLE 2.1 Developmental milestones in the early childhood years

Development in relation to age	Physical	Intellectual	Linguistic	Emotional	Social
2	Runs with confidence. Can build a tower of six blocks. Pushes trike. No steering. May do and undo own buttons.	Enjoys role play and imaginative play. Can point to major body parts. Recognises self in photographs.	Asks many questions. Listens to answers. Chats continuously at play. Obeys simple requests.	Is prone to temper tantrums. Still requires adult reassurance. In need of constant love and attention.	Plays near but not with others. Is unable to share toys. Likes outside environments but unaware of dangers.
3	Walks upstairs unassisted. Uses spoon and fork. Pedals and steers trike. More competent in locomotion.	Asks questions constantly. Short-term memory has increased. Can relate past and present.	Talks in sentences of four or five words. Carries out simple oral instructions. Asks meanings of words.	Fewer tantrums. Is more confident in new situations. Still emotionally vulnerable.	Enjoys helping adults. Can be part of a small group. Keen to please adults.
4	Builds a tower of ten blocks. Can use scissors. Accomplished trike rider. Shows agility in locomotion. Can throw and catch a ball.	Able to compare two objects. Well developed imaginative play. Enjoys practical work.	Able to draw houses and people. Mostly uses correct grammar. Often has difficulties with w, f, th.	Inclined to be cheeky. Developing a sense of humour. Takes some responsibility for personal hygiene.	Likes the company of other children. May boast and boss others. Has learned to share.
5	Skilled in climbing on apparatus. Responds well to music. Good pencil control. Kicks and throws with some accuracy.	Drawings become more recognisable. Distinguishes between truth and lies. Enjoys games with rules. Clear sense of humour.	Speaks correctly. Able to write own name. Recognises some printed words. Knows over 2000 words.	Shows care towards others. Understands the need to have rules. Overall balanced.	Chooses own friends. Separates well at nursery or playgroup. Can co-operate with others.

TABLE 2.2 Developmental milestones in the primary years

Development in relation to age	Physical	Intellectual	Linguistic	Emotional	Social
6	Has self-dress skills. Displays confidence in movement skills. Active. Enjoys rough and tumble play.	Has an active mind but easily distracted. Tends to think before making decisions. Interested in learning.	Reading is developing. Speech is socially useful. Sees relationships in stories.	May look to adults for direction. Capable of physical temper outbursts.	Friendships appear and reappear quickly. Becoming part of the 'gang' is important.
7	Body balance skills improved. Takes part in games with defined rules.	Mathematical skills involve more abstract concepts. Deploys memory strategies.	Has an interest in poetry. Written stories are longer and more detailed.	Personality now clearly evident. Less boisterous as absorbs more.	Likes to help. Less dependent on family for reassurance.
8	Better hand–eye co-ordination. Able to practise skills for longer time periods.	Shows understanding of cause and effect. Finds it easier to process more than one task at a time.	All speech sounds are established. Uses compound and complex sentence structures.	Less overt aggressive behaviour. More self-reliant. Is aware of own shortcomings.	Is more sociable. Being popular and successful outside the family is important.
9	Fine motor skills well developed. Particular strengths in PE and sports become apparent.	Uses strategies for remembering more effectively.	Very few lapses in grammar, tense, plurals, etc. Reading with ease.	Self-motivated. Develops sense of self-worth.	Can appear shy in new situations. Prosocial behaviour is generally increased.

continued on next page

TABLE 2.2 continued

Development in relation to age	Physical	Intellectual	Linguistic	Emotional	Social
10	Shows good fine motor control. Has a wide repertoire of physical skills.	Long-term knowledge base extends. Adds, subtracts, multiplies and divides easily.	Understanding of syntax and sentence structure is developed.	Able to take into account other people's viewpoints.	Conflicts with siblings develop skills of conflict resolution.
11	Able to apply skills in various contexts. Agility, speed, balance, power and accuracy increases.	Able to sustain attention for extended periods. Able to think logically.	Marked increase in written output. Increases in language and numerical skills	Settled. Accepting of adult authority.	Begins to want privacy. Establishes deeper friendships.

Children's movement capabilities

Movement is an integral part of the human condition. We only have to look around us to see movement in everything we do. In our primitive past it was expressed in everyday living and the rituals and traditions of different cultures. We have inherited this legacy today: our daily domestic and professional lives play host to a myriad of movements, many of which we take for granted. Movement in modern life is very much a tool for life. It has been described as 'a product of being alive' (DES, 1972, p. 3). Simply, the more efficiently one moves, the more meaningful one's life becomes. There is a wonderful versatility too about the ways in which we move. In PE and sport, witness the elegance and grace of the dancer, the control of the gymnast or the explosive power of the athlete in motion.

Movement is a natural part of childhood. Babies communicate their needs and feelings through movement. What was until quite recently considered by many as being unimportant twitching of limbs, we now know as one way that babies communicate their needs to adults around them. Movement provides a form of immediate response to their surroundings and within a matter of months a vital means of exploring this environment. The pre-school child's movements are driven by a desire to find out more and enquire. Maturation of the brain and nervous systems, alongside increases in body strength, encourage exploration of what the body can do and an eagerness to test it out. Children of this age enjoy the thrill of running, jumping and climbing. Vital experiments into body balance, heights to jump on to and from, speeds and directions to run in are constantly being investigated and new limits set. Progression into the primary years sees the same almost limitless energy and enquiring disposition where there is further delight in the accomplishments of how the body is capable of moving. In this desire for knowledge, movement remains a child's principal medium of discovery.

Movement (and its development) is a key concern of physical educators. Movement has been linked to an enhancement of learning, the promotion of health and increased self-esteem. A key role for educators is to help children move more efficiently and to increase the quality of their movement performance. This is achieved in the Foundation Stage by capitalising on the natural movements of childhood and guiding their explorations of different types of movement and movement contexts. Movement is at the heart of PE in the primary years and intrinsic to the areas of activity in Key Stages 1 and 2. Each area of activity has a different stress and taxes the body's capacity to move in different ways. (Further discussion and practical guidance on the kinds of movement experiences for children in the Foundation Stage will be given in Chapter 4 and for primary children in Chapters 5 and 6.)

Movement education is an important aspect of PE programmes, especially in primary schools. It exploits the science of movement and is designed to help young children become more aware of their bodies and how to move more efficiently (Bucher, 1979). The characteristics of movement education are that it:

■ is child centred;

■ involves problem-solving;

■ is less formal than traditional PE;

■ involves equipment;

■ facilitates the learning of motor skills;

■ seeks to produce a feeling of satisfaction in movement;

■ encourages an analysis of movement.

Arnold (1988) proposed four reasons why movement merits a place in the curriculum. First, it articulates movement as a field of study that has academic interest and is worthy of study in own right. Second, it fulfils an instrumental role if it can be demonstrated that other educational or desirable ends are served. The third reason is that it is an intrinsic and valued part of culture that should be transmitted on to future generations and finally, it is the only area of the curriculum directly concerned with the experiences of moving which form an integral part of what it is to be a person. These dimensions of movement provide an excellent basis for curriculum development and are the basis for our next discussion here.

Education *about* movement

This first aspect refers to enquiry into movement itself and poses questions about learning to move and theories of motor learning that underscore this enquiry. It is also concerned with how the body is organised to support movement, ways of moving and how to classify and analyse movement. There is a knowledge connection here, predominantly of the type Hirst (1974) labelled 'propositional knowledge', or 'knowing that'. Reid (1998) suggests that this form of knowledge functions as technical knowledge. How this form of knowledge relates to movements of young children is through their knowledge of rules, procedures and concepts within their PE experiences. It is the type of knowledge that is embedded in the natural play of young children and also in later structured PE experiences such as gymnastics. Consider the following three scenarios that demonstrate children's theoretical knowledge in PE.

Children demonstrating learning *about* movement

Knowledge of concepts

Maria, in a Year 3 gymnastics lesson is learning to balance on three points. She needs to have some theoretical knowledge about bases, stability and centre of gravity to balance properly.

Knowledge of procedures

Carla in the Nursery with help from the practitioner is attempting to monkey travel across the climbing frame. She knows that she should hold on to the bar with one hand and take all her weight before letting go and placing her other hand.

Knowledge of rules

Tom in Year 5 is playing an opposed sending and receiving game based on netball. He is aware that he cannot travel with the ball so he uses this knowledge of the game and its strategies to put himself in a position to receive a pass from his team-mates and to move to a position on court that gives him the best chance of scoring.

Propositional knowledge is acquired predominantly through information provided by the teacher but also through working in a cross-curricular way. The popular topic of 'Movement', with its early years emphasis on the ways in which animals, humans and machines move, presents valuable sources of theoretical knowledge about movement as more scientific work on forces and levers through science taught in Key Stage 2. Observation and the type of knowledge gleaned through observation is important so that children can make reasoned judgements about the movements they observe. These can be their own, the movements of their peers or expert performances of top athletes watched on DVD or on video.

In order that children develop their knowledge and understanding about movement, it is necessary that they know the range and character of the different activity areas in PE. A curriculum that is broad and balanced provides all pupils with the best opportunities to experience the demands and challenges of different practical activity areas. Bailey makes the point that a narrow interpretation of a competitive team-games curriculum alienates a large number of pupils and robs them of valuable learning experiences. He states that 'an adequate education *about* movement, therefore, introduces the full range of movement experiences, and offers each pupil the opportunity to excel' (2001, p. 8).

Education *through* movement

This refers to the use of physical activities as a means to achieve educational aims that may not be intrinsic to those activities. They relate to the broader aims of education in two ways. They can *illustrate* a point that has arisen, for example, in another curriculum area or they can *refer* to a question that has arisen, for example, from earlier work or work elsewhere. The illustrative function, suggests Arnold, is best understood in terms of a question such as, How can I (as the teacher) help my class learn by actively using movement? The referent function he suggests might be understood in a question from pupils such as, Why is it necessary to have rules in games?

These two questions might well arise during the course of normal classroom situations or through PE lessons as is illustrated below.

Children demonstrating learning *through* movement

■ Year 1 pupils Yasmin and Gethin practise letter formations p and d by tracing out letters in the air which will assist in writing activities.

■ Ben and Matt in Year 2 measure the length of their classroom by pacing it out. Their teacher will follow this up with a discussion on standard units of measurement later.

■ In a PE lesson with Year 4, the class are using a warm-up game called North, South, East and West that involves them running and touching different areas of the hall. This helps their understanding of compass points.

■ As part of a Year 6 games lesson, the teacher takes some time to talk about fair play after witnessing some unsporting behaviour from two pupils

---

This aspect highlights how movement can contribute to learning in other areas of the curriculum by working in a cross-curricular way. Hopper and colleagues suggest that the potential for this type of learning is nowhere more evident than in interpreting movements into the spoken word. They suggest that language offers 'a treasure chest of descriptive, directional and action words for children to explore and experience' (2000, p. 91). With older children, the use of score sheets, reading from work cards, writing instructions for games and marking movement performances of others provide many rich opportunities to enhance learning elsewhere in the curriculum.

Education *in* movement

Education in movement is the most fundamental dimension of the physical education curriculum (Doherty and Bailey, 2003). This is because learning occurs through active participation in movement activities. A different type of knowledge is required here which is expressed in practical ways. This is practical knowledge or 'knowing how'.

For Arnold (1988) this is essentially concerned with mastering skills and being able to participate in activities successfully with understanding. He writes that its distinctive features are that it involves practice and not just theory; action, not just thought or belief and intentionally doing something, rather than providing information about it or speculating about it (ibid.).

If we agree with the proposal in Chapter 1 that PE is part of the wider process of education, then by offering children opportunities for movement and physical activity, we introduce them to a physical dimension that brings its own intrinsic worth and enjoyment. Children of all ages love to move and demonstrate their physical skills and therefore to deny them this important part of their education is to deny them something that is fundamental to the whole human experience.

Education in movement involves participation that provides a unique opportunity to enjoy it 'from the inside'. A broadly based PE curriculum from 3 to 11 can provide children with experiences that are valuable and worthwhile in their own right. Here are some examples from such a curriculum that offers a range of movement experiences.

Children demonstrating learning *in* movement

- Matti and Harry are enjoying exploring the outside area around their school nursery.

- Ali in Year 3 has learning difficulties. He looks forward to when his class go swimming as he loves to feel the water on his skin and move freely around the shallow end.

- Mrs Taylor has brought a visitor into her Year 5 class who will teach the children a traditional Asian hand dance.

- This term Bev and Jon in Year 6 have been improving their striking and fielding skills and have been excited to take part in a Kwik Kricket game against another local school.

Clearly there are overlaps between the three components of movement. This is inevitable and their interrelationship should be promoted if children are to achieve their full potential in PE. A planned physical education curriculum from 3 to 11 with multiple learning outcomes is required. If based upon key principles, with movement as its cornerstone, it will help young children become more aware of their bodies and move more effectively. In the next section we consider the concepts that form such a movement education.

Adopting a movement approach

In his comparison of the alphabet as a function of formal language with the concepts pertaining to movement, Buschner (1994) coined the phrase 'movement alphabet'. Where the traditional alphabet has twenty-six letters, the movement alphabet contains twelve movement concepts and eighteen movement skills that also require mastery. Drawing upon early work of Melograno (1979), he links movement concepts and movement skills (considered later in this chapter) as organising centres that give co-hesion to the curriculum in a sequential and progressive way. Buschner argues that these should be placed at the centre of the PE curriculum to allow for applications into sports, dance, exercise and gymnastics later in a sequence of developmentally appropriate learning. This mirrors the progression from early years and primary through to more complex and applied movements in the secondary phase. References elsewhere in the literature to movement concepts and skills under other labels are also to be found (Kirchner, 1992; Nichols, 1986; Thomas *et al.*, 1988). Let us now turn to look at movement concepts.

We might wish to consider Graham and colleagues' useful description of movement concepts as the adverbs that modify the skills in such an alphabet (1993). Distinguishing between the two, movement concepts describe *how* a skill is performed. A practical example of this should aid clarification. If we take a movement skill such as running, this can be altered. I can run fast, slow, backwards, sidewards, lightly or alongside another person. I can change the skill in these ways and many others just as I can with any other movement skill! A framework comprising four features is commonly used to describe movement. The influence of Rudolph Laban's work in this country in the 1930s can be seen in much of the work today in school educational gymnastics and dance. The four factors below are all observable in bodily movement in spontaneous play and in structured PE lessons.

Body awareness

It was stated earlier that movement is readily observed in babies and continues throughout childhood as a natural expression of living. Pre-school children and those in Key Stage 1 have remarkably little awareness of what their bodies are doing as they move. Early teaching should concentrate on children being able to name and identify parts of the body and becoming aware of their bodies moving and forming different shapes. Dance is a particularly good medium for developing this capacity in young children, who enjoy activities of the type, 'Make your body as wide as an ocean' or 'Make your body as tall as a tree'. Older children will benefit from exploring symmetrical and asymmetrical shapes in gymnastics. Understanding balance and bases of support challenge pupils but are essential for fuller understanding of this concept.

There are various non-locomotor movements including body flexion, extension and rotation which are commonly described as bending, stretching and twisting and which appear in various forms in PE. Others in this category include the contribution of actions themselves such as spinning, stepping or travelling and those of different body parts that lead movement or support it. Once again these are commonly seen in gymnastics and dance lessons throughout the primary years.

Space awareness

Since all movements take up space, children should be aware of their bodies in space (self-space). As they move around and engage in different activities and in different situations, the need to understand the space around them becomes more marked (general space). One reason why primary children should not play full-sided games is because their awareness of general space is not developed sufficiently to know where to move to on the pitch or court. With experience this will happen but games lessons with large numbers on large areas of play should be avoided with primary pupils. Movements can also involve the six directions of upwards, downwards, left, right, backwards and forwards. They can be at three different levels: high (the space above shoulder height), middle, and low (below the knees). Pathways are either straight, curved or zig-zag. Finally, movements may be made near to the body or far from it, such as catching a ball with the arms beside the body or extended away from it.

Effort

This aspect considers how the body moves. Its abstract nature can make it a concept that is often forgotten in gymnastic or dance lessons but its inclusion is vital. If we were to observe elite athletes in action this quality would be immediately apparent in their movements. Can we say the same about a class of movers in primary school? Three elements define this concept. The first is *time*, which if fast suggests quickness, suddenness and explosiveness. Ballistic movements such as starting off in a sprint or throwing in athletics typify fast movements. In contrast, the movements of a 5 year old walking across a beam in gymnastics are characterised by slowness and sustained effort. The *force* component has two opposites: strong and light. Both may be witnessed in dance lessons where children are encouraged to move like a giant (strong) or like snowflakes (light). *Flow* is also commonly represented in dance lessons. It can be bound where movement responses are robot-like, jerky and restricted, or free and show fluidity, continuity and smoothness.

Relationships

This concept is associated with whom or with what the body moves. With younger children, since their interest is primarily about themselves, lessons to identify their own body parts are essential. With older children they should be encouraged to note the position of their limbs in executing movements. In games, attention might be drawn to the position of the arms in performing a tennis serve action or the position of the supporting foot in preparation for kicking a ball.

Relationships to objects include balls, hoops, mats, gymnastics equipment or line markings on the ground. Relationships to others are often seen in the Key Stage 2 gymnastics lessons working on a theme of 'Partners'. This provides children with ample opportunities to explore concepts such as meeting and parting, following and leading or mirroring and matching. The four concepts of movement can be described in diagram form as in Figure 2.1.

The acquisition and development of movement skills

Alongside movement, physical skills are intrinsic to the physical education experiences of all children. Physical skills take many forms and are very much part of children's

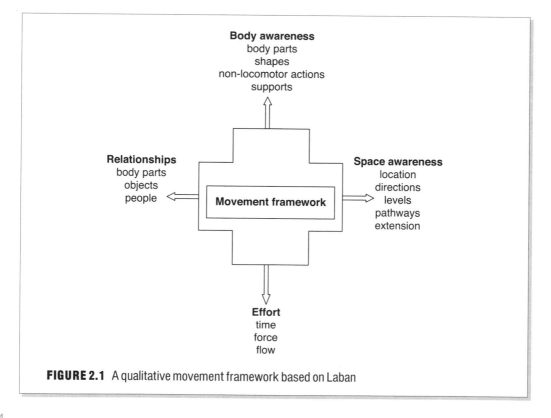

FIGURE 2.1 A qualitative movement framework based on Laban

everyday lives. Reading and writing, using a knife and fork, tying shoelaces, and walking to and from school are essential to normal living. Other skills are evident in the PE and movement experiences of children in school, and an understanding of the process through which children learn and improve their skills is essential for those who teach them. In the previous chapter we highlighted that the child who is physically educated displays competency in a variety of movement skills and in this chapter we outline some of the processes involved in acquiring and developing movement skills. (For the purposes of this book we shall use the term movement skills and motor skills interchangeably.)

Although the term *skill* has been variously defined by many writers, several common features can be identified. McMorris in his book, *Acquisition and Performance of Sports Skills* (2004) discusses four features that are common in most discussions on how skill is represented. First, skill is *learned.* The execution of all skills involves complex learning processes. It occurs either implicitly, such as in many of the skills in early childhood like crawling, or explicitly and involves some formal instruction, such as how to execute the drive shot in cricket. It is not inherited but performance is dependent upon practice and experience. The second feature is that skill is *consistent.* A one-off shot into a netball ring is not characteristic of skilled performance if the majority of other attempts have been unsuccessful. Such consistency will inevitably involve economy of effort. Skilled movements look the same each time. They are efficient in terms of the performer's time and expenditure outlay. Third, it is *specific.* Chipping a football and kicking a ball for distance are examples of two particular skills that are required in the game of soccer for different purposes, over and above being merely able to kick the ball. Finally skill is *goal-oriented.* In other words there is an outcome or end result. Learning to accelerate at the start of a sprint race is important in order to improve one's running time. It has a clear purpose and direction. The goal can only be achieved by learning to carry out the action.

Task 6 Categorising motor skills

One way to categorise skills (Schmidt and Wrisberg, 2000) is according to their most important characteristics. Taking a task perspective, physical skills can be categorised as being *closed* (performed in an environment that does not change) or *open* (where the environment is constantly changing). Another system classifies skills according to their organisation. *Discrete* skills are those with a distinct beginning and end. In contrast, *continuous* skills have neither and are usually repetitive in nature. Use this information to give examples from physical education for these ways of categorising motor skills.

continued on next page

continued from previous page

Closed skills
e.g. performing a forward roll

Open skills
e.g. playing a game of basketball

Discrete skills
e.g. catching a ball

Continuous skills
e.g. swimming

It may be useful at this point to briefly introduce another term closely related to skill but which is distinctly different. The term *ability* is more general than skill and refers to the innate actions that underlie skilled performance. Unlike a skill which is a learned response, abilities are genetically endowed and can only be improved marginally through practice because of genetic limitations. The ability to aim at a target, to react quickly to a stimulus and to maintain a steady hand are all examples of innate human abilities that will show little improvement regardless of the amount of time practising! Skills and abilities do interact though. The skill of throwing a ball for example, commonly seen in school halls and playgrounds everywhere, requires the thrower to possess a number of different abilities – balance, hand–eye co-ordination, kinaesthetic awareness, arm speed – for successful execution. It is also important to note that children (and adults) may perform the same skill differently because they possess different abilities and that these abilities can change over time. Given that everyone has different abilities, it raises the question of the appropriateness of teaching everyone to perform skills according to a standard 'textbook technique'.
Diversity is the stuff of life!

Children learning movement skills

In order to understand how children acquire movement skills, it is necessary to make reference to the theories relating to motor learning. Research into motor learning and performance can be traced back to the early part of the last century where association (stimulus–response) and cognitive approaches competed for acceptance as the solution to how skills are acquired and developed. The period from the1950s onwards heralded changes in thinking and many new advances in this area. Today there are still many unanswered questions and no single theory has been able to provide the solution. Questions like, How are new movements performed? What cognitive

TABLE 2.3 Key points of recent theories of movement learning and performance

Information-processing theory *Welford (1968)*	Closed-loop theory *Adams (1971)*	Schema theory *Schmidt (1975)*	Dynamic systems theory *Thelen and Smith (1994)*
Original idea proposed the Black Box model. Allies information processing to a computer with input and output. *Input* refers to the information available in the environment. Internal processes (perception, organisation, decision-making) lead to movement output. Emphasises internal and external feedback. Information is stored in motor programmes.	Dissatisfaction with stimulus–response theory. Did not explain 'why' movements are produced. Movements initiated by a memory trace, e.g. experience. Movements controlled by a perceptual trace, e.g. a reference that compares feedback from the movement. Skill arises from matching perceptual trace and feedback through practice.	Believes that every movement is different (unlike Adams). Model emphasises experience, feedback and error correction. Proposed that our brains cannot contain a memory for every single movement action. Memory stores contain relationships (schemas) rather than specific movements. Practice cements these relationships.	Rejects idea of skill development in predetermined stages. Perception is direct and does not require memory. Perception and action combine. Movement is self-organising. Joints, muscles and nerves work together to create movement. Is functionally specific, e.g. kicking a ball. Goal achievement is connected to affordances (opportunities in the environment).

processes are involved in controlling fast and slow actions? What is the role of the environment in movement skill learning? remain hotly debated. What is certain is that the combined wisdom of these different approaches has increased our knowledge of this area considerably.

The key points of four recent theories are presented in Table 2.3. Rather than view these as four separate and competing 'manifestos', readers are encouraged to consult the recommended further reading at the end of the chapter for more detailed information.

Earlier in this chapter the concept of a movement alphabet was introduced and movement concepts were likened to adverbs. The second component of this alphabet are movement skills which in turn may be likened to verbs. Both movement concepts and movement skills are essential in a quality programme of physical education: movement skills define *what* actions children perform in PE lessons and movement concepts characterise *how* these may be performed. Using running as an example to illustrate this point, a child may run (skill) but may do so in a variety of ways, e.g. forwards and alongside a partner (concept). By itself, the skill of running is bland but, by colouring it with one or more movement concepts, it becomes interesting, varied and challenging for the performer.

What are the typical movement skills which children up to the age of 11 display in PE? Knowledge of child development informs that young children need to master three prime categories of movement for survival and effective interaction with the world around them (Gallahue, 1993). In their first two years of life they need to strive towards an upright sitting and standing posture (*stability*); be able to move with efficiency (*locomotion*) and have meaningful contact with objects with hands and feet (*manipulation*). These rudimentary movements are part of a continuum of movement that progresses through the years of schooling from fundamental movement skills in the Foundation Stage and Key Stage 1 to specialised sports skills in Key Stages 3 and 4.

Stability

This is the building block of all future movement. It involves children establishing and maintaining their bodies' relationship to gravity. From the outset it has direct association with posture and how they support their bodies as the centre of gravity is changed. A fine example of this is in gymnastic movements that extend from the base of support in static balances such as stork balances, arabesques and handstands to dynamic balances like cartwheels, where the centre of gravity shifts as limbs move away. Stability is also needed for axial movements that involve the body bending and twisting in a stationary position. As children's movement skill repertoire increases, these axial movements are intrinsic to actions in diving, swimming and tumbling activities.

Locomotion

This aspect is concerned with the body moving through space. The body is projected in space by changing its position in relation to fixed points. Typically, children in the Foundation Stage have achieved some degree of competence in a skill like running, but require opportunities for practice and improvement for progress in the skill alone or so that it can be linked with other skills, such as bouncing a ball. Curriculum requirements at Key Stage 2 for games demand some level of competency in many of the locomotor skills and a lack of proficiency will impede enjoyment and progress in activities such as soccer, netball, hockey, basketball, etc.

Manipulation

For younger children, skills here provide meaningful contact with objects in the immediate world. Manipulation itself is characterised by the relationship to the object in terms of applying force to it or receiving force from it. Hands and feet therefore

TABLE 2.4 Categories of movement showing fundamental movement skills

Stability skills	Locomotion skills	Manipulation skills
Bending	Walking	Handling
Stretching	Running	Ball rolling
Twisting	Chasing	Kicking
Turning	Vertical jumping	Throwing
Reaching	Distance jumping	Catching
Swaying	Hopping	Trapping
Pushing	Galloping	Striking
Pulling	Sliding	Punting
Swinging	Leaping	Dribbling
Dodging	Skipping	Volleying
Rolling	Bouncing	Stopping
Balancing	Climbing	

become the most frequent manipulators. Propulsion is involved in sending an object such as a ball or beanbag with different degrees of force, and absorption is involved in cushioning the impact of an object in receiving it. There need to be plentiful opportunities for children to engage in PE lessons in throwing and catching activities with a variety of different sizes, shapes and weights to develop competency in manipulation. Examples of skills within each of the three movement categories are shown in Table 2.4.

Children developing movement skills

Movement skills and their development are intrinsic to the whole PE experience. Factors including developmental readiness, clear and informed instruction, teacher feedback, adequate practice time and motivation contribute to skill learning and improvement. The literature also suggests that proficiency in movement development occurs sequentially (Wickstrom, 1983; Graham *et al.*, 1993; Bailey, 2000). David Gallahue (1982), for instance, proposes two concepts upon which improvement in movement skill learning depends:

(1) Movement skills progress from simple to complex.
(2) Skills proceed gradually from general to specific.

In considering the first of these, it is obvious that children need to master skills such as balancing, hopping, skipping, throwing and catching before more complicated and activity-specific skills such as passing, dribbling, shooting at a goal in games and various specific gymnastics actions are tackled. With regard to the second point, it also follows that when early skills such as walking and running are acquired, children need time and proper instruction to enable them to refine and perform these and other physical skills with increased control and fluency (Haywood and Getchell, 1993). This progression in Gallahue's model establishes a hierarchy that mirrors progression in children's movement skills from the Foundation Stage through to the end of Key Stage 2. Its five stages are presented below and are returned to later in the book, under guidance on teaching skills. For the present the stages are:

1. *Exploration* – a pre-control stage where children try to understand the pattern or skill and form a general framework of it.
2. *Discovery* – an early stage involving learning through indirect means such as watching others rather than formal instruction.
3. *Combination* – involves experimentation with isolated movements in various ways.
4. *Selection* – smoothes out the whole of several skill-related tasks through lead-up games and informal challenges.
5. *Refinement* - selected movements are refined and often performed formally in competition. Skills are automatic by this stage.

(Gallahue, 1982, p. 45)

The development of movement skills, from the reflexes and reactions of the newborn to the increasingly refined and specialist movement patterns used in various sport and PE activities, provides this progression. Figure 2.2 shows a way of conceptualising movement skills for children 3–11 that draws upon a number of similar models.

At the base of the diagram are the first movements in the womb and those the child makes as a newborn baby. Newborns possess a repertoire of early movements such as head turning, grasping, performing 'swimming' type actions with arms and legs and even recognisable stepping. Because of neurological immaturity, complete control of voluntary action is not yet possible and so many other actions are reflexive responses. Extending their arms outward when the head is moved forward (Moro reflex), gripping tightly on to an object (Plantar grasp) and the Symmetrical and Asymmetrical Tonic Neck reflexes, allowing flexion and extension of limbs in response to head turning, are exhibited along with other reflexes. As the brain develops, most of these reflexes are replaced by voluntary actions of turning, rolling and twisting movements and the child gains more postural control. By the second year this has advanced considerably, leading to the child being able to sit upright, stand, balance and walk, shown in the diagram as rudimentary movements.

From age 3, children have achieved a great deal of important motor milestones and from this stage onwards display the movement skills that are at the very heart of physical education – skills such as skipping, dodging, throwing, bouncing, etc. This is a gradual increase and occurs at different times for individual children. In the early stage of running, witness the flat-footed action with little knee-bend, legs swinging

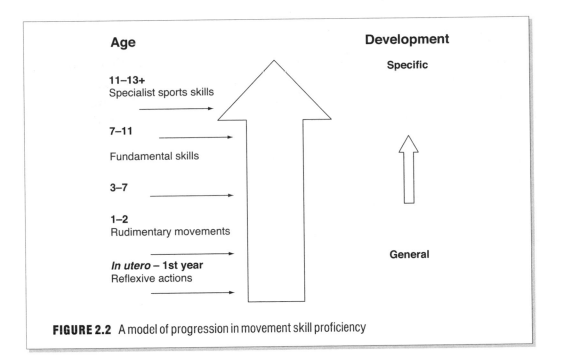

FIGURE 2.2 A model of progression in movement skill proficiency

out and minimal involvement from the arms, and time off the ground being very limited. By the mid to late primary years, the skill (as a consequence of maturation and experience) has developed considerably. At this stage we can observe the length of the stride increasing, enabling greater speed, greater flexion of the knee, more involvement from the arms and greater overall extension of the whole body. Even to the untrained eye, the child at this more advanced level has much greater proficiency in this skill.

The fundamental skills (e.g. running, jumping, skipping, balancing, etc.) are those that children from 3 to 11 are principally concerned with acquiring and developing. It is these skills that form the basis of the physical education programme in the Foundation Stage curriculum and all NCPE activity areas in Key Stages 1 and 2. Helping children to progress these skills is therefore a prime concern for physical educators.

Task 7 Skills

Take one skill from any of the three movement categories (stability, locomotion and manipulation). Observe two children performing the *same* movement skill at different levels of proficiency (they may or may not be the same age). Child A is learning the skill. Child B has achieved some proficiency in the same skill. Record what you see for both children.

The following prompts should help your observations:

■ What was your overall impression of how this skill was performed?

■ Describe what the leg action was.

■ Describe what the arm action was.

■ How would you describe the overall body shape?

■ How well was the skill being performed?

■ As a physical educator, what suggestions can you make for *both* children to improve?

Chapter summary

In this chapter three important components of physical education experiences were discussed. Information about the overall development of children in the early years and extending through to age 11 was given, and links were made between all areas of development. Second, movement was presented as a cornerstone of PE as well as very much as part of the whole human condition. There followed a discussion on the role of movement and education with examples from the three categories given. Factors allied to skill were presented and four recent theories in motor learning were summarised. The chapter concluded by showing how movement skill is progressed from birth to 11, highlighting that improvement in movement skill progresses from simple to complex and from general to specific movements.

Questions for reflection

■ Do you think it is important that all physical educators have knowledge of child development?

■ Is it necessary to know about other aspects of development or have knowledge of physical development only?

■ In this chapter, movement was presented as a cornerstone of physical education experiences. Is this reflected in all phases of PE? Is it equally reflected?

■ What priority is given to children learning motor skills as they progress through the primary school PE curriculum?

Further reading

Buschner, C. (1994) *Teaching Children Movement Concepts and Skills.* Champaign: Illinois: Human Kinetics.
Chapters 1 and 3 give a very sound rationale for embedding movement into the PE curriculum.

Gallahue, D.L. and Ozmun, J. (1998) *Understanding Motor Development – Infants, Children, Adolescents, Adults.* Dubuque, Iowa: McGraw-Hill.
A classic text in motor development but one that makes good links to PE. Theoretical, but a really good text.

Schmidt, R.A and Wrisberg, C. (2000) *Motor Learning and Performance.* Champaign, Illinois: Human Kinetics.
Technical book that goes into skill and skilled performance in depth. Some prior knowledge of theories of motor learning might be needed. Adopts an information-processing approach to motor learning.

Sharp, B. (1992) *Acquiring Skill in Sport.* Eastbourne, UK: Sports Dynamics.
For those who wish to find out more about skill and performance. It is not a curriculum book but is an accessible read full of useful information.

Thomas, J.R., Lee, A.M. and Thomas, K.T. (1988) *Physical Education for Children.* Champaign, Illinois: Human Kinetics.
Part 1 has general chapters on development and skill which are very readable.

Issues in physical education today

Chapter objectives

By the end of this chapter you should be able to:

■ Identify key issues with regard to contemporary PE;

■ Understand how these wider issues relate to teaching and learning in school-based PE;

■ Appreciate how these broader issues raise questions about the future of PE in primary schools.

The wider picture

THIS CHAPTER IS AIMED AT providing as wide a perspective on PE as possible by introducing some of the key issues relevant to the teaching and learning of the subject in schools. We believe that it is important and healthy for practitioners to reflect on and debate core issues that impact upon the way we think about, plan and deliver PE in our schools. The following topics are selected on the basis that they raise important questions about the place of PE in school, both currently and in future:

■ Inclusion of all learners;

■ Equal opportunities – gender;

■ Accountability in PE;

■ High quality PE;

■ PE and Sport Education;

■ Physical literacy;

■ Addressing the needs of the more able pupil.

Physical education for *all* pupils

The introduction of the National Curriculum established that it was a statutory requirement for all state schools to provide *all* children with a broad and balanced curriculum including physical education. The most recent revision of the National Curriculum for Physical Education (1999) featured a new explicit emphasis on schools ensuring that their practices are inclusive. However, Penney (2002) warns that, for many, the terms 'inclusion', 'inclusive practice', 'equality' and 'equity' are most often treated as dealing with 'the same things' (p. 111). Whilst recognising that there are important and subtle differences in meaning between these terms, we argue that catering for the needs of all pupils in physical education and school sport requires schools, and the teachers within them, to reflect on the extent to which they address the challenges of 'difference' and 'fairness'. Some key questions are:

- How well does our PE curriculum meet the needs of those pupils performing *below*, *at* or *above* the expected levels?

- Do *all* learners enjoy the same opportunities to participate, learn and improve in curriculum PE and extra-curricular activities?

- How well does the PE curriculum and extra-curricular programme of the school reflect the needs and interests of all learners?

- In PE and school sport terms, can we distinguish one 'group' of learners from another (*girls, boys, minority ethnic pupils, motor elite/motor impaired, developmentally mature/immature, overweight/underweight,* etc.)?

- How concerned are we to develop strategies that target the participation and improvement of specific groups of learners in PE and school sport?

Searching for answers to these questions is likely to reveal uncomfortable truths about the extent to which curriculum PE and extra-curricular activities provide *some* pupils with access and opportunity to participate in *certain* activities in *certain* ways. The traditions of physical education and the architecture of schools are clearly influential factors here and present significant barriers to progress. Yet change is underway and progress is being made. In this chapter we highlight some of the key challenges facing physical education in our changing world and provide examples of the ways in which teachers and schools are developing practice in physical education to the benefit of all.

Boys and girls come out to play – gender issues in PE

From birth, children are unwitting participants in a process of differentiation that determines appropriate and expected behaviours dependent on sex. The ways in which physical education and sport can contribute to and challenge gender identity construction is the subject of this section. A quick glance at the structure and practices of the PE curriculum from the Foundation Stage through to the end of Key Stage 2 reveals a gradual parting of the ways between the sexes. Whilst early organised physical activity experiences are conceived of and delivered as 'gender-free', with pupils changing together, playing and learning together and using the same equipment, by the end of Key Stage 2 pupils may well be changing separately and playing different activities in single-sex groups.

In examining today's physical education curriculum, Fernandez-Balboa has forced us to re-examine our practices. With the intent to raise awareness on the part of physical educators, he contends that there are existing taken-for-granted patterns of behaviour and features of what is referred to as the hidden curriculum (content, pedagogy) that dramatically contribute to the inequities and social injustices of society. These behaviours and curriculum features reinforce an ideology, which ultimately serves the interests of the status quo. The hidden curriculum communicates social values, norms and beliefs that students learn, perhaps more than anything else. Fernandez-Balboa's analysis (1993) of the hidden curriculum in physical education is convincing and insightful. He argues that through the hidden curriculum in physical education powerful messages are sent out to both girls and boys which have a lasting impact throughout their adult lives on their interactions with one another. While there are many educationally sound physical education programmes, there are still many that have inequities and that continue to promote gender-role stereotyping.

In the area of NCPE Games for instance, strong gender traditions have meant that boys' experience within and outside school serve to channel them towards football and rugby whilst girls will be channelled towards hockey and netball. Such processes are now, rightly, subject to question on the grounds of fairness. The result of challenging 'natural' assumptions has been liberating, particularly for girls. It is now increasingly common for mixed groups of pupils to participate in the revised introductory versions of, for example netball (High Fives netball) and rugby (TAG rugby) in primary schools whilst the nationwide growth in popularity of girls' football speaks volumes about the potential momentum generated when a shift in attitudes facilitates access and opportunity in specific activities. Accompanying the long overdue review of gender marking of activities has been a greater sensitivity towards the gendered nature of language used in PE. Unless the language of PE can become more equitable, children will continue to receive subliminal messages during PE and school sport that privilege particular forms of masculinity, regardless of the activities that they experience.

> ## Task 8 Gender labelling
>
> Sort the following activities into three gender-assigned lists: 'Female', 'Neutral' and 'Male'.
>
> - Ice dance, rugby, hockey, football, rounders, lacrosse, volleyball, archery, gymnastics, tennis, skiing, rally driving, kick-boxing, aerobics, surfing, skateboarding, cycling, triathlon, judo, badminton.
> - What are the common characteristics of activities that have become marked as essentially 'male' or essentially 'female' or gender neutral?
> - Why are some activities more difficult to assign than others?

Creating fairer access to activity opportunities, however, does not guarantee fairer access to learning. Irrespective of whether mixed or single-sex grouping is employed, or novel or traditional activities pursued, not all pupils will necessarily access the same quality of learning experience in PE lessons. Ability is recognised as being a key variable shaping pupils' experiences of PE and school sport and their potential to access the opportunities on offer. Differentiation through structuring the learning experience according to the needs of learners and designing tasks to promote learning and enjoyment for all is fundamental to inclusive practice. Recognising and catering for difference in PE should not be targeted at attaining equal outcomes (Talbot, 1993) but at ensuring that all pupils have the opportunity to access the knowledge, skills and understanding that is appropriate to their different levels of learning.

It is quite simple really: if there are no opportunities for a pupil to be successful, then they are not fully included and the activities need adapting in the future. As will be seen in the chapters that follow, modifications to the equipment used, the playing areas and/or the rules to make tasks easier or more difficult are a good starting point. Focusing on what the pupils *can* do, negotiating challenging, transparent and achievable targets for all pupils, and celebrating pupils' success when such targets are achieved, represent significant positive steps towards becoming more inclusive in PE.

The issue of accountability

Ever since Labour Prime Minister James Callaghan's Ruskin College address in 1976 sparked a healthy and urgent review of the role of school 'subjects' there has been a tendency to make extravagant claims for the benefits accruing from participation in PE and school sport. By way of illustration, Armour (2006) questions the aims of the United Nation's International Year for Sport and Physical Education (2005) as a means to promote education, health, development *and peace*, suggesting that such claims can only be made because rarely, if ever, is anyone actually held accountable for failing to attain such lofty goals. Teachers of PE are not immune from such proclamations. Armour and Yelling, (2004) report that teachers identified an ambitious mix of health and social goals as the intended learning outcomes from their PE programmes. Furthermore, claims made for the outcomes of professional development for PE teachers can also be rather optimistic. For example, the new National PE Continuing Professional Development (CPD) Programme for teachers in England specifies five key outcomes, including the claims that it will raise the attainment of *all* pupils and enhance links between PE and physical activity/health. Such claims are made precisely because it is unlikely that any teacher, or CPD provider, will ever be held fully account able for them. The likelihood that the attainment of *all* pupils will rise as a direct result of this programme is extremely difficult to evidence and thus the issue of accountability, according to Armour, is fudged. By engaging in such rhetoric, Armour suggests, practitioners and policy makers neatly avoid having to make the kinds of dramatic changes to curriculum and pedagogy that meeting such claims demand. One of the key issues therefore, that practitioners and policy makers for PE need to address is what is PE to be held accountable for – physical activity rates of young people, the number of Olympic medals won, the girth of the nation's waistlines? Physical activity rates of young people are clearly likely to be influenced by the experiences that pupils receive whilst in school but are too heavily dependent on a wide range of factors outside the control of teachers in school (such as transport, economics and opportunity) for teachers to legitimately be held accountable for this measure. Similarly the journey from 'first taster' session to Olympic champion is long and complex, and whilst in some cases a seed may be sown during PE experiences, drawing a direct connection between PE in school and elite international sporting performance is unacceptably tenuous. The fact that in PE teachers promote the health benefits of exercise and equip pupils with the essential knowledge, skills and understanding to exercise safely and appropriately does not mean that teachers would wish to be held accountable for a pupil's subsequent lifestyle choice of inactivity. This, after all, may be much more in tune with their domestic and cultural influences than their educational experiences. So what of the role of PE in tackling the reported obesity 'epidemic' (Evans *et al.*, 2003)? It is widely accepted that attempting to encourage young people to be physically active as part of a strategy to tackle obesity or overweight is far from straightforward. Accepting responsibility for the popularity of physical activity amongst young people is one thing but accountability for food choices surely falls collectively on a number of groups, including parents, manufacturers, retailers, advertisers, legislators at all levels and students themselves.

The key feature that emerges from this discussion is that by focusing on accountability, physical educators are presented with a difficult choice. Surely we are to be held accountable, for something and it would seem sensible to us that we should be accountable for activity rates/choices amongst young people during the school day.

If it is not the role of physical education to inspire young people and equip them to take up activity, then what is its role? As Armour (2006) points out, the challenge associated with being accountable is that we are forced to confront the consequences of our actions. In PE this means facing up to the harsh reality that continuing with a traditional programme and traditional pedagogy in the face of a changing world is not sustainable. In a climate in which young people expect to exercise choice, exhibit sophisticated tastes and have a huge array of interests competing for their limited leisure time, a traditional PE programme is rendered meaningless for the vast majority of young people. Accepting the challenge of accountability ultimately means that PE will in the medium to long term have to change what it claims, what it does, or both. To ensure that we make the right decisions, the challenge for the short term is to nurture a culture of evidence-based practice within PE and embed systems for collecting evidence of the impact of the PE programme on pupils' lives.

Task 9 School documentation and accountability

Take a look at the prospectus/general information/policy documentation of your school.

- Are any specific claims for physical education *made* here?
- Are any specific claims *implied* here for physical education?
- Are you happy to be held personally accountable for these claims in relation to the pupils you teach?

List some of the issues that are likely to assist/hinder meeting the claims made implied.

It seems fair to us that PE practitioners should be held partially accountable for young people's activity choices and they should be more diligent in collecting data to evidence the impact of PE provision on pupils' activity rates. This data could then be used to analyse who takes up which opportunities and, more crucially, who does not. We argue that this type of evidence-based reflection is vital if we are to ensure that PE remains relevant to young people. The experiences offered through a school's PE and sport programmes should therefore be sensitive to the interests and experiences of all pupils and be more reflective of the dynamic society in which we now live.

High quality PE and school sport for *all* children

Until recently, subject leaders for physical education fought a lonely struggle over access to curriculum time and resources. The identification of a national standard of a minimum of two hours high quality physical education (Public Service Agreement,

2002) has shifted the debate from *time* to *quality* of provision. Whilst governors and head teachers ultimately carry the responsibility for making adjustments to the curriculum allocation to facilitate meeting the time-allocation target, PE subject leaders and their colleagues carry accountability for the provision of high quality experiences in this time. The first step towards meeting the challenge of providing high quality physical education (HQPE) for all pupils is agreeing what the phrase means in practice. The Qualifications and Curriculum Authority identify ten outcomes to aid teachers, parents and school authorities to assess the quality of the experience offered. The outcomes for HQPE in brief are:

- Pupils are committed to PE and sport and make them a central part of their lives, in and out of school.
- Pupils know and understand what they are trying to achieve and know how to go about doing it.
- Pupils understand that PE and sport are an important part of a healthy active lifestyle.
- Pupils have the confidence to get involved in PE and school sport.
- Pupils have the skills and control they need to take part in PE and school sport.
- Pupils willingly take part in a range of competitive, creative and challenge type activities.
- Pupils think about what they are doing and make appropriate decisions for themselves.
- Pupils show a desire to improve and achieve in relation to their own abilities.
- Pupils have the stamina, suppleness and strength to keep going.
- Pupils enjoy PE, school and community sport.

(For further guidance go to: http://www.qca.org.uk/pess/7.htm)

Whilst the achievement of these outcomes will help to determine whether provision in any context has been of high quality, practitioners may need further guidance along the way. For this reason, accompanying each outcome is a series of performance indicators and suggestions to help teachers, head teachers and other providers to compare their provision against. The recognition that teachers, administrators and outside providers share joint responsibility for ensuring that the quality of provision is maintained and that they need to work together towards achieving the goal of HQPE and school sport is a significant step forward. Table 3.1 identifies some of the key issues that both schools and sports organisations should be working towards in order to deliver the ambition of providing all pupils with access to a minimum of two hours HQPE during curriculum time and a further two to three hours high quality school sport during out of school hours learning (OSHL).

TABLE 3.1 Key issues in the delivery of high quality PE

1. Creating the vision

Head teachers	Sports club leaders/administrators
■ recognise what PE and school sport can achieve for each pupil and the whole school;	■ recognise what their sport can achieve for each young member and the whole club;
■ set high expectations of what individual pupils/ participants and the whole school/club can achieve in and through PE and school sport;	■ set high expectations of what each young member and the whole club can achieve in and through their sport;
■ explain the value of PE and school sport to learning, health and well-being in a way that pupils, teachers, parents and governors can understand.	■ explain the value of their sport to learning, health and well-being in a way that young members, coaches, parents and the local community can understand.

2. Inspiring young people to learn and achieve

Teachers	Sports coaches
■ show commitment and enthusiasm and provide positive role models;	■ show commitment and enthusiasm and provide positive role models;
■ show confidence in their pupils' ability to make progress and achieve;	■ show confidence in their young members' ability to make progress and achieve;
■ listen to their pupils and value what they say and do;	■ listen to their young members and value what they say and do;
■ raise their pupils' aspirations and increase their determination to make progress and succeed;	■ raise their young members' aspirations and increase their determination to make progress and succeed;
■ have pride in and celebrate their pupils' successes;	■ have pride in and celebrate their young members' successes;
■ let pupils' parents/carers know what they have learnt and achieved in PE and school sport;	■ let young members' parents/carers know what they have achieved;
■ improve their own subject expertise.	■ improve their own knowledge of how to work with young people of different ages.

3. Helping young people to learn and achieve

Teachers	Sports coaches
■ have a clear plan that sets out steps towards meeting the school's vision and expectations for PE and school sport;	■ have a planned programme of activities that sets out steps towards meeting the club's vision and expectations for the sport;
■ share with pupils what they expect them to achieve in a way that they can understand;	■ share with young members what they expect them to achieve in a way that they can understand

continued on next page

TABLE 3.1 continued

■ take into account what pupils have already learnt within and beyond school;	■ take into account what young members have already learnt within and beyond the club;
■ identify the next steps in progression and communicate them to pupils and their parents/carers;	■ identify the next steps in progression and communicate them to young members and their parents/carers;
■ give each pupil relevant learning activities and authentic contexts that interest, excite and motivate them;	■ give each young member relevant learning activities that interest, excite and motivate them;
■ provide opportunities for pupils to analyse, assess and evaluate their own and others' work;	■ give young members opportunities to analyse, assess and evaluate their own progress and achievement;
■ give pupils time to think, reflect and make decisions for themselves;	■ give young members time to think, reflect and make decisions for themselves;
■ allow pupils time to wrestle with problems, while giving well-timed advice and support to advance learning and avoid frustration;	■ allow young members time to wrestle with problems, while giving well-timed advice and support to advance learning and avoid frustration;
■ ensure that they use time, staff, equipment and resources in ways that keep pupils interested and learning.	■ ensure that they use time, staff, equipment and resources in ways that keep young members interested and learning.

(Source: Adapted from DfES/DCMS (2004) *High Quality PE and Sport for Young People* available at http://www.qca.org.uk/pess/pdf/high.quality. guide.pdf)

The theme of working in partnership is picked up again in Chapter 10 and will be an important feature of physical education as we look forward to key national events in the early twenty-first century, not least the Olympic Games in London in 2012. Perhaps the time is right to consider alternative approaches to the design and delivery of physical education programmes in order to ensure that pupils are fully equipped to take advantage of the activity opportunities they will be presented with throughout their post-school lives. For this reason some schools are remodelling their PE programmes along the lines of sport education.

Sport education

Sport education is a curriculum model designed for delivery in physical education Key Stages 2, 3 and 4. It is intended to provide children and young people with more authentic and enjoyable sport experiences than those typically offered in traditional physical education classes. This model was developed and introduced in the USA by Daryl Siedentop in 1984 and has since been adapted and successfully implemented for pupils of varying ages in many different countries.

Starting from the premise that sport is different from other types of physical activity, Siedentop (1994) suggests that there are six distinguishing features of competitive sport. These are that:

1 Sport is played in seasons.

2 Participants affiliate to named teams.

3 Competition and practice sessions blend together throughout a season.

4 Records of individual and team performance provide feedback to participants and encourage goal setting for improvement.

5 Individual and team performances are recognised and celebrated through a concluding festival event (as in a World Cup/championship tournament).

6 Sport is exciting, unpredictable and meaningful to participants and spectators alike, and this is reflected in a sport season.

In an effort to recreate the essence of sport in an educational context, sport education involves the equitable arrangement of participants into teams for the duration of a 'season', which is typically longer than the normal PE unit of work. Throughout this period pupils take an active role in their own sport experience by serving in varied and realistic roles that we see in authentic sport settings. In addition to serving as players, pupils decide on the allocation of other roles and responsibilities such as captains, coaches, trainers, statisticians, officials, publicists, and members of a sports council. Teams develop camaraderie through team uniforms, names, and cheers as they work together to learn and develop skill and tactical play.

The three underpinning goals that guide the sport education process are for pupils to become *competent, literate,* and *enthusiastic* players. Siedentop (1994) defines these as follows:

- A *competent player* has sufficient skills to participate satisfactorily, can execute strategies that are appropriate for the complexity of the game being played, and is a knowledgeable player.

- A *literate player* understands and values the rules, rituals, and traditions of sport, and is able to distinguish between good and bad sport practices in a variety of sport settings.

- An *enthusiastic player* is one who preserves, protects, and enhances the sport culture through participation, involvement, and appropriate behaviour.

To achieve these goals, participants in sport education programmes must:

1 Develop skills and fitness specific to particular sports/activities;

2 Appreciate and be able to execute strategic play in sports;

3 Participate at a level appropriate to their stage of development;

4 Share in the planning and administration of sport experiences;

5 Provide responsible leadership;

6 Work effectively within a group towards common goals;

7 Appreciate the rituals and conventions that give particular sports their unique meanings;

8 Develop the capacity to make reasoned decisions about issues that arise in sport contexts;

9 Develop and apply knowledge about umpiring, refereeing, and training;

10 Decide voluntarily to become involved in after-school sport.

Table 3.2 identifies what a sport education season may look like in a Key Stage 2 context.

TABLE 3.2 Understanding sport education in a Key Stage 2 context

Season week	Content
1	Teachers observe and assess ability of pupils' individual skills.
2	Further teacher observation and assessment of pupils' team skills.
3	Meet with all Year 5 pupils to explain and discuss sport education. Pupils informed of teams and encouraged to discuss and agree a team name. Introduction of portfolios and team display boards.
4–7	Pre-season training – teacher-led. Pupils encouraged to practise the role of reporter, warm-up coach, scorekeeper and equipment manager whilst also being active playing members of their teams.
8–11	Round-robin formal competition (5 v 5). Team T-shirts designed and printed.
12	Festival Day. All teams play one match (5 v 5) to decide their finishing position. Medals awarded to all students as well as the winning team, most improved team and most improved player.

(Source: MacPhail *et al.*, 2005 p. 125)

Task 10 Assessing the value of sport education

Consider some of the risks and benefits associated with adopting a sport education model for physical education in the primary school.

Risks	Benefits
	Pupils experience the demands of roles other than player.
Longer 'seasons' would disrupt the timetable.	
	All pupils experience the excitement of team competition.
Participation in sport becomes the principal focus of physical education lessons.	
	Pupils are keen to participate in extra-curricular activity to continue their involvement.

Is sport education the future for physical educataion? What do you think?

Sport education offers an interesting alternative to the typical physical education programme offered in schools in the UK. It can be adapted to accommodate participation in each of the six named activity areas of the National Curriculum and to take account of younger pupils' relative inexperience. Whilst sport education casts pupils as active participants in their own learning it relies upon the teacher successfully modelling the roles and responsibilities that pupils are required to adopt in order to be effective. For all but the most confident and experienced teachers, the challenge of trialling this form of innovation in isolation could prove a step too far. Whilst we see enormous potential in the sport education model we also argue that it is likely to work best in schools with large classes, with ample PE equipment/facilities, where the class teacher is able to access additional 'adult' support during lesson time and where two or more colleagues collaborate in its introduction. Adopting a sport education approach in PE should not be seen as an all-or-nothing decision. We suggest that it can be successfully deployed alongside a conventional physical education programme. Trialling a sport education approach in the teaching of athletics throughout the summer term might be a good introduction to the process for teachers and pupils alike and could culminate in a celebration of achievement in an inter-year group athletics festival.

Providing a varied menu of experience for pupils both in terms of activities studied and pedagogy selected is, we argue, more important than advocating one approach as being preferable to any other. What sport education does offer practitioners is an unequivocal articulation of goals, something which physical education has seemingly been unable to offer teachers despite many years of discussion and debate. The goals of physical education vary according to time, place and source, serving often to leave classroom practitioners bemused. More recently, Whitehead has attempted to shift the debate to another level entirely. Her attempt to work towards a clear definition of the concept of physical literacy may ultimately prove more helpful in determining the goal of a physical education programme.

Physical literacy

Whitehead (2006) (with Murdoch) describes physical literacy as the 'motivation, confidence, physical competence, understanding and knowledge to maintain physical activity at an individually appropriate level, throughout life'.

Thus a physically literate individual will:

- move with poise, economy and confidence in a wide variety of physically challenging situations;
- be perceptive in 'reading' all aspects of the physical environment, anticipating movement needs or possibilities and responding appropriately to them, with intelligence and imagination;
- have a well-established sense of self;
- show an ability to identify and articulate the essential qualities that influence the effectiveness of his/her own movement performance;
- have an understanding of the principles of maintaining their health, in relation to exercise, sleep and nutrition.

The process of acquiring physical literacy, Whitehead (2006) argues, stretches across the lifespan. She identifies six stages of development in which the individual is likely to be presented with opportunities and experiences which will contribute to their confidence and competence as well as their knowledge and understanding of movement. These stages are broad approximations and are categorised as follows:

1 Birth to 4 years old;

2 Early childhood (the Foundation Stage and primary school years);

3 Adolescence (the secondary school years);

4 Early adulthood (the period following compulsory education);

5 Adulthood;

6 Older age.

For our purposes it is appropriate to consider in more detail the first stages in this process. In the first stage, the pre-school period, the foundations for the development of physical literacy are laid. It is important that at this stage all those with responsibility for the care of the child should seek out, encourage and support opportunities for movement development. The child should be exposed to movement opportunities in a range of different environments – in and around the home, the local environment, child care settings and activity clubs – conducive to developing a broad repertoire of movement experience. Developing physical literacy at this stage is significantly in the hands of the child's extended family.

In early childhood (the Foundation Stage and primary school years), the fundamentals of physical literacy need to be further developed and embedded (see Table 3.3). This is a crucial period when competences are developed and attitudes formed, none so important as motor competence and self-confidence in physical activity contexts. Burgeoning physical literacy can be seen in the young child's ability to co-ordinate the whole body in activities such as running, jumping, climbing and swimming and in the manual dexterity needed to thread, tie knots, colour-in and write. Developing physical literacy at this stage is significantly in the hands of teachers conducting physical education lessons, but also with adults leading activity clubs, sports coaches, parents, grandparents, siblings and peers. Environments that are

TABLE 3.3 Developing physical literacy from 3–11

Initial stages in attaining and maintaining physical literacy	
Motor development fostered, supported, encouraged	Development of physical literacy as a fundamental goal of physical education
	Fundamentals of physical literacy developed: motor competence, knowledge and understanding
Personnel influencing the attainment and maintenance of physical literacy	
Parents, family, significant others	Teachers, LSAs, parents, family, peers, coaches, club and local facility personnel
Contexts in which physical literacy can be encouraged, established and maintained	
Home, local environment, day care, nurseries, pre-school activity clubs	School physical education, extra-curricular opportunities, sports/activity clubs, home, local environment, local facilities

Adapted from www.physical-literacy.org.uk/plchart2006.doc

needed to support this stage of development include the school, the home, local clubs and open-access recreational facilities such as parks, cycle ways and woodland trails.

Catering for the most able in PE

The Department for Education and Skills (DfES) recognises that schools could do more to cater for the top 5–10 per cent of the ability range both within and outside curriculum time. Defining this small but significant cohort as gifted and/or talented the following definitions are usually cited: *Gifted* pupils are the most academically able in a school. *Talented* pupils are those with high ability or potential in art, music, performing arts, physical education or sport.

Raising the achievement of the most able pupils is likely to have an impact on all pupils within a school environment. Renzulli's (1998) analogy in relation to able, gifted and talented provision that 'a rising tide lifts all ships' is supported by Ofsted's Chief Inspector of Schools who argues that schools willing to deal effectively with the needs of able pupils will raise the achievement of all pupils.

Initially launched as part of the Excellence in Cities (EiC) initiative in 1999, the provision of specific programmes for gifted and talented pupils has since become an expectation of all schools. So far as addressing the needs of the gifted and talented in PE is concerned the PE school sport and club links strategy (PESSCL), launched in 2002, identifies provision for gifted and talented pupils as one of its eight core strands of development. Working in partnerships with local sports organisations and national governing bodies of sport, this strand suggests that schools should work collaboratively to provide, amongst other things, access to:

- Local multi-skill academies;
- National performance camps (organised by governing bodies);
- Web-based resources for teachers, parents and coaches;
- A support programme for teachers of talented pupils;

(For further information visit http://www.talentladder.org and http://www.talent matters.org)

The ambition of this programme is to raise the attainment, aspirations, motivation and self-esteem of talented pupils through improving the range and quality of teaching, coaching and learning that takes place in school and during out of hours learning.

Talent development

The role of classroom practitioners in schools and early years settings in the development of talent in sport is not entirely clear. Whilst most models of talent development are based on the assumption that curriculum PE lays the foundation for sports performance, how well schools are doing in meeting the needs of the talented can be measured against the quality standards for physical education. Morley and Bailey (2006) argue that these standards provide a series of outcome statements that reflect the different degrees of good practice, from the basic to the exemplary and are supplemented by strategies and tools that can help schools to improve their provision. The quality standards are organised around six core themes: policy, professional development, identification and selection, teaching and provision, supporting talented pupils and managing talent in physical education. This framework should prove useful in future in enabling schools to prioritise areas for development and providing tangible standards to aim for. Table 3.4 illustrates the way in which the standards can be used for schools to audit their current provision and aspire to move to the next level.

TABLE 3.4 Auditing gifted and talented pupils through the standards

Quality standards for physical education

Theme: Teaching and provision for G&T pupils

Guiding principles	Requisite standards	Improving standards	Exemplary standards
Planning for talented pupils in PE considers progression across key stages, activity areas, core strands and other subject areas.	There are opportunities for observation and discussion with colleagues in other age phases and subject areas.	There are regular opportunities for PE teachers to observe and discuss good practice in provision for talented pupils both within their own and partnership schools.	There is a structured programme of opportunities for PE teachers to observe good practice in providing for talented pupils both in other schools and other subject areas.
	Talented pupils are offered opportunities to work with either other G&T pupils within their own school or talented pupils in PE in other schools.	Talented pupils in PE have opportunities to work alongside pupils with gifts and talents in other subject areas and in other schools.	Talented pupils in PE engage in a structured programme of activities in which they work alongside pupils with gifts and talents in other subject areas and in other schools.
Effective provision for talented pupils has a positive impact on the education of all pupils.	There are opportunities, within both curricular and extra-curricular time for providing for talented pupils in PE.	Provision for talented pupils is an embedded feature of curriculum PE.	The focus of provision in schools for talented pupils in PE is firmly located within curricular PE, and reflects NC requirements.
	Pupils regard gifts and talents as positive attributes.	Pupils celebrate their talents and those of others.	Pupils regard talent development in PE as part of an over-arching philosophy of achievement and aspiration for all pupils.

(Source: Adapted from Quality Standards for Physical Education available at http://www.talentladder.org/tl.supp.curr.qs.html)

Morley and Bailey (2006) point out that despite there being little evidence to demonstrate that PE actually does provide an appropriate base for the development of sports performance, many of the existing national sports development systems have PE at the base of a pyramid-shaped model. More recently, two important models for talent development have emerged from the academic literature and from research with sports organisations. Balyi's (2001) Long Term Athlete Development model recognises the importance of playing at lots of different activities in the early stages but, whilst conceding that different sports require different stages of specialisation, it identifies five key stages of development, which we summarise here:

1 The *FUNdamental* stage is characterised by structured fun, games activities designed to help develop core movement skills, agility, balance and co-ordination. At this stage children are encouraged to play.

2 The *Learning to Train* stage is characterised by the teaching of specific movement skills to lay the foundation for sports specificity. Children are introduced to basic strength, flexibility and speed development activity and participate in structured age-appropriate competition.

3 During the *Training to Train* stage children will learn about their fitness and how it can be improved whilst also developing sport-specific techniques.

4 In the *Training to Compete* stage, learning to prepare for competition is the key. By this stage, young people will be engaged in a structured intensive training programme planned around an agreed competitive season.

5 In the final stage, *Training to Win*, the maturing athlete learns to apply their physical and psychological training to best effect in a competitive arena.

The model proposed by Cote and Hay (2002) suggests that pupils experience a 'sampling phase', between the ages of 8 and 14, in which they engage in a wide range of sporting activities.

Chapter summary

The message emerging from these more recent developments is that schools and teachers need to provide sufficiently stimulating and interesting physical education programmes to nurture pupils' interests, skills and competencies early on. Enabling pupils to develop their full potential however involves working in partnership with outside providers and creating pathways for progression for those that seek to specialise or merely recreate in their own time.

Questions for reflection

- How do the issues raised in this chapter relate to your own teaching context?

- These are some contemporary issues. What 'new' issues might arise in the foreseeable future?

Web links and further reading

For practical ideas relating to inclusion in PE, try the 'Success for All' CD-ROM which is free from the DfES through Prolog (email dfes@prolog.uk.com). The section on the Inclusion Spectrum details a variety of methods which can be employed to create an effective inclusive setting.

National Association of Gifted Children http://www.nagcbritain.org.uk/www.sportengland.org

Good site with policy documents accessible and easy to download.

Balyi, I. and Hamilton, A. (2000) 'Key to success: long term athlete development', *Sport Coach* 23 (1), 10–32.

Cote, J. and Hay, J. (2002) 'Children's involvement in sport: a developmental analysis' in J.M. Silva and D. Stevens (eds) *Psychological Foundations of Sport*. Boston, MA: Allyn and Bacon.

MacPhail, A., Kirk, D. and Kinchin, G. (2005) 'Sport education in Key Stage 2 games' in D. Penney, G. Clarke, M. Quill and G. Kinchin (eds) *Sport Education in Physical Education*. London: Routledge.

Morley, D. and Bailey, R. (2006) *Meeting the Needs of Your Most Able Pupils: Physical Education and Sport*. London: David Fulton.

Renzulli, J.S. (1998) *A Rising Tide Lifts All Ships: Developing the Gifts and Talents of all Students*, available at http://www.gifted.uconn.edu/sem/semart03.html, accessed August 2006.

Siedentop, D. (1994) *Sport Education: Quality PE through Positive Sport Experiences*. Champaign, Ill: Human Kinetics.

Whitehead, M. (2006) Physical Literacy and Physical Education Conceptual Mapping, http://www.physical-literacy.org.uk/conceptualmapping2006.php, accessed August 2006.

The curriculum

Physical education in the Foundation Stage

Chapter objectives

By the end of this chapter you should be able to:

- Know the requirements for physical development in the Foundation Stage curriculum;

- Understand the role of physical play in indoor and outdoor environments;

- Contextualise the importance of physical skills for children between 3 and 5 in the curriculum;

- Reflect on differences between PE in the Foundation Stage and PE in the National Curriculum.

WHAT IS INSTANTLY RECOGNISABLE about young children between the ages of 3 and 5 is their sheer delight in being active. We know from Chapter 2 of their advances in physical, cognitive, social and emotional development and they arrive in early years settings with a zest to move, to develop physical skills, explore their new surroundings and interact with others. Early movement experiences are crucial in helping to establish and maintain the desire to be active and to use their bodies both for fun and learning. As babies they will become aware of their immediate physical surroundings through their senses. They have learned where their body ends by flicking fingers and toes. Control of neck and head has improved, as has general body strength, and the perceptual mechanisms to enable hand–eye coordination established. As toddlers, movement explorations allow navigations of a wider area that develop their awareness of space, fully integrate both sides of the body and begin a host of new movement patterns. Between 3 and 5, running, jumping and climbing are sources of real enjoyment for children and their sense of accomplishment and confidence performing these and many other activities is to be easily seen written all over their faces! The challenge for early years practitioners is to respond to this need for children to move in purposeful and challenging ways. In this chapter we look at the Foundation Stage curriculum and how it, and specifically its physical development component, can be interpreted to achieve this.

The Foundation Stage in England and Wales begins when children are 3 years of age and extends to the end of the Reception year at age 5. Established in 2000, this phase is distinct in its own right and established a curriculum separate from that followed by primary aged pupils (5–11). As a major milestone in education policy, it identified the very particular needs of children attending nurseries, playgroups and childminders as well as Reception classes in schools, and laid down a common framework to meet these needs with a separate philosophy and underlying principles. It articulated the process through which children learn in terms of knowledge, skills, concepts and attitudes in six areas of learning, as contained in the *Curriculum Guidance for the Foundation Stage* (DfEE, 2000):

- Personal, social and emotional development;
- Communication, language and literacy;
- Mathematical development;
- Knowledge and understanding of the world;
- Physical development;
- Creative development.

By the end of the Foundation Stage, the majority of children will have reached the goals linked to each of these areas. Because of different maturational levels, some will have exceeded the goals and some not yet reached them but will be progressing along 'Stepping Stones' towards them. We now turn our attention to the goal linked to children's physical development.

Physical development in the Foundation Stage curriculum is concerned with improving pupils' co-ordination, control, manipulation and movement skills. It also recognises that increases can be expected in confidence levels, self-esteem and in developing a sense of well-being. This in particular extends *A Strong Child* and *A Healthy Child* aspects of the Birth to Three Framework (DfES, 2002) although it has connections to all four identified aspects. Eight statements comprise the goal for physical development in the Foundation Stage which states that most children by the end of the stage will be able to:

- move with confidence, imagination and in safety
- move with control and co-ordination
- show awareness of space, of themselves and of others
- recognise the importance of keeping healthy and those things which contribute to this
- recognise the changes that happen to their bodies when they are active
- use a range of small and large equipment
- travel around, under, over and through balancing and climbing equipment

■ handle tools, construction objects and malleable materials safely and with increasing control

(DfEE, 1999, p. 39)

The challenge for practitioners is to interpret this curriculum framework and respond to the needs of young children. Translating the eight statements into practical activities, we offer the following:

Moving with confidence, imagination and in safety

■ Exploring moving in different ways, e.g. skipping, galloping and climbing;

■ Adjusting speed and direction to move around safely;

■ Performing stories and action rhymes through movement;

■ Moving freely to music, showing pleasure and expression.

Moving with control and co-ordination

■ Playing board games with dice and counters;

■ Performing basic actions on the spot and then moving;

■ Holding a shape or remaining in a fixed position;

■ Moving around safely on wheeled vehicles.

Showing awareness of space, themselves and of others

■ Moving fingers, hands, feet and elbows;

■ Performing action songs with an emphasis on various parts of the body;

■ Exploring personal space. 'Pretend you are in a bubble. . . .';

■ Playing 'Follow my leader' type games.

Recognising the importance of keeping healthy

■ Understanding the importance of hand-washing and keeping clean;

■ Knowing that exercise is important to keep the body healthy;

■ Distinguishing between 'healthy' and 'unhealthy' foods;

■ Recognising the need for rest after being active.

Recognising the changes to their body when active

■ Not over-exerting physically;

■ Recognising that the heart beats faster after exercising;

- Appreciating that they may be out of breath after being active;
- Beginning to talk about changes after exercise 'My legs feel heavy!' 'I feel hot!'

Using a range of small and large equipment

- Enjoying playing on bikes, trikes and other wheeled toys;
- Experiencing activities with balls, bats and simple games equipment;
- Exploring indoor and outdoor climbing apparatus;
- Participating in parachute games with the whole class.

Travelling around, under, over, through equipment

- Using indoor and outdoor apparatus to scramble, slide and jump on and off;
- Showing various skills on the above apparatus;
- Moving on and off equipment arranged at different heights.

Handling objects safely and with increasing control

- Practising (un)dressing skills;
- Using knives, forks. Using chopsticks. Using paint brushes and crayons;
- Playing with jigsaws, construction sets and small toys;
- Practising skills like cutting and pasting. Practising skills of moulding, threading, posting.

In this chapter we will draw out three factors of significance within this goal: the role of play, the importance of physical skills, and the positive effects of being healthy, and active, and it is these that form the basis of the next discussion.

The role of play

Play is intrinsic to all cultures for children and adults. It is an essential part of the human experience and contributes to our social, intellectual and physical development. It is generally agreed by early educators that play is central to the experiences of young children and fulfils a vital learning function. The early pioneers of early childhood education such as Froebel, Steiner, Montessori, Isaacs and MacMillan viewed play as central to their respective curricula. More recently there is strong evidence to support this in the contemporary early years curriculum in this country (Sylva *et al.*, 1980; Hutt *et al.*, 1989; DfEE, 2000; Siraj-Blatchford, 2002). In their book *Developing Early Years Practice*, Linda Miller and colleagues strongly link play and learning, and provide the following in support:

Play is the child's means of living and of understanding life.

(Isaacs, 1954, p. 32)

Play is not only crucial to the way children become self aware and the way in which they learn the rules of social behaviour; it is also fundamental to intellectual development.

(ACCAC, 1996, p. 3)

Children in the Foundation Stage learn best through play, experience and conversation.

(ECEF, 1998, p. 52)

Many of the developmental milestones outlined in Chapter 2 are achieved in informal ways that include exploration, discovery, watching others, and trial and error. Central to all of these is play. In an early years setting it is often very difficult to separate what is play and what is learning. Consider the example of a 4 year old playing with a set of plastic shapes of different colours and sizes. By observing closely it becomes apparent that vital sorting, classifying and comparing skills are being developed here. Play or learning? Children play in a variety of situations, and terms such as 'role play', 'constructive play', 'fantasy play' are in common use. We know that the nature of children's play changes as they grow older. Children under 2 play alone and scarcely interact with others, whereas children from 3 to 5 engage in associative play where there is some interaction, usually in mixed-sex groups. This leads to co-operative play with shared goals, normally in single-sex groups, as they enter primary school (Miller *et al.*, 2005). It may be helpful to categorise play in two forms: free play or structured play. In free play, children set their own agenda and pace as well as control-ling it themselves. For example, a 4 year old on a trike may choose to roam quite freely inside a safe area and has control over speed, direction or distance. Structured play, in contrast, is play directed by the practitioner who structures the learning environment for the child and is clear about the engagement of the child in this process. An example of this type of play is a 5 year old throwing a beanbag at a target cone. Here, it is the practitioner who controls the object to be thrown, the target, the distance to be thrown, the number of throws and so forth, and directs the child's learning. Both are valid and both have their place in an early years curriculum.

Connecting physical play to the development of physical skills, Trish Maude has this to say, 'play provision should take account of play limitations as well as capabilities, the power of play in facilitating motor skill acquisition and in providing endless oppor-tunities for practice, repetition and refinement of physical skills' (2001, p. 29). Play that promotes physical development can be seen in a child's spontaneous urge to try out physical activities for enjoyment and a sense of mastery in the gross motor skills of running, jumping and climbing and in the fine motor skills of building blocks, mark making and posting shapes in boxes (Anning, 1991). Such play can occur in both indoor and outdoor environments. Wetton (1988) cites two early observational studies (Cooper, 1972; Hutt, 1972) that advocate children having freedom to climb, slide, run, chase and be involved in rough and tumble play. She proposes six requirements for indoor physical play:

1 A multi-purpose climbing frame;

2 Wheeled toys;

3 Large building blocks;

4 Freedom to walk around without restriction;

5 A space for rough and tumble play;

6 A space for teacher directed activity.

Other complementary apparatus for indoor use includes mats, ladders, barrels, a see-saw, boxes, balance boards. She recommends due consideration be given to the equipment being safe, in providing different challenges, and being colourful and made of a mixture of wood, metal and plastic to provide interesting tactile experiences for children.

Outdoor learning is given a high status in various international approaches to the early years curriculum. It is a strong feature of the Reggio Emilia curriculum (originating in northern Italy but also observed in schools in the UK) where the physical environment and how it is resourced are embedded in its philosophy (Dudek, 2000). Recently in the UK, Growing Schools set out to make better use of outdoor environments where the use of the garden as a stimulating outdoor learning environment is prioritised (Garrick, 2004). The *Curriculum Guidance for the Foundation Stage* (DfEE, 2000) also advocates that the outdoors is as much a child's learning environment as the indoor one and encourages practitioners to 'make good use of outdoor space so that children are enabled to learn by working on a larger, more active scale than is possible indoors' (ibid., p. 15). A quality outdoor environment contributes to a number of aspects of children's development. Drawing upon a wide literature, the following is a list of the benefits of outdoor play for young children:

■ assists in developing children's spatial abilities;

■ is a rich sensory experience;

■ develops language capability in connection with concepts such as speed, length and size;

■ fosters independence;

■ allows independence from adult control;

■ provides a valuable change of scale;

■ helps with learning about themselves and the world around them;

■ assists in the development of dramatic play (amongst boys in particular);

■ offers unique opportunities for learning.

There is a view among some educators that the outdoor environment is a potentially dangerous one and therefore they are reluctant to engage children fully in it. Safety is of course a prime concern for all those responsible for children, and indeed there are risks involved with this type of physical play. Whilst many children seek exciting and challenging play that has inherent risks, practitioners need to balance this with sound risk assessment and management. When outdoor environments are created that give opportunities for children to be adventurous and to test out what they can do physically, this is actually where learning about themselves begins. It also provides excellent contexts for them to begin to learn about assessment of risk for themselves. Recent research (Thomas and Thompson, 2004) found that risk assessment was children's top priority when asked to think about different environments. If children are under-challenged in physical play, they find their experiences boring and it can result in using equipment in inappropriate or dangerous ways.

There is much anecdotal evidence to suggest that as educators we over-protect children in the outdoors and by doing so limit the learning and development of the children we are seeking to protect. Ouvry (2005) reports that children with disabilities are at times over-protected and kept inside unnecessarily. She argues that this environment has benefits for all children and that children with a disability have the same right to be independent learners as able-bodied children. In an earlier (1990) study of outdoor-play nursery schools over the course of one month (Ouvry, 2005) the few accidents that were reported were all minor, and included grazed knees and minor bruises. It is when outdoor activities are limited that children get over-excited and tend to use this time rushing about, but when it is a familiar and regular time they use the time actively but also sensibly. Again, the call is to adopt a balanced approach that offers stimulating and challenging outdoor play environments for children but where the level of risk involved is identified and managed and there is no exposure to unacceptable risks of serious injury. Such a view is endorsed in the position statement of the Play Safety Forum (2002). Further guidance is available to inform practical decision-making from many sources; for example, the European Standards and the Health and Safety Executive provide clear standards for safety of playground equipment (National Children's Bureau, 2002).

Task 11 Managing risk in outdoor play

- Staff in your setting are concerned about children's safety in outdoor play. Together you meet to discuss this issue

- List the factors you feel are important in risk management in outdoor play.

- In what ways will you reassure parents that this provision is safe but also challenging?

Careful planning and monitoring are required to make children's learning outdoors safe, enjoyable and purposeful. Planning outdoor provision with an emphasis on physical development can take a variety of forms, including intended observations of individual children, a general class topic, a story, or spontaneously responding to children's enthusiasm and interests. Most Foundation Stage settings have clear policies on outdoor learning. The use of staff rotas allows all staff to be involved in this enterprise. Flexibility of provision mixed with clarity of roles and a strong commitment to outdoor play is essential. Having clear rules for safety outside, that all children are aware of and adhere to, is essential. Involving parents in this is highly desirable. Parents, for example, may be consulted as to what risks of danger they see in the use of the outdoor environment and how the staff are involved in this provision. A set of safety rules could be drafted which will have involved parents, staff and children together in the process and these could be posted in prominent places in the setting.

Since children need sustained periods of time to develop their movement skills, frequent use of the outdoor area is needed and preferably on a daily basis. In resourcing outdoor physical play, the following might well appear:

- A space large enough for children to run around freely that promotes vigorous heart fitness;
- Large apparatus that offers challenging climbing opportunities – tyres, tunnels, a climbing frame, planks, etc.;
- A space for wheeled toys – prams, trikes, trucks, trolleys, etc.;
- Small apparatus such as beanbags, quoits and hoops to develop co-ordination and balance;
- Different surfaces such as grass, tarmac, bark;
- Quiet areas for reflection with blankets or mats;
- Places to hide such as natural areas or even large cardboard boxes;
- A wild area to explore freely;
- A garden area.

Task 12 Providing for outdoor play in a setting

- Analyse the provision for outdoor play in your own setting.
- Compile an inventory of equipment currently in use.
- What other equipment might be required to supplement the current provision? Make a list.

Outdoor physical play has a great deal to offer children. It contributes to all areas of children's development and to all areas of the early years curriculum. With careful planning, links can be made between indoor and outdoor learning so that children view it as not just a time to 'let off steam'. Creative practitioners can make stimulating environments that are rich with opportunities to promote physical skills and enjoyable, purposeful activity. Table 4.1 lists some practical suggestions that emphasise physical development through outdoor play.

TABLE 4.1 Maximising physical development through outdoor play

Type of outdoor activity	Examples to use in practice
Class games	■ What time is it Mr Wolf? ■ The farmer's in his den ■ Grandma's footsteps ■ Hide and seek ■ Ring-a-ring o' roses
Large apparatus	■ using swings ■ using slides ■ playing on see-saws ■ free play on climbing frames ■ moving through tunnels
Small apparatus	■ handling beanbags, balls, quoits and hoops ■ bouncing large balls ■ throwing and catching, kicking ■ rolling a small ball or beanbag to a target ■ balance boards ■ using skipping ropes
Parachute games	■ passing it around the group ■ passing it around at different levels ■ making waves ■ changing places with a friend inside the canopy ■ bouncing a teddy on top of the chute ■ moving the chute while reciting nursery rhymes

continued on next page

TABLE 4.1 continued

Type of outdoor activity	Examples to use in practice
Wheeled toys	■ steering bikes along straight lines on the ground
	■ pedalling trikes or go-carts around curves
	■ exploring the use of wheelbarrows, trolleys, prams, push-me pull-me vehicles and buggies on the flat and up/down slopes
	■ loading materials on to trailers
	■ setting up traffic systems that include roundabouts, traffic lights and road signs
Trails and courses	■ take the children on a walk around the local park
	■ simple activity circuits to include running, jumping, balancing skills
	■ playground markings, e.g. compass points, snakes and ladders, stepping stones, etc.
	■ treasure hunts
	■ obstacle courses with tunnels, slides, tyres
Other equipment	■ using space hoppers
	■ practising with stilts
	■ building with large crates of different sizes and different materials
	■ moving on pogo sticks
	■ exploring a tree house or disused boat
	■ supervised play in a paddling pool

Physical skills in the Foundation Stage

Another way to promote children's physical development is by developing their gross and fine motor skills. In Chapter 2, we looked at what skill is and how it is acquired and improved. In this section we consider the development of gross and fine motor skills specifically in the context of Foundation Stage pupils.

Developing good motor skills is crucial to children's overall development but it also has a vital role to play in their learning. Nowadays children of 3 come to schools or other early years settings with very variable experiences physically. For those who have difficulty in dressing and the more common everyday curriculum tasks that have a motor component such as mark-making, holding a paint brush, beating a drum, manipulating jigsaw pieces, holding books correctly or sand and water play, deficits in physical skills are real barriers to their learning. This also impacts upon their view of themselves and the view that others have of them. Early work by Tansley (1967) showed that a young child's self-concept, stemming from an understanding of the body and its capabilities, was closely linked to how they feel about themselves. A deficit in physical skills has implications for the expectations of teachers and parents as well as for their sociability and acceptance by other children.

Before the age of 3, young children need ample opportunities to use large muscle groups and build up muscle strength, balance, suppleness and confidence. Floor-based activities such as lying on backs, turning over on to fronts, rolling and belly-crawling lay excellent foundations for the development of gross motor skills later. By 3, more complex activities like stepping, skipping and jumping, plus sitting astride and steering wheeled toys provide excellent workouts for leg muscles. Stretching up and down and from side to side, bending and twisting actions strengthen backs and promote flexibility. Arms and shoulders receive benefits from hanging, swinging and climbing on large apparatus and by pushing and pulling larger vehicles such as wheel-barrows and trolleys. Children's confidence and abilities to balance are increased through dynamic balance activities such as spinning, using hoppers or stilts or moving and carrying objects like beanbags or balls. Static balance is improved in exploring body shapes, using different body parts to balance upon, both on the floor and on apparatus. Smaller muscle groups require equal attention. As babies, holding rattles and other toys, turning their wrists and hands, clapping two hands together are important ways to develop dexterity and manipulative abilities. When they enter the Foundation Stage, handling objects of different sizes and shapes should continue, and sand and water play promotes understanding of applying variable pressures and builds up finger strength. Although lateral dominance is not always fully established by this age, practitioners should encourage children to use both hands in these and other tasks but not intervene if a child tends to opt for a preferred hand at this stage. Manipulation also involves feet, and activities that encourage wiggling and cur-ling or uncurling of toes or feet rotation are helpful. Perceptual–motor development continues to increase around this age and can be enhanced by integrated activities like manoeuvring around obstacle courses on foot or on moving vehicles, aiming balls at targets and playing lotto and matching games. Some practical suggestions to develop gross and fine physical skills are given below.

Promoting physical skills in the Foundation Stage

Gross motor

- Walking (in straight lines, changing direction, speed)
- Marching like a soldier
- Running and dodging
- Running and freezing on a signal

Fine motor

- Sand play
- Water play
- Tying shoe laces
- Buttoning clothes
- Using a knife and fork

continued on next page

Gross motor

- Jumping up and down on the spot
- Hopping – both legs. Hopscotch
- Statues – keeping still
- Bending and stretching with different body parts
- Imitating animal movements (e.g. flutter, strut, gallop)
- Hanging and swinging
- Using a climbing frame
- Action songs and rhyme
- Sliding and spinning on tummies and bottoms
- Stories to music (e.g. *Three Little Pigs*)
- Pushing, pulling and steering wheeled toys
- Throwing and catching
- Kicking, rolling different objects
- Parachute games

Fine motor

- Role-play activities (e.g. using a till, stamping)
- Modelling with plasticine, play dough or clay
- Cutting out with scissors
- Baking tasks – rolling out, kneading, shaping
- Cutting with simple tools
- Mark-making. Colouring
- Painting
- Doing jigsaws
- Building with cubes
- Using large construction materials (duplo, lego, etc.)
- Glueing and sticking
- Keyboard skills
- Using a computer mouse
- Threading beads
- Finger wriggling. Extensions
- Copying own name on paper

Physical skills permeate the whole of the Foundation Stage curriculum. New skills are introduced and others build upon earlier acquisition in the period from birth to 3 years. It is essential that opportunities are presented in a range of activities in indoor and outdoor environments to provide breadth of experience for all children. Practice is a vital ingredient for success and this can be achieved through repetition as well as variety of practice situations. A well-planned curriculum in the Foundation Stage provides an excellent framework to offer activities for children in all six areas of learning and to emphasise skill development in the area of physical development.

Being healthy and active

In recent years concerns have been raised over the lack of exercise and physical activity of young children. The popular press abounds with articles that lay blame for this lack of activity and the increase of childhood obesity at the door of the PE profession for not engaging children in relevant curriculum physical education. This has also been fuelled by concerns over the selling-off of playing fields, alarm over adventurous activities offered by schools, mixed messages about school sport and two hours a week curriculum PE, and so on. As Libby Purves quotes, 'we are all choking on our own fat due to insufficient netball and the demise of the vaulting horse. Woe, woe, doom, doom!' (TES, 18 June 2004, p. 32). What does the evidence really tell us in relation to 3–5 year olds?

In this country, levels of obesity have tripled over the past twenty years for adults and children. From the early 1980s the numbers of overweight and obese children in the UK have risen at an alarming rate. In an extensive study of 2600 children, researchers found so many children in the categories of overweight and obese in all the age categories they studied that they described their findings as nothing less than an 'epidemic of obesity in children in the UK' (Reilly and Dorosty, 1996). We now estimate that one in every three children is overweight and one in every five defined as obese. The number of obese children starting school is currently one in ten (Doherty, 2004). In the UK as a whole, the scale of the problem is such that for the first time in history, some of the current generation of parents can be expected to outlive their children (ibid.). There are two *main* causes for this: increases in food consumption (in particular foods high in calories and/or saturated fats) and a reduction in physical activity, and what is very alarming is that this is a problem that involves children between 3 and 5 in our nurseries and schools. The early years are crucial to laying down proper foundations for lifelong physical activity and in combating the rise in childhood obesity.

Changes to our lifestyles mean that children are experiencing uncharacteristically inactive lifestyles from a very early age. A good deal of research points to the low levels of physical activity in children and a decline in the activity levels of children (Armstrong, 1998). Hypokinetic diseases (i.e. those related to a lack of physical activity) such as coronory heart disease, raised blood pressure, depression and obesity are now becoming evident in young children. Findings from Whitaker *et al.* (1998) suggest that the early years represent a 'critical period' for the development or otherwise of life-long obesity. We know that young children readily adopt lifestyles of their parents. Children whose parents are physically active are twice as likely to be active themselves. If both parents are physically active, they are six times more likely to be active. Pressures of everyday life have meant a reduction in opportunities for many families to be active. Children ride in car seats to and from nursery or playgroup and are driven to friends houses or to the shops. There has been a decline in the number of children walking or cycling to school. In 1986 the numbers of children walking to school was 67 per cent. By 1996, it had fallen to 55 per cent. For those who cycled, the number was 1 per cent which fell to zero in 1996 (DETR, 2000). There appears less time for playing out of doors and self-selected physical play activities. With parental concerns over safety, children spend less time outside playing. Television and the new technologies like video and computer games condition children to be less active and to be indoors with, on average, children spending about twenty hours a week watching TV (Central Statistical Office, 1994).

An alarming picture for educators and parents and yet there is strong evidence of the positive values of being healthy and active in early childhood. Although most studies have concentrated on older children, the wealth of evidence in support of the many positive effects of 'a healthy mind and a healthy body' is unequivocal (Pollatschek and O'Hagen, 1989; Mutrie and Parfitt, 1998; Sallis and Owen, 1999). These positive benefits include:

- Overall psychological good health;
- Improvement in self-esteem;
- Reduction in stress;
- Reduced anxiety;
- Enhancement in social development;
- Increased moral reasoning;
- Mood change regulation;
- Increased motivation;
- Cognition increased;
- Reduced aggression;
- Improvement in academic performance.

In order to counter the alarming trend of physical inactivity and increased weight gain, educational practice needs to embrace the seriousness of the problem and seek ways to provide rich and varied opportunities for movement activities in the curriculum. Even before their children enter the Foundation Stage, parents have much to offer by way of home-based movement from a very early age. In school or other settings practitioners can be good role models themselves and ensure that movement and activity permeate the curriculum.

Task 13   Promoting physical activity in the early years

Research findings (Armstrong and Wilsman, 1997) suggest that when children begin regular physical activity at an early age, the effects are more pronounced and last longer. As a Foundation Stage practitioner, consider

a) what are the barriers to promoting physical activity in your setting?

b) how do you think you can overcome these?

Moving towards the National Curriculum

The Foundation Stage curriculum goes further than setting out what children should know, do and understand across six areas of learning. It sets out a philosophy based on principles of good practice. The document, *Curriculum Guidance for the Foundation Stage* (DfEE, 2000) offers a strong rationale with clear statements about the value of working with parents as partners, play and inclusion, and views such a curriculum as underpinning all future learning (p. 8). There is growing recognition from many teachers that its principles and practice have much to offer later years of school. Approaches to learning and teaching in the Foundation Stage are relevant to Key Stage 1 and Key Stage 2, and many teachers welcome the interface between the Foundation Stage and Key Stage 1 in particular.

In physical education, however, this interface has highlighted a number of differences in teaching and learning which has resulted in some confusion as to what physical education children between 3 and 5 years should be receiving. Some of the differences in approaches to teaching and learning in PE between the Foundation Stage and Key Stage 1 are neatly summarised by Lavin (2003) and are presented in Table 4.2.

Lavin's findings are worrying. As a profession we do need to agree on how our subject is defined and communicate that message to others both inside and outside the profession. An immediate stumbling block is in the framework (or indeed our interpretation of this framework) that shows obvious differences in *what* and *how* the subject should be taught. The questions for reflection at the end of the chapter ask you to consider this with regard to lack of consistency between PE in the early years curriculum and PE in the National Curriculum.

TABLE 4.2 Teaching and learning in PE in the Foundation Stage and Key Stage 1

Foundation Stage Physical Development			National Curriculum PE Key Stage 1		
Play-centred	Exploration	Experimentation	Skill focus	Teacher-directed	Subject-based
Wide range of equipment	Creativity	Autonomy	Developing, selecting and applying skills	Limited equipment/ apparatus	Co-operative working
Manipulation	Co-ordination	Confidence	Exercise and health notions	Compositional ideas	Evaluate and improve performance
Increasing control	Respond to rhythm, safety, music, story	Understanding	Watching and listening	Express feelings through movement	Remember and repeat simple skills and actions

Source: Lavin (2003)

Chapter summary

Effective physical education for children from 3 to 5 years is centred around having knowledge of children's development and knowledge of how they learn, and matching this to appropriate curriculum content. The Foundation Stage curriculum is a holistic one and serves to progress children's knowledge, skill and understanding in six broad areas in an interrelated way. It identifies physical development as one of these areas and is concerned with movement, co-ordination, control and manipulation but stresses that physical development is inseparable from all the other areas of development because children of this age learn through being active and interactive (DfEE, 2000, p. 101). In this chapter we have shown that by combining free and structured play (indoors and outdoors), developing physical skills and encouraging children to be active and healthy, the building blocks of future physical education are laid. This broad base provides a vital foundation for the more structured requirements of NCPE in Key Stage 1 (and beyond) through dance, gymnastics and games activities. The chapter concluded with a plea that the profession needs to aim for seamlessness and consistency, so that the good practice identified in this chapter is taken forward into later years and modified and enhanced to meet the changing learning and development needs of primary children in PE.

Questions for reflection

- Do you think children perceive the Foundation Stage curriculum as different from the Key Stage 1 curriculum with regard to their physical education?

- Is there a balance to be struck between the play element in the Foundation Stage and the structure of NCPE in Key Stage 1?

- Does the term *physical development* adequately portray the essence of physical education?

- As it stands currently, does the *physical development* early learning goal adequately prepare children for the activity areas of gymnastics, dance and games in Key Stage 1?

Further reading

Bilton, H. (1999) *Outdoor Play in the Early Years.* London: David Fulton Publishers.
This is an excellent rationale on playing outdoors. Practitioners in the Foundation Stage will find this a very welcome text indeed.

Doherty, J. and Bailey, R. (2003) *Supporting Physical Development and Physical Education in the Early Years.* Buckingham: Open University Press.
A comprehensive text dealing with PE from 3 to 7. Combines theory and many practical ideas.

Doherty, J. and Whiting, M. (2004) 'All about . . . tackling childhood obesity'. *Nursery World*, April.
An eight-page article on the childhood obesity issue. Deals with the role of exercise and offers good advice on eating healthily.

Miller, L., Cable, C. and Devereux, J. (2005) *Developing Early Years Practice*. London: David Fulton Publishers.
An early years text. Chapter 2 is good on learning through play.

Ouvry, M. (2005) *Exercising Muscles and Minds*. London: National Children's Bureau.
An easy read. Short sections full of relevant information on outdoor play and the early years curriculum.

Pre-school Learning Alliance (1998) *Physical Development through Play*. London: Pre-school Learning Alliance.
Short and easy to read booklet. Gives practical suggestions for gross and fine motor skills. Many ideas also on children's play.

Wetton, P. (1988) *Physical Education in the Nursery and Infant School*. London: Croom Helm.
Although preceding the current curriculum in Foundation Stage, the book remains a standard. Chapter 4 has a useful discussion on play. Many practical ideas included.

CHAPTER

5

Physical education in Key Stage 1

Chapter objectives

By the end of this chapter you should be able to:

■ Understand the breadth and scope of PE at Key Stage 1;

■ Develop your knowledge of delivering successful learning experiences through the core activity areas of dance, games and gymnastic activities;

■ Understand how the four aspects of learning can be used as a focus for teaching, learning and assessment at Key Stage 1.

PE in the National Curriculum at Key Stage 1

BUILDING UPON THEIR EXPERIENCES of movement and physical activity in the Foundation Stage, pupils' formal physical education in the National Curriculum begins as they enter Key Stage 1. At this early stage in the PE curriculum our primary concern should be to ensure that all pupils enjoy the experience of being physically active. Teachers should exploit pupils' natural exuberance for movement and their curiosity about the world in assisting them to become *confident, competent* and *co-ordinated* movers. Pupils make best progress when they have *regular, high quality* and *successful* activity experiences. These should be planned to ensure that *all* pupils are suitably challenged and participate in a range of tasks, which should include *doing, observing* and *discussion*.

Whilst the activity areas have been selected to make different demands of pupils and dictate the nature of the experiences that the pupils will face, at all Key Stages, teachers need to help pupils to develop their knowledge, skills and understanding in PE through the following four aspects of performance (first introduced in Chapter 1):

■ Acquiring and developing skills;

■ Selecting and applying skills tactics and compositional ideas;

■ Evaluating and improving performance;

■ Developing an understanding of fitness and health.

The four aspects of knowledge, skills and understanding help teachers to move beyond simply developing pupils' techniques in a variety of contexts towards enhancing pupils' knowledge *and* understanding of physical activity. This is vital if we are to help pupils to make the connection between what takes place in PE in school and those sport and activity opportunities that are available outside school.

At Key Stage 1 pupils should participate in a range of activities selected from the areas of dance, games and gymnastics activities (and swimming where this is feasible) (see Table 5.1). In each activity area, teachers should plan for a progressive and purposeful programme of experiences that stretch pupils physically and intellectually taking account of their developmental needs. Just as all good teachers adjust the level of challenge according to the needs of the pupils in the classroom, in PE all pupils should be set tasks that are appropriately challenging. Teachers should therefore familiarise themselves with simple strategies for differentiating their teaching accordingly. Using the STEP framework is one such strategy. The acronym STEP (space, task, equipment, people) can be a useful reminder to help teachers differentiate activities to help all pupils successfully participate. An example of applying STEP to practical activity in gymnastics is shown in Table 5.2.

In the remainder of this chapter, we outline the rationale for each of the activity areas included at Key Stage 1 in the National Curriculum for PE. Following an introduction to the basic principles associated with teaching and learning in each activity area we suggest some activities that you might like to try with your pupils. Guidance on delivering knowledge and understanding of fitness and health is provided towards the end of the chapter.

TABLE 5.1 Knowledge, skills and understanding in PE at Key Stage 1

	Acquiring and developing skills	Selecting and applying skills, tactics and compositional ideas	Evaluating and improving performance	Developing knowledge and understanding of fitness and health
Pupils should be taught to	explore basic skills, actions and ideas with increasing understanding; remember and repeat simple skills and actions with increasing control and coordination.	explore how to choose and apply skills and actions in sequence and in combination; vary the way they perform skills by using simple tactics and movement phrases; apply rules and conventions for different activities.	describe what they have done; observe, describe and copy what others have done; use what they have learnt to improve the quality and control of their work.	understand how important it is to be active; recognise and describe how their bodies feel during different activities.

TABLE 5.2 An example of applying STEP to practical activity

Practise and repeat a sequence that includes two jumps, a turn and a balance

STEP	Easier	Harder
Space	In own space	Sharing the space around the room
Task	Copying a set pattern	Invent your own routine
Equipment	On the floor only	Using a mat and a bench
People	Working on own	Working alongside or with a partner/group

Dance activities

Through dance, teachers can develop pupils' non-verbal communication skills, aesthetic appreciation and artistic expression through movement.

The National Curriculum advises that, at Key Stage 1, pupils should be taught to:

a. use movement imaginatively, responding to stimuli, including music, and performing basic skills [for example, travelling, being still, making a shape, jumping, turning and gesturing]
b. change the rhythm, speed, level and direction of their movements
c. create and perform dances using simple movement patterns, including those from different times and cultures, express and communicate ideas and feelings.

Through experiencing a range of dances from different times and places, by the end of the key stage, pupils should be equipped to create and perform simple dances with confidence. To meet this goal, the teacher needs to have a clear understanding of the dance process. During Key Stage 1, pupils will acquire and develop dance skills through experimenting with a wide range of actions. They will acquire and develop knowledge of basic dance structure and composition through remembering and performing teacher-led dances. As their repertoire of movement skills grows, they will be able to select and apply movements and simple compositional ideas to make changes to dances and eventually create their own dance phrases and simple dances. Through observing dances performed by their classmates they will develop an understanding of high quality movement and begin to recognise what makes a good dance. In so doing, they will develop an appreciation of movement and the effort required to make a dance performance special. The key to good dance composition is the selection of a *theme* that is meaningful to and excites the imagination of the class. Having identified a topical theme, the quality of the *stimuli* selected, and the discussion that they elicit, provides the foundation upon which the dance can be constructed. Introducing one or two stimuli at the start of each lesson to spark ideas and encourage the sharing of thoughts about movement possibilities initiates the composition process.

Task 14   Dance themes and dance stimuli

Select a theme and identify as many different **stimuli** for it as you can.

KS1 theme ideas	Stimuli
■ Nursery rhymes	Visual – pictures, video, colours, shapes
■ Toys	
■ Holidays	Auditory – music, poetry, sound effects, percussion
■ Mini-beasts	
■ Pirates	Tactile – textiles, textures, props
■ Dinosaurs	Kinaesthetic – motif, steps
■ Bob the Builder/Fireman Sam	Ideas – stories, characters, emotions

Teaching tip

In the early stages use flash cards with words and/or pictures to help pupils respond to a stimulus. Spread the flash cards out on the floor and ask the pupils to choose the words/pictures which help to describe the stimulus. Later, as pupils discuss a stimulus in small groups, ask them to write their key words on mini whiteboards to share with other groups. Over a period of several lessons, collect and display the dance vocabulary in the hall to act as a reminder for pupils as they work.

To begin with, pupils need to be helped to develop an enhanced awareness of various body parts and how they can move separately and in combination to express a theme or idea (see Table 5.3).

TABLE 5.3 Enhancing awareness of body parts

Body part	Practise
Head, neck and face	Nodding (up and down), shaking (side to side), ear to shoulder, circling/spiralling action with forehead, move eyebrows, eyelids, cheeks and lips.
Trunk	Bending (forwards, backwards, side to side), twisting, 'snaking' or 'popping' (wave-like action passing through trunk).
Arms	Try each of the following with arms working together or in opposition – swinging, circling, swimming, shaking, 'popping', flapping.
Hands and fingers	Squeeze together, stretch apart, rub, wring, shake and clap hands. Point, drum, walk and crawl with fingers.
Legs	Bend, straighten, kick, cross and shake legs whilst standing, sitting or lying.
Feet and toes	Circle toes and heels. Point and pull toes. Wriggle each toe. Stand on toes, heels, insides, outsides and balls of feet. Practise stepping from heel to toe.

Using combinations of the above, pupils can begin to move in more controlled, imaginative and thoughtful ways. By developing a wall of images and words (Douglas, 1999) pupils can be challenged to try to move in ever more expressive ways (see Table 5.4).

TABLE 5.4 Expressive ways of moving

Prowl	Picture of cat	Leap	Picture of flea	Jump
Picture of lion	Pounce	Picture of tortoise	Crawl	Picture of eagle
Slide	Picture of wader bird	Creep	Picture of rabbit	Bound
Picture of snake	Stride	Picture of giraffe	Scurry	Picture of squirrel
Slither	Picture of snail	Gallop	Picture of elephant	Sway

Once pupils get to know their bodies they can extend these movements further by experimenting with the elements shown in Table 5.5.

TABLE 5.5 Elements of movement

Size	Direction	Level	Pathway
Large, small	Forward, backward, sideways, towards, away from	High, low, medium	Straight, diagonal, L-shaped, zig-zag, curved

To create a dance phrase pupils need to select appropriate actions and order them using simple choreographic ideas. A dance phrase can be easily constructed by selecting a response to each of four key questions:

■ WHAT is the body doing?

■ HOW is the body moving?

■ WHERE is the body being moved?

■ WHO (or what) is involved in the movement?

Table 5.6 shows some examples.

TABLE 5.6 Illustration of the four key questions

What	How	Where	Who
Skipping	lightly	around	a hoop
Creeping	slowly	in and out of	the group
Turning	sharply	away from	a partner
Sinking	gently	towards	a marker

Teaching tip

'What's in the bag?'

Once pupils have developed a repertoire of movement experiences, create a *what, how, where,* and *who* bag with a selection of terms in each. Ask four pupils to select one word from each bag and arrange these on a board for the class to see. Pupils try to move according to the instructions. This can be developed into a guessing game where a group of pupils have to guess the words on the cards from the movements alone.

A good dance theme is one that draws upon pupils' experience and fires their imagination. Try using some of the suggestions listed in Table 5.7.

Learning to appreciate movement begins in Key Stage 1 with learning to sit attentively and quietly during a performance. Practising this skill in the hall while other pupils perform their dances can be quite a challenge. Structuring pupils' observations of one another is the key to making progress in the skills of observing and evaluating

TABLE 5.7 Suggested dance themes

Theme	Movement ideas	Stimulus ideas
Nursery rhymes	*Incey Wincey Spider* – crawling, creeping and climbing spiders, tumbling and falling.	
	Hickory Dickory Dock – scurrying mice, short sharp changes of direction, jerking, rhythmic clockwork actions.	
Animals	Pets – bounding dogs with wagging tails, swimming and shaking dry. Slinky cats, quietly creeping, curling and sleeping. Hamsters busy, collecting, nibbling, trundling.	
	Wild animals – prowling, slumbering big cats, chasing, roaring. Gliding, snapping, snaking crocodiles. Swinging, scratching, climbing, falling, playful monkeys.	
	On the farm – chickens pecking, flapping, scratching and nesting; lambs suckling, jumping and chasing; pigs wallowing in mud and feeding from the trough; horses pull carts, gallop, jump and rear up.	
Stories	*Jack and the Beanstalk* – growing, climbing, creeping, giant heavy strides, swinging the axe. Other examples such as *Hansel and Gretel* and *The Gingerbread Man*	

performance. Following these simple guidelines will improve pupils' chances of becoming a better audience:

- Make sure observers are sitting comfortably and have a clear view.
- Reduce distractions by setting performers against a plain backdrop.
- Sit the audience in a circle in the middle of the room facing outward while dancers dance around the outside.
- Encourage observers to watch only one dancer or pair of dancers (dancing nearest to them).
- Ask the observer to look for particular changes – e.g. in level or direction.
- Question the audience after the performance.
- Show appreciation to the performer by smiling or clapping when they have finished.

Try using these questions to focus the observer's attention:

- Does the dance have a clear beginning, middle and ending?
- Does the dancer control their movements well?
- Can you see the pathways used?

Games activities

Games activities provide multiple opportunities for pupils to work co-operatively and competitively, to develop a sense of fair play and to learn to appreciate the qualities of being 'a good sport'. When taught well, regular games play promotes normal, healthy growth and can foster positive social, emotional and moral development.

The National Curriculum advises that, at Key Stage 1, pupils should be taught to:

a. travel with, send and receive a ball and other equipment in different ways
b. develop these skills for simple net, striking/fielding and invasion-type games
c. play simple, competitive net, striking/fielding and invasion-type games that they and others have made, using simple tactics for attacking and defending.

Learning to play games requires the development of both co-ordination skills and thinking skills. As the guidance suggests, the National Curriculum for Physical Education currently requires that pupils should be introduced to three types of games: *striking and fielding games; net/wall games;* and *invasion games*. Table 5.8 describes the key features of these game families.

TABLE 5.8 Classifications of games in the National Curriculum

Game category	Key features
Striking and fielding	Players take turns to either strike or field. When striking the aim is to score as many points as possible. When fielding the aim is to limit the score of the striking team.
Net/wall games	Players from opposing teams are separated by a barrier and take it in turns to try to score points against their opponents. Points are scored when players fail to keep the object in play.
Invasion	Players share the playing area and compete to gain and then retain possession of the object. They try to invade their opponents' territory to score points.

These three categories by no means represent all game forms but collectively draw upon certain fundamental skills which underpin all games play. These are the skills of *sending, receiving* and *travelling,* and in those games that permit it, *travelling with* the object (see Table 5.9). We agree with Bunker's (1994) suggestion that, in the early stages of games skill development, participation in *target* games offers pupils the opportunity to develop an understanding of game play in an unopposed context. In target games, pupils have the opportunity to rehearse the core skills of travelling and sending before learning the more complex skill of receiving.

TABLE 5.9 Fundamental skills of games

Sending	Throwing, rolling, kicking, striking, batting, padding
Receiving	Catching, fielding, trapping, blocking
Travelling	Stepping, jumping, running, sliding, turning
Travelling with	Dribbling a ball with feet or a stick

Establishing a framework for teaching and learning core games skills is made easier when the individual actions, and their interdependence, are well understood. Figure 5.1 identifies the core actions to be introduced, rehearsed and developed throughout the key stage. As the overlapping circles suggest, each skill set can be rehearsed and performed in isolation and, through games play, in simple combinations.

Rather than spending too much time rehearsing these core actions through drills, we recommend that, where possible, skill development should be embedded within fun games. It is important to recognise, however, that some games are inherently more complex and demanding than others. Developing Bunker *et al.*'s (1994) framework for the introduction of games in the primary school, we suggest that, at Key

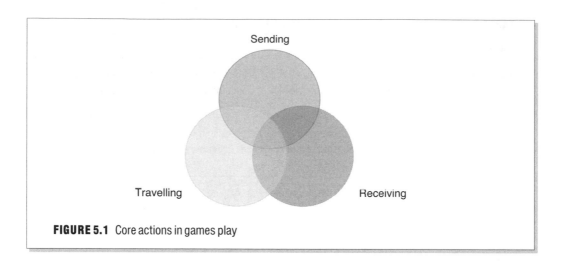

FIGURE 5.1 Core actions in games play

Stage 1, pupils be provided with opportunities to play individual and paired versions of target games, net/wall games and striking and fielding games (see Table 5.10).

It is important to remember that pupils will need regular practice if they are to improve. In addition to trying these activities during lesson time, pupils should be encouraged to practise the skills during active playtime and at home (see Table 5.11).

TABLE 5.10 A framework for the phased introduction of games at Key Stage 1

Game type	FS	KS 1		KS 2
	R	1	2	3
Target				
Striking and fielding				
Net/wall				
Invasion				
Games making				

█████ Proportion of curricum time

Source: Adapted from Bunker *et al.* (1994)

TABLE 5.11 Developing game skills through practice activities

Activity	Adaptations	Technical tips	Signs of success
Balloon bashing – keep a balloon up in the air for a minute. Hit it up and turn around before hitting it again. After three hits, catch the balloon with two hands.	Less air in the balloon/ use a beach ball. Increase the time to keep it up. Use different parts of your body to keep it up. Catch at head height, waist height, knee height.	Keep eyes on the balloon. Move feet to get underneath the balloon. Wait for balloon to arrive.	Pupils become more relaxed and appear to have more time between hits. Pupils hit up with palm of hand. Pupils complete more complex between-hit challenges.
Sliding and skimming – slide or skim a beanbag or quoit along the floor towards a target.	Target further away/ smaller.	Bend knees to get close to the floor. Finish with hand pointing towards target.	Increasing accuracy and consistency over different distances. Pupils can explain how to do it.
Rolling – roll a quoit or ball to a target. 'Under the Bridge' In threes, one player stands with legs wide apart to form a bridge. The other two players count how many times they can roll the ball under the bridge without it touching the sides.	Target further away/ smaller.	Bend knees to get close to the floor. Finish with hand pointing towards target.	Increasing accuracy and consistency over different distances. Pupils can explain how to play the game.
Throwing – throw a beanbag to a target.	Target further away/ smaller	Palm facing upwards. Opposite foot forwards. Finish with hand pointing towards target.	Increasing accuracy and consistency over different distances. Pupils can explain how to do it.
Kicking – kick ball to a target.		Use instep. Place non-kicking foot to the side of the ball. Follow through to the target with kicking leg.	

continued on next page

TABLE 5.11 continued

Activity	Adaptations	Technical tips	Signs of success
Bouncing – count how many times you can bounce a ball in a hoop using two hands to send and receive.	Bounce using alternate hands/one hand only. Bounce from side to side. Bounce ball whilst walking around the room.	Push ball down to the ground with fingers.	
Review questions	Can you describe how to catch/throw/roll/kick/bounce?		

The review question at the foot of the table focuses on evaluating and improving performance.

Early travelling games such as tag provide a good introduction to the principles of game play and allow pupils the opportunity to develop travelling skills (running, dodging, avoiding, accelerating, decelerating and turning) and awareness of space (see Table 5.12).

TABLE 5.12 Tag games

Activity	Adaptations (applying STEP)	Technical tips	Signs of success
'Count tag' Nominated chasers score points by touching runners trying to escape.	S – Reduce/increase working space. T – Chasers have longer/shorter time limit to score points. E – Introduce hoops as a safe zone for runners. P – Increase/decrease number of chasers/ reduce number of runners – tagged runners become chasers.	Run on the balls of your feet. Push harder with one foot to help change direction. Make small steps and bend your knees when turning.	High-scoring chasers. Pupils run lightly on feet showing change of pace and direction. Chasers and runners remember the rules.
'Bag tag' In groups of eight, two chasers use a beanbag to tag runners. Chasers pass the beanbag between them.			
Review questions	Do you know why you were caught? What can you do to avoid being caught as quickly next time? What makes a good chasing team? Can you describe how you feel before, during and after a chasing game?		

Target games provide a good opportunity to rehearse core skills and challenge pupils to improve their accuracy and consistency. They also introduce pupils to 'turn taking' which is an important feature of both striking and fielding and net/wall games (see Table 5.13).

TABLE 5.13 Target games

Activity	Adaptations (applying STEP)	Technical tips	Signs of success
Beanbag skittles – players knock over/move skittles by sliding bean bag/kicking a ball to a target. **Throw golf** – players count how many throws to land your beanbag in the 'hole' (target hoops) spread around the playground/field.	S – Target further away/smaller. T – Try with your other hand. E – Substitute beanbag for a quoit/slightly deflated ball/large foam ball. P – play on own/in pairs.	Look at target. Step towards target with opposing foot. Swing arm in a smooth motion.	Increasing accuracy and consistency over different distances.
Review questions	Can you explain why you sometimes miss the target? Why is it harder to hit a target that is a long way away?		

In the example of a striking and fielding game described in Table 5.14, the focus is on developing an understanding of attacking a space. In this game, pupils will discover that by sending the ball accurately to a space, and far from their partner, they will have more time to score points.

TABLE 5.14 Kicking rounders

Activity	Adaptations (applying STEP)	Technical tips	Signs of success
Kicking rounders Played in pairs. Players take turns to be the 'kicker' and/or the 'fielder'. 'Kicker' kicks stationary ball and runs between cones. Each cone touched counts 1 point. 'Fielder' collects and puts ball in hoop as quickly as possible. Kicker has three turns to score as many points as possible, then players swap roles. Equip: Ball, 2 x cones and hoop	S – increase/decrease distance to cone. T – ball can be thrown instead of kicked. E – play with different types of ball. P – play with two fielders.	For more distance take two steps into the kick/throw. Hand/foot should finish pointing where you want it to go. Move straight away after kicking/throwing the ball. Fielder, wait on your toes ready to move quickly.	Increasing distance kicked. Introduction of basic disguise. Fielder anticipates/predicts which way the ball will go.
Review questions	When kicking/throwing/hitting, where should you send the ball to score as many points as possible? When fielding, how can you keep the kicker's score low?		

In early net/wall games (see Table 5.15) pupils begin by playing *co-operatively* to score as many points *with* their partner as they can. When they have had plenty of practice and established a *personal best* score, they will enjoy competing *against* their partner, who then becomes an opponent. The shift from *beating your record* or best score to *beating your opponent* is an important transition in games and one that increases the motivation to play once the skills necessary to play have been acquired.

TABLE 5.15 Beanbag ball bash

Activity	Adaptations (apply STEP)	Technical tips	Signs of success
Beanbag ball bash In pairs, stand opposite your partner, behind a set line, with a large foam ball placed in the space between you. Take it in turns to throw three beanbags at the ball to try to move it over your partner's line. Reset game after a line has been crossed and a point scored.	S – Play on a short wide court or a long narrow court. T – Take alternate throws. E – increase/decrease number of beanbags. P - Play 'doubles' with two players behind each line.	*See earlier tips on throwing.* Move along your line to keep ball directly in front of you before throwing. Try to hit the middle of the ball.	Effective throwing – ball rarely missed. Longer 'rallies' – ball is moved backwards and forwards before a point is scored.
Review questions	Can you make your partner go the wrong way? What do you need to improve to play this game better?		

Gymnastic activities

Whilst most people would accept that a physical education would not be complete without some form of gymnastics experience, the nature and scope of gymnastics in schools is contested and subject to much debate. From personal experience of working with students and teachers in schools we find ourselves in agreement with Reynold's (2000) view that, 'for many teachers, confusion may persist over what actually constitutes the make-up of the various approaches to gymnastics' (p. 156).

Our focus however is the quality of the experience rather than the application of a label to the form of experience offered to pupils. In gymnastic activities, pupils strive to improve gross motor control through engaging in activity experiences on the floor and with apparatus. This context provides children with an opportunity to create, control and link movements in increasingly complex patterns and in which the central challenge remains the replication of high quality movement.

Gymnastics is distinct from other activity areas in that pupils are required to think about how to create, perform and replicate actions, agilities and sequences as accurately as possible. We now turn our attention to what should be taught in gymnastics at Key Stage 1.

The National Curriculum advises that, at Key Stage 1, pupils should be taught to:

a. perform basic skills in travelling, being still, finding space and using it safely, both on the floor and using apparatus
b. develop the range of their skills and actions [for example, balancing, taking off and landing, turning and rolling]
c. choose and link skills and actions in short movement phrases
d. create and perform short, linked sequences that show a clear beginning, middle and end and have contrasts in direction, level and speed.

Building on pupils' experiences of movement in the Foundation Stage described earlier, at Key Stage 1 teachers should continue to provide pupils with a variety of gymnastic challenges. This is achieved by providing pupils with opportunities to ask and then find answers to the following four key questions:

■ What can we do?
■ Where can we move?
■ How can we move?
■ Who can we move with?

The gymnastics curriculum emerges out of finding increasingly inventive and creative answers to these questions.

In the next section we suggest ways in which the teacher can develop a high quality and well-rounded programme of gymnastics that addresses the aspects of learning.

Teaching pupils the skills associated with gymnastics is made easier when the actions to be introduced are classified. Developing the work of Smith (1994), we recommend a simple classification system as shown in Figure 5.2.

These are the building blocks of successful gymnastic performances. Each can be rehearsed and developed in isolation from the others but a sequence of many actions is likely to involve two or more domains.

Teaching tip

For each new action or combination, ask the pupils to describe where it would fit on the model (Figure 5.2) to encourage them to look for and describe travel, balance, shape and rotation. Placing the names of, or a picture of, the action on a chart in the classroom helps to develop pupils' understanding of gymnastic skills.

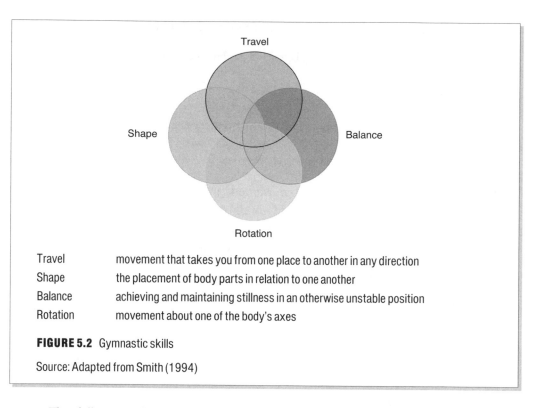

Travel	movement that takes you from one place to another in any direction
Shape	the placement of body parts in relation to one another
Balance	achieving and maintaining stillness in an otherwise unstable position
Rotation	movement about one of the body's axes

FIGURE 5.2 Gymnastic skills

Source: Adapted from Smith (1994)

The following charts illustrate some of the skills that pupils should rehearse at Key Stage 1.

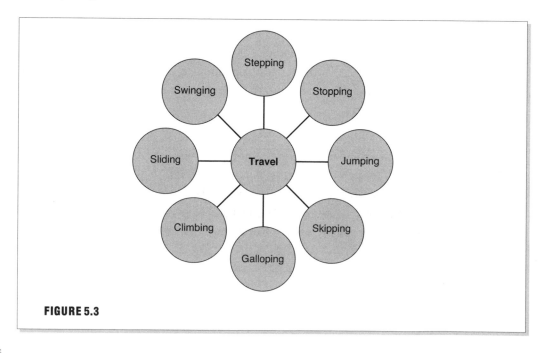

FIGURE 5.3

Teaching tip

After introducing each of the 'travel' actions to pupils, give them time to practise on their own, on the spot or in a small space. Then try the following simple pattern: start from being still, perform the action on the spot to the count of eight and be still again. When they can repeat this consistently, increase the space they are allowed to work in and the length of time they repeat the action for.

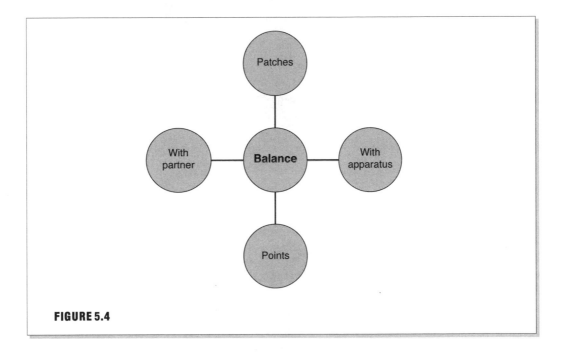

FIGURE 5.4

Teaching tip

It is important to provide pupils with a visual guide to help extend their thinking in relation to what body parts they could try balancing on. Trying to keep still in new positions develops pupils' core stability. Presenting pupils with high quality example images to copy will enhance their performance and improve their accuracy in both performance and observation.

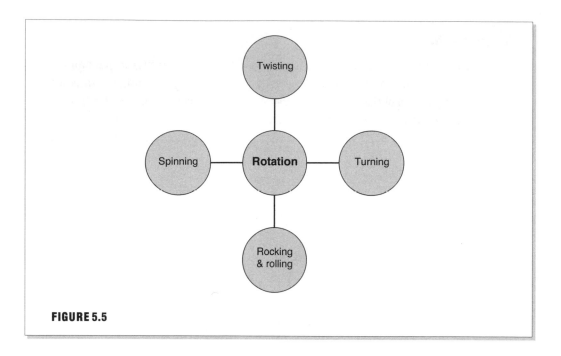

FIGURE 5.5

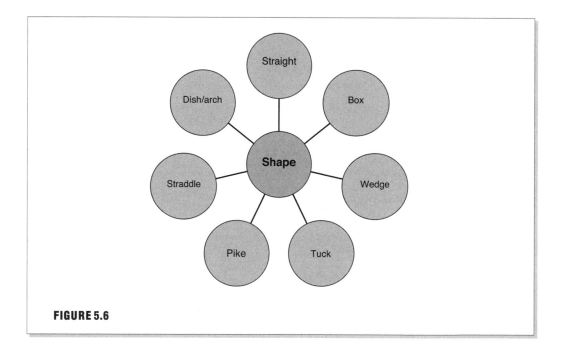

FIGURE 5.6

One of the key challenges of gymnastics is learning how to link a series of actions together into a continuous and fluid sequence. At Key Stage 1, helping pupils to link movements together involves developing their use of pathways, direction, level and speed.

Having practised and repeated a simple skill in isolation, pupils should then be encouraged to create an 'action sandwich' where the new action is sandwiched between two others. Pupils will enjoy creating their own simple action sandwiches and can then start to add additional and more challenging 'fillings'. Try variations on the following activity:

The Special Double Deluxe Gym Sequence Sandwich

Using a balance as the 'bread' in your gym sandwich, choose three fillings from this list to squeeze in between:

Turn, slide, jump, roll, twist, hop, skip, gallop, crawl. My Special Double Deluxe Gym Sequence Sandwich:

> Balance
> Slide
> Balance
> Jump
> Balance
> Skip
> Balance

Teaching tip

When helping pupils to remember simple movement patterns it is a good idea to write down the pattern or draw it on a board. Not only does this help to remind pupils what is coming next but it will also help to extend their movement vocabulary.

The next challenge is to learn to perform the movement pattern along a specified pathway. Try the following example patterns:

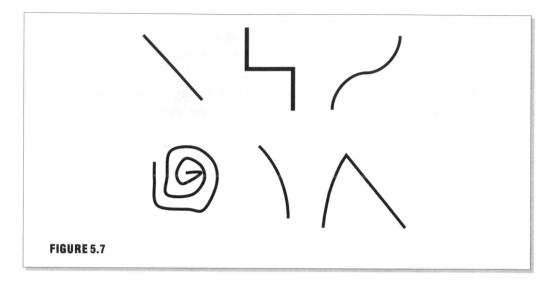

FIGURE 5.7

Then use recognisable letter shapes:

A   K   G   H   Q

Using apparatus to develop pupils' skilfulness and confidence is an important part of gymnastics. The different surfaces and levels that the introduction of apparatus brings to the working environment helps to extend pupils' repertoire of actions and challenges their composition skills. Pupils need to be taught how to handle mats, benches, trestle tables and climbing frames. Whilst integrating apparatus time into every lesson may not be feasible, within each block of gymnastics lessons pupils should have the opportunity to try out their skills with low-level apparatus combinations.

By providing pupils with the opportunity to assemble patterns of movement from a series of separate parts they will get better at visually unpicking patterns when they see them performed by others. Thus through the processes of selecting, ordering, reordering, practising and performing movement patterns, pupils will intuitively develop an understanding of composition. The act of observing and then describing individual actions, and then simple patterns of movement, will assist pupils to develop a gymnastic vocabulary. This can be helped by the use of flash cards.

Teaching tip

Once pupils are changed for PE but whilst still in the classroom, show images of gymnasts and ask them to describe what they see. As pupils' gymnastic vocabulary develops hand out large photographs of gymnasts in action to small groups and ask pupils to describe what the gymnast has just done, is doing and will do next.

Once confident in describing movement from still images they can then practise on live action by observing each other. More able pupils can then be challenged to make suggestions for improvement.

Swimming and water-based activities

Bath time at home and early play experiences in wet play areas should provide pupils with experience of pushing and pulling motions through water, developing their knowledge of what floats and sinks, and how water pours, splashes and fills containers. Changing to get into a paddling pool or larger pool of shallow water should be a natural extension of these experiences and provide children with the opportunity to play with water using their legs and feet.

The QCA recommend that where swimming is introduced at Key Stage 1 pupils should be taught to:

a. move in water [for example, jump, walk, hop and spin, using swimming aids and support]
b. float and move with and without swimming aids
c. feel the buoyancy and support of water and swimming aids
d. propel themselves in water using different swimming aids, arm and leg actions and basic strokes.

The guidance assumes that pupils may have had limited experience of swimming in pool environments. Pupils will, of course, arrive in Key Stage 1 with varying degrees of water confidence and competence. Following an initial assessment, teachers will need to select appropriately challenging experiences and draw, where necessary, from the curriculum activities planned for pupils in Key Stage 2 (see Chapter 6).

Since only very few primary schools have their own pool, in the majority of cases going swimming involves a journey to an unfamiliar site, with unfamiliar faces, smells, sights and sounds. For this reason we recommend arranging a 'dry run' class visit to the pool venue prior to starting the swimming programme. If pupils also pack their swimming kit to take with them on this visit, the whole experience provides good practice for the real thing. Pupils will need to know:

- Where they change;
- Where to leave their clothes;
- Where the toilets are;
- The rules for safety and hygiene at the pool;
- How to get from the changing rooms to the poolside;
- Where to wait prior to entering the water;
- Where the shallow water and deep water is;
- Where to get in and out of the water;

- What equipment they will be using;
- How to behave when in the water;
- What the various whistles, alarms and signals mean;
- Where to congregate at the end of the lesson.

Teaching tip

Devising a question sheet for pupils to complete during the visit can be a good way to focus pupils' attention on the information they need to know.

Prior to developing pupils' knowledge and competence in the recognised swimming strokes (see Chapter 6), it is important to develop their confidence in the water so that they can relax and allow the water to support them. Whilst many pupils will welcome the opportunity to get into the pool, there will be some for whom it is a frightening experience. For this reason, teachers should try to make the water as inviting as possible. By distributing toys, floats, 'noodles', flips and hoops in the water, pupils will be much more inclined to enter the space. The activities listed below provide some initial ideas for building water confidence in the pool environment. Pupils can work with or without buoyancy aids as necessary.

Walking practices

Holding the rail

- slide feet along the bottom;
- lead with only one foot, then alternate feet;
- try the above whilst moving up and down in the water.

In pairs

- walk holding a partner's hand;
- walk sideways facing your partner holding both hands (remember to look where you are going);
- holding hands walk around in a circle;
- try the above whilst moving with your shoulders in the water.

With equipment

- push a ball across the pool with your hands/shoulders/knees/chin/nose;

- push a ball across without touching it;

- pass the ball between you and a partner whilst walking forwards/sideways/ backwards across the pool;

- climb in and out of a floating hoop (push the hoop down to step in and out).

Regaining feet

- hold a ball/float/noodle for support and practise lifting both feet off the bottom;

- looking down to the bottom of the pool, stretch one leg out behind you (arabesque), lean forwards with your weight on the ball/float/noodle, lift the other leg to meet it. Bend at the knees and at the waist to regain feet.

- as above but start looking up at the ceiling;

- walk forwards/backwards and repeat the above.

Floating practices (use buoyancy aids as necessary)

Keeping shoulders under the water

- hold a float under each arm or wrap a noodle around your back and hop from one leg to the other;

- jump feet off the bottom and hold them up as long as you can;

- jump feet off the bottom and make a tuck/straddle/pike shape;

- with a partner supporting you under your shoulders let your head lie on the surface and look up at the ceiling;

- in this position, can you push your tummy to the surface?

- how long can you keep both feet off the bottom for?

- can you lie parallel with the side of the pool holding on to the side with the nearest hand and with a float under the other arm? Gently let go of the side and lie still before regaining your feet.

Propulsion with arms

As pupils play these games and move through the water with growing confidence and speed they will automatically begin to rehearse the arm actions similar to those used in breast stroke, front crawl and butterfly. To develop and refine these actions try the following activities:

With shoulders beneath the surface

■ walk along the bottom of the pool, pulling yourself along with bent arms/straight arms;

■ recover arms out of the water, at first together and then alternately;

■ try feeling the difference when fingers are closed tightly/spread wide;

■ walk sideways with one arm pointing where you want to go and pull with the other arm only, recovering out of the water;

■ hop along the bottom, pulling arms together or alternately;

■ count how many times your feet touch the bottom.

Having tried 'alternating' and 'simultaneous' actions, label these 'front crawl', 'back crawl', 'breast stroke' and 'butterfly' to extend pupils' vocabulary and for easy reference in the future.

Propulsion with legs

When learning to kick it is fun to make a big splash, but too much splashing can be intimidating for less confident pupils. Pupils should aim to create some 'white water' turbulence where their feet are, bringing their feet up to, but not breaking, the surface. Try the following:

■ Hold on to the side of the pool, look down towards the bottom of the pool and kick your feet up and down with bent legs. Try the same but with straight legs. Which feels harder?

■ Wrap a noodle around your back (or hold a float under each forearm) and push your tummy up towards the surface. Try drawing big circles with your heels, first one way and then the other way. Can you do the same but with your feet turned away from each other?

As with the arm actions, having tried 'alternating' and 'simultaneous' actions, label them accordingly.

Games

Once pupils have gained experience of moving in the water, playing games is a good way of consolidating their movement skills and provides them with opportunities to select and apply skills. The following examples are good to start or conclude lessons:

■ The Lighthouse Keeper's Lunch – In groups of three or four, spread out in a line across the pool and, on the signal, pass items from one side to the other without them getting wet.

■ Lifeboats – spread a range of floating toys/swimming aids on the surface. Pupils have to 'rescue' one item at a time and place it on the side.

■ Overboard! – like 'Simon Says' but using actions with a nautical theme such as 'climb the rigging', 'scrub the decks', 'duck the boom', 'bail out', etc. On the command, 'Overboard!' pupils have to jump up, submerge, resurface and wave both arms in the air.

Before and after swimming lessons, encourage pupils to talk about how they feel when they are in and around the water. Sharing thoughts about their feelings can alleviate concerns and can also ensure that pupils are supportive of each other when in the water. Show pupils pictures of different water sports (swimming, sailing, scuba diving, water skiing) and talk about what is happening. Ask pupils to set personal targets for each lesson and share them with their swimming 'buddy'. Ask buddies at the end of the lesson if the target has been achieved.

Developing knowledge and understanding of fitness and health

At Key Stage 1 pupils should be taught:

a. how important it is to be active
b. to recognise and describe how their bodies feel during different activities

From getting to know their bodies through naming and labelling body parts to recognising that lots of energetic activity makes us tired, there are a number of opportunities in any PE lesson to focus pupils' attention on the impact of activity on their bodies.

Teaching tip

It is a good idea to establish a regular warm-up/cool-down 'routine' that pupils can be introduced to in stages and which provides them with an opportunity to learn and improve a simple movement pattern.

As the lesson draws to a conclusion, pupils should be offered opportunities to show what they can do. Allowing time for showing and sharing provides a natural slowing down of pupils' activity rates. Following brief discussion of a range of performances, pupils could repeat a variation on actions carried out in the warm-up at a reduced intensity. Engaging pupils in warming up and cooling down activities provides good opportunities to discuss how exercise makes us feel different. Recognising and being able to describe the changes that take place is one of the key indicators that pupils are developing knowledge and understanding of fitness and health appropriate to their key stage.

Chapter summary

This chapter has provided a rationale for the inclusion of each of the activity areas making up the PE curriculum experience for pupils at Key Stage 1. Through identifying the distinctive nature of each of the activity areas we have sought to demonstrate how each makes an important contribution to a pupil's initial experience of physical education. By outlining a framework of understanding for each activity area we hope to have contributed to your understanding of the potential for learning about, in and through each domain. The four aspects of learning have been introduced as the glue which binds the activity areas together and provides coherence to what may otherwise appear to be a rather eclectic set of experiences. Keeping these in the forefront of your thinking is the key to moving beyond occupying pupils in activities to helping pupils to learn through those activities. Furthermore, we have encouraged you to think about ways in which, just like in classroom-based activities, you can differentiate the level of challenge in each of the activity areas in order to address the needs of all pupils. We hope that the suggested activity ideas are useful and serve as a catalyst to inspire further thinking, discussion and planning.

Questions for reflection

■ Do you think that the activity areas suggested for inclusion at Key Stage 1 represent a 'complete' experience? If not, what would you add/take away?

■ What do you identify as the key barriers, if any, to delivering the recommendations for PE at Key Stage 1?

■ Thinking about a PE lesson you have recently taught or observed, which of the four aspects of learning was most prominent? Which, if any, were absent?

■ How well does your teaching in PE accommodate the needs of pupils with different levels of experience?

Web links and further reading

www.peprimary.co.uk
A subscription site but with free access areas brimming with advice and ideas for enhancing the PE programme for pupils in Key Stage 1.

www.nc.uk.net/safeswimming/
An excellent, easy to navigate site with a host of swimming activities addressing the needs of the non-swimmer to the accomplished swimmer.

Bailey, R. and MacFadyen, T. (eds) (2000) *Teaching Physical Education 5–11*. London: Continuum.
Chapters 10–16. Very readable collection of chapters with a clear focus on pupils' learning in each of the activity areas. Includes a chapter on teaching health-related fitness discretely as a 'seventh' activity area.

Bunker, D., Hardy, C., Smith, S., and Almond, L. (eds) (1994) *Primary Physical Education: Implementing the National Curriculum*. Cambridge: Cambridge University Press.
Packed with useful activity ideas for each of the six activity areas.

Douglas, M. (1999) *Hodder Primary PE: Dance*. London: Hodder and Stoughton.
A really easy read, packed with exciting ideas for developing creative movement experiences.

Physical education in Key Stage 2

Chapter objectives

By the end of this chapter you should be able to:

- Understand the breadth and scope of PE at Key Stage 2;

- Develop knowledge of delivering successful learning experiences through the core activity areas of dance, games and gymnastic activities and the additional areas of athletic activities, outdoor and adventurous activities and swimming;

- Understand how the four aspects of learning can be used as a focus for teaching, learning and assessment at Key Stage 2.

PE in the National Curriculum at Key Stage 2

COMMON SENSE WOULD SUGGEST that PE at Key Stage 2 will involve more of the same, but with a greater level of challenge, providing pupils with the opportunity to consolidate and extend their repertoire of skills. As explained in Chapter 5, for teachers and pupils to make sense of the National Curriculum it is important to take every opportunity to draw connections between the four aspects of knowledge, skills and understanding (see Table 6.1).

During the key stage, pupils should be taught the required knowledge, skills and understanding through five areas of activity:

    a) dance activities

    b) games activities

    c) gymnastic activities

    and two activity areas from:

    d) swimming activities and water safety

    e) athletic activities

    f) outdoor and adventurous activities.

TABLE 6.1 Knowledge, skills and understanding in PE at Key Stage 2

	Acquiring and developing skills	Selecting and applying skills, tactics and compositional ideas	Evaluating and improving performance	Developing knowledge and understanding of fitness and health
Pupils should be taught to	consolidate their existing skills and gain new ones; perform actions and skills with more consistent control and quality.	plan, use and adapt strategies, tactics and compositional ideas for individual, pair, small-group and small-team activities; develop and use their knowledge of the principles behind the strategies, tactics and ideas to improve their effectiveness; apply rules and conventions for different activities.	identify what makes a performance effective; suggest improvements based on this information.	understand how exercise affects the body in the short term; warm up and prepare appropriately for different activities; understand why physical activity is good for their health and wellbeing; understand why wearing appropriate clothing and being hygienic is good for their health and safety.

Swimming activities and water safety must be chosen as one of these areas of activity unless pupils have completed the full Key Stage 2 teaching requirements during Key Stage 1.

In practice, despite the statutory orders, most schools endeavour to provide pupils with learning experiences in all six areas of activity at Key Stage 2. In the absence of statutory guidance relating to the allocation and distribution of curriculum time however, decisions about how much time to spend on each area within each year are taken at the school level. Many schools adopt a pragmatic approach, allocating the bulk of curriculum time to activity areas that are more readily accommodated during the normal school week (dance, games, gymnastics) whilst delivering the programme of study for athletic activities, outdoor and adventurous activities and swimming at convenient times throughout the year.

In the next section we begin by considering ways in which to develop pupils' knowledge, skills and understanding in the activity areas introduced in Chapter 5 and then consider the contribution of athletic and outdoor and adventurous activities to PE at Key Stage 2.

Dance activities

Davies (2000) suggests that dance makes a unique and distinctive contribution to pupils' physical education, posing the performer the challenge of finding meaning in movement. Douglas (1999) argues that dance is not only interactive but also an integrating medium in which pupils are provided with the opportunity to increase their movement vocabulary, practise decision making and problem solving and exercise aesthetic judgement (p. 2).

Through their dance experiences in Key Stage 2 pupils should be encouraged to develop an awareness of quality and beauty in their immediate environment, to describe what they see, to discuss how they feel and to enjoy objects and events for what they are, 'the way they look, sound or feel . . . for their qualities of line, pattern, dynamics, colour, texture and shape' (Davies, 2000, p. 127). Since dance is the only art form in the PE curriculum, through creating, performing and evaluating dances pupils experience what it is to be an artist. Just as all art forms evolve over time, the dance curriculum in school is able to draw upon a wide range of traditional and contemporary styles for inspiration. We contend that the dual location of dance, in the PE curriculum and in the expressive arts domain, represents an opportunity to explore movement from a dual perspective. On the one hand, pupils can enjoy the physicality of dance as a movement form and experiment with the mechanics of motion, the challenge to their physical fitness, control and co-ordination and the discipline of choreography that any dance performance demands. On the other hand, pupils can enjoy the intellectual and emotional demands of the creative process through devising, performing and appreciating dances. Approached from either direction, in our experience, teaching dance is an exciting, stimulating, infinitely varied process that is full of surprises and which so often produces truly memorable results. The four key components of movement in dance are action, space, dynamics and relationships.

Building on their experiences in Key Stage 1, at Key Stage 2 pupils should be encouraged to increase their use and understanding of each component and in so doing become more confident, skilful and appreciative dancers.

The three key phases in this process are composition, performance and appreciation. Dance composition involves the selection, ordering and pacing of movements to communicate an idea or story to an audience. During performance, the dancer attempts to present their work to an audience. Prior to this, plenty of practice is essential. Practising a performance enables the dancer to refine the movements, the quality of expression, the use of space and each other to convey their ideas most effectively. Showing dances, or parts of dances, to the rest of the class is an important experience and serves as a useful stepping stone to developing the confidence to perform in school assemblies, to parents and the wider public.

> **Teaching tip**
>
> It is a good idea to increase the frequency of performance opportunities in dance lessons as a dance unit progresses. An audience can consist of one other pupil and need not be a large group.

The act of dance appreciation involves looking, contemplating and making judgements. To assist this process, pupils should be provided with key questions to ask. At Key Stage 2 these should extend beyond whether they 'liked' the dance, to explaining the reasons behind their response to the dance. As pupils acquire experience of being an audience and develop their knowledge and understanding of what makes a good dance, the feedback they offer can be used to improve and extend the performance. It is important to remind pupils to be sensitive and constructive when commenting on others' work.

The National Curriculum advises that at Key Stage 2 pupils should be taught to:

a) create and perform dances using a range of movement patterns, including those from different times, places and cultures
b) respond to a range of stimuli and accompaniment.

To fulfil this requirement Robertson (1994) helpfully sees four clear stages to work through:

- Learning to tell stories;
- Developing those stories;
- Composing and performing dances;
- Experiencing other styles of dance.

The first stage requires that pupils acquire and develop an extensive movement vocabulary.

A precursor to effective communication in any new language is accurate pronunciation. When learning the language of movement this equates to learning to use the body, as a whole or in part, to convey a word or idea convincingly. This takes much practice and will always be open to misinterpretation. In order to minimise error, dancers use repetition and amplification. By exaggerating and repeating key aspects of a movement idea, the novice dancer increases their chances of being understood.

Dance lessons should provide opportunities for pupils to rehearse each of the four key components through a range of stimulating themes (see Table 6.2).

TABLE 6.2 Components of movement applied to dance

Action	Dynamics	Space	Relationships
Whole body – jump, leap, hop, skip, shiver, fall, shake, collapse, roll, stamp, twist, spin, twirl; Body parts – hands, feet, head, knees, elbows, above waist, below waist.	Time – hurried, quick, hectic or relaxed slow, calm; Weight – heavy, firm, strong, powerful or light, fine, gentle, delicate; Pathway – direct and decisive or indirect and faltering; Flow – the rhythm or continuity of a movement, predictable or unpredictable.	Direction – forward, backward, sideways; Level – high, medium, low; Proximity – near to, far from; Pathway – curling, angular, diagonal; Size – big, small.	Solo, duo, duo + 1, trio; Unison or canon; 'Question and answer'; Mirroring/shadowing; Symmetry/asymmetry.

Teaching tip

Before introducing a theme with pupils, complete a table such as Table 6.2 with specific terms that relate to your theme. This will provide you with a bank of ideas to help pupils when their ideas dry up.

Each time you introduce a new theme to your pupils add their ideas to a word wall (see Figure 6.1). This will help pupils to develop an ever-expanding movement vocabulary.

During Key Stage 2, pupils should be challenged to compose longer dance phrases that:

■ have a clear beginning, middle and end;

■ can link to other dance phrases;

■ show progress along the four key components.

Stimulating pupils' imagination, creativity and story-telling capability relies on the selection of appropriate themes (see Table 6.3).

Teaching tip

Make mini whiteboards available for pupils to sketch and record their ideas. This helps them remember what they were doing and can be a useful focus for discussion with a partner, small group or the teacher.

Where	What			
Straight	Freeze	Hop	Stride	Spin
Square	Shudder	Melt	Writhe	Cower
Diagonal	Heave	Flick	Crumble	Expand
Triangle	Turn	Twist	Rise	Slide
Curling	Scamper	Spiral	Leap	Fall
Circle	Roll	Zip	Swoop	Pounce
Zig-zag	Glide	Wheel	Contract	Skip
Spiral	Drip	March	Float	Extend
Crescent	Envelop	Retreat		
Jagged				
Smooth				

	Who	How	
	Alone	Effort	
Forwards	In pairs	Strong	Light
Backwards	In groups	Heavy	Weak
Sideways	Lead and follow	Smooth	Free
In front	Together	Jerk	Hesitant
Behind	Meeting	Sudden	Sustained
Alongside	Parting	Speed	
Above	Going around	Accelerating	
Below	Encircle	Decelerating	

FIGURE 6.1 An example of a word wall

TABLE 6.3 Stimulus and movement ideas for KS2 dance

Theme	Movement ideas	Stimulus ideas
Work	Farmer – driving, stacking, milking, fencing;	Pictures, toy animals;
	Mechanic – lifting, hammering, winding and washing;	Toy cars, lorries;
	Fire fighter – cleaning, sliding down the pole, hosing down, chopping;	Fireman Sam;
Seasons, e.g. autumn	Gusts of wind, leaves detach, fall, tumble, drift, settle, swept up;	Dried leaves, sweeping brush, dustbin bags;
	Fireworks – patterns created by different types of firework – rocket, Catherine wheel, Roman candle;	Tchaikovsky's 1812 overture, patterns;
	Halloween – witches bent over cauldrons, making potions, curious cats, swooping on broomsticks, gliding ghosts, flapping bat's wings;	Pumpkins, masks, witches hat, rubber bats;
The Olympic Games	Faster – higher – stronger;	Video excerpts from an opening/ closing ceremony;
	Preparing, competing, celebrating;	
	Different activities at different sites – makes for a good whole class dance.	Olympic picture icons for each sport.

Teaching tip

By selecting a theme with the potential for multiple activities performed simultaneously, the teacher can choreograph an effective whole-class dance, as in the Olympic Games example below.

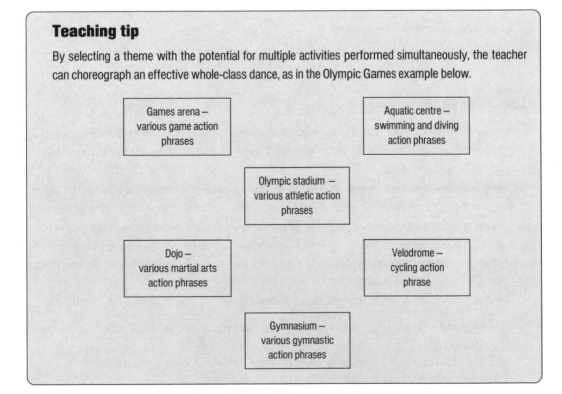

Drawing on a range of dance styles from different times and cultures adds a further dimension to pupils' dance experience. This will also provide an opportunity to discuss similarities and contrasts between dance styles and the significance of costume, staging, make-up and music to dance experience.

Teaching tip

Show pupils pre-recorded dance performances of professional dance artists or companies. This will motivate pupils and help develop the skills of observation and appreciation (see key questions below) as well as being a source of compositional ideas.

Key questions for the audience

- Does the dance have a clear beginning, middle and ending?
- Is there variety in the movement?
- Does the dancer control their movements well?
- Does the dancer show good extension of the body?
- Can you see shapes in the movement – in the body or in the pathways used?
- Do the movements flow from one to the other?
- Is the dancer convincing?
- How does the dance make you feel?

Games activities

Across the ages many games have appeared, been developed and become popular. Where some have endured and now enjoy long histories and rich traditions, others have disappeared only to be replaced by new games. Amidst all this change one thing remains constant – our insatiable desire to play! Through the energetic use of large muscle groups and the subsequent heavy demand on the cardiovascular system, games can provide excellent opportunities for physical growth and development. The requirement to co-operate, compete, and abide by rules and conventions in the pursuit of arbitrary goals have also long been associated with the development of social and emotional skills.

The National Curriculum advises that, at Key Stage 2, pupils should be taught to:

a) play and make up small-sided and modified competitive net, striking/fielding and invasion games
b) use skills and tactics and apply basic principles suitable for attacking and defending
c) work with others to organise and keep the games going.

At Key Stage 2 pupils should build upon their learning of core skills in Key Stage 1, then experience and create games drawn from selected categories or families of games. Games can be classified into different groups in many ways. The most common approach, however, classifies games according to their structural features and presents us with several family groups that include combat, invasion, net/wall, striking/fielding and target games. By developing our understanding of how games work, we should be better placed to help pupils develop an understanding and appreciation of games play, in addition to helping them to play well.

All games have structural, strategic and technical components.

The game structure determines the overall aim, playing boundaries, time limits, number of players, the equipment to be used and the playing rules. Structural components are usually fixed and upheld by independent officials.

Specific game strategies evolve over time and determine how the game is played. Players selectively employ strategy to try to outwit their opponents and be successful in achieving their aim.

Players put into practice their game strategy through employing techniques at the appropriate time. Some techniques are very complex and highly specific to individual games (such as the golf swing) but others are more generic and are useful in a multitude of games (such as running, catching, throwing).

Thus whilst several games may share common rules, apply common strategies and certain generic techniques, it is in the unique mix of structure, strategy and technique that each named activity remains distinct.

As pupils enter Key Stage 2, they are still developing consistency and accuracy in sending, receiving and travelling skills. In invasion games however, pupils are denied sufficient time and space to rehearse and refine these skills in context. Thus, games experiences should be selected on the basis that they provide an environment where pupils have as much time and space as they need, and in which they can be protected from interference. In this context, pupils are more likely to be successful and develop a sense of achievement. Whole-class invasion games (such as bench ball) break all of these rules and consequently are unlikely to be productive in helping pupils to develop their skilfulness or strategic thinking.

With this in mind, we suggest that during Years 3 and 4 children are exposed in equal measure to target, striking and fielding and net/wall games. Having had the opportunity to rehearse and combine their sending, receiving and travelling skills in these formats, children should be sufficiently skilful to try simple small-sided invasion games towards the end of Year 4. Throughout Key Stage 2, children should be encouraged to make up, revise and adapt their own games in order to assist their understanding of how games work. Rather than teaching and refining pupils' technical proficiency in isolation, we advocate developing pupils' proficiency in games through the 'games for understanding' model.

The traditional approach to teaching games involves teaching 'how' followed by teaching 'why'. In other words, pupils are taught games skills in small, progressive steps and then asked to put these into practice in games. Learning technique takes precedence over learning tactical or strategic understanding. The Teaching Games for Understanding (TGfU) model (Bunker and Thorpe, 1982) uses sequences of game-like scenarios in which pupils can work on game strategies, and on the skills needed for the task, in a developmentally appropriate manner. TGfU follows six basic steps:

Step 1: Learners are introduced to the game and allowed to play.
Step 2: Following play, the conventions of the game are explained.
Step 3: Learners reflect on their experience of playing the game and think about the major tactical problems that the game presents.
Step 4: Learners practise using game-like tasks to develop their tactical knowledge and to learn to apply strategies to specific situations.
Step 5: Learners are encouraged to use new and existing skills/tactical awareness in game-like situations.
Step 6: Learners refine their skills so that game play is based on tactical knowledge, game appreciation and game strategies.

This process encourages pupils to develop higher-order cognitive skills and social skills through problem solving, analysing, evaluating, decision making, and social inter-action, which are crucial to success in games play. The learning of skills, whilst no less important, is relegated to later in the process.

In Tables 6.4 and 6.5, which show some examples, the review questions are designed to start conversations in lessons about what makes a good performance and how performances can be improved.

When using the TGfU model, teachers and pupils can work together to create games that develop understanding of the principles of games play. At a later date, the strate-gies employed in these games can be put into practice in modified versions of adult games. Pupils will not be disadvantaged by delaying their introduction to adult games in curriculum time. On the contrary, their performance in these games is likely to be enhanced by their increased understanding of how the game works. Table 6.6 identifies key features of families of games that could be used as a starting point in creating new games.

TABLE 6.4 Games involving travelling activities

	Adaptations	Technical tips	Signs of success
Stuck in the mud Nominated 'catchers' tag 'runners'. Caught runners stand still until tagged by free runners.	Number of catchers. Playing time.	'Catchers' plan how to work together. 'Runners' change speed and direction.	Catchers working as a team. Runners avoiding being caught.
Raiders In a divided playing area, 2 teams of 4 players try to 'raid' beanbags/balls from their opposition's end zone. Defenders are not allowed in their own end zone. Having captured a beanbag the 'raiders' have to return to their own half, avoiding being tagged by the opposition.	Number of players. Court size.	Plan strategy before a raid.	Continuous game.
Review questions		Can you describe three ways of avoiding someone trying to catch you? How do you use your feet when changing direction?	

TABLE 6.5 Games involving striking, throwing and catching activities

Striking, throwing and catching activities	Adaptations	Technical tips	Signs of success
See 'Kicking rounders' p. 93 but add a striking implement.	Size of bat/ball. Strike from tee.	*Batters* Stand sideways on to ball. Take bat back. Swing through the ball to follow through in the direction of travel. *Fielders* Line up with direction of ball. Scoop ball with both hands. Stand sideways on to target for throw.	Consistency of contact. Accuracy in direction.
1, 2, 3, 4 Number players 1–4. Pass ball in order whilst moving around a nominated space. Score 1 point every time the ball gets back to No. 1 without being dropped.	Playing time. Number of players.	Move near to passing player. Show a target for thrower to aim at.	Number of dropped passes decreases.
Review questions		Give three tips to help a partner throw/hit with accuracy.	

TABLE 6.6 Features of games at KS2

Game type	Distinctive features	Common features
Striking and fielding	Players take turns to accumulate points. Consistency of hitting/throwing for distance and accuracy. Speed around bases/over short distances.	Players use/invent strategies to outwit opponents.
Net/wall	Barrier divides court. Consistency of hitting for accuracy/power. React quickly to opponent's hit to develop a rally (repeated 'turn-taking').	Players use/invent strategies to dominate the playing space. Players try to anticipate what opponents will do next.
Invasion	Players share same playing space. Gaining and retaining possession. No 'turn-taking'.	Players make decisions individually and collectively.
Review questions	In a striking and fielding game how do fielders decide where to stand? In a net game what are the advantages and disadvantages of playing close to the net? When you have possession in an invasion game, when should you run and when should you pass?	

Gymnastics activities

In Chapter 5, we identified four core themes that underpin all skill development in gymnastics – travel, balance, rotation and shape. Even when performing very complex tumbling combinations the most accomplished gymnast draws on these same fundamental principles. Thus during Key Stage 2, pupils should be encouraged to consolidate their performance and understanding through revisiting these themes, through repetition and through differentiated challenges.

The National Curriculum advises that, at Key Stage 2, pupils should be taught to:

a) create and perform fluent sequences on the floor and using apparatus
b) include variations in level, speed and direction in their sequences.

With such broad guidance, identifying what pupils should be taught, and in which order, can be a perplexing problem.

The key performance goal of gymnastics is to enable pupils to create and perform aesthetically pleasing patterns of movement that use the whole body. In the Foundation Stage pupils will establish basic movement and control competencies. In Key Stage 1 these will be refined and consolidated. As pupils become more experienced in Key Stage 2, their knowledge, performance and composition skills will develop further along what we refer to as the PACE continuum (see Table 6.7).

TABLE 6.7 The PACE continuum

P	Presentation	Developing awareness of an audience and performing movements in an aesthetically pleasing manner for that audience.
A	Accuracy	Developing greater control over the body and accuracy in movement through repetition.
C	Combination	Linking movements together in increasingly inventive and challenging ways.
E	Extension	Building an ever increasing repertoire of repeatable actions using both floor and apparatus.

Teachers can identify that learning in gymnastics is taking place when they see evidence of pupils' progression along the continuum (see examples in Table 6.8).

Using the PACE continuum is one way in which teachers can help pupils to remain focused on producing high quality work in gymnastic activities.

The structure of a gymnastics lesson should normally consist of:

- Warm up – gentle preparation for thinking and moving with control and poise;
- Floor work – exploration of a theme with open-ended and skill-based tasks;
- Apparatus work – development of movement ideas from floor work section on and around apparatus;
- Conclusion – reflection and review of achievements, revision of some aspects of floor work.

Shorter lessons, however, may be structured differently, as shown in Table 6.9.

TABLE 6.8 Examples of progress

	Examples of progress		
PACE	KS1	Early KS2	Later KS2
Presentation	Little or no awareness of audience, occasional use of starting or finishing position.	Regularly uses starting and finishing positions for a movement sequence.	Performer is conscious of the audience throughout all stages of a movement sequence.
Accuracy	Movements performed differently each time.	More consistency in the way in which some movements are performed.	Consistently accurate in the performance of the movement repertoire.
Combination	Can link two movements together smoothly in a repeating pattern.	Can remember and link up to four movements together smoothly in a repeating pattern.	Can remember and link more than four movements together smoothly.
Extension	Work on the floor and mats only.	Performs floor work on apparatus.	Uses apparatus to develop and extend floor work.

TABLE 6.9 Structuring shorter lessons

Lesson 1	Lesson 2	Lesson 3	Lesson 4
Warm up	Warm up	Warm up	Warm up
Floor work	Apparatus work	Floor work	Apparatus work
Conclusion	Conclusion	Conclusion	Conclusion

When pupils are regularly challenged to learn new skills, to incorporate those skills in ever expanding sequences of movement and given regular opportunities to perform, their hunger for new material grows and their enthusiasm for the activity increases. Teachers should not shy away from challenging pupils to work at their skill threshold and this will require a seamless blending of open-ended tasks with formal (named) skill teaching (see Table 6.10).

Remembering to adhere to the principles of differentiation, outlined in Chapter 5, individuals and groups should be working at a level of challenge that is appropriate. Thus whilst all pupils will be working on the same theme in a lesson, some will be working on open-ended tasks whilst others will be learning specific named skills under closer supervision.

Once pupils have developed a repertoire of movement ideas, they should be challenged to pick and mix these actions to create interesting patterns and combinations. Providing an action word bank is a really useful device to both develop pupils' vocabulary and their organisation skills. Doing this collaboratively (in small groups or as a class) adds a further interesting dimension in which pupils learn to share their movement thoughts and pick up ideas from each other. To begin with, pupils should be encouraged to copy and repeat appropriately challenging patterns that have been devised for them. Once they are sufficiently experienced in remembering and repeating patterns with consistency and accuracy they can start to assemble their own from an action word/image bank. This not only encourages pupils to develop, then select and apply their knowledge of actions and sequences but also provides a sound framework for beginning to describe and comment on the performance.

TABLE 6.10 Blending open-ended tasks with named skills

Theme	Open-ended challenge	Named skill(s)
Travel	Find three ways of leaping from one foot to the other.	Stag leap
Balance	Find three ways of balancing on two body parts.	Handstand
Rotation	Find three ways of rotating close to the floor.	Forward roll
Shape	What shapes can you make in the air when you jump from a bench to a mat?	Straddle, pike and tuck jumps

Integrating the use of apparatus in gymnastics is vital for pupils' progression. Not least, teaching pupils how to lift, carry and place large objects are important transferable skills. Through the process of planning, assembling, using and dismantling apparatus pupils will develop their confidence and awareness of safe practice in gymnastics.

Teaching tip

Distribute apparatus around the edge of the school hall to make it accessible and reduce assembly/dismantling time.

Check that apparatus:

■ is complete (rubber feet, plastic knobs, etc.);

■ can be placed on a firm footing;

■ is clean and non-slip (including mats);

■ coverings are not ripped or surfaces splintered;

■ locking devices can be fully secured;

■ can be accessed easily;

■ can be assembled by the pupils.

Teaching tip

Encourage pupils to visualise the layout of separate apparatus 'stations' and to work together in assembling apparatus through the use of apparatus cards (see examples in Figures 6.2 and 6.3).

Take the time to teach pupils how to carry and place equipment. It is helpful to establish simple guidelines for the pupils to follow:

■ Always face the direction of travel.

■ Ensure sufficient pupils are in position to lift the apparatus easily.

■ Lift with bent legs and a straight back on a count of '1, 2, 3, lift'.

■ Move to new position and place apparatus on the count of '1, 2, 3, down'.

For each apparatus 'station'

■ Large items out first (boxes, benches, tables and frames).

■ Small items out last (mats, skipping ropes, hoops).

■ Ensure adequate entry and exit points to avoid queues.

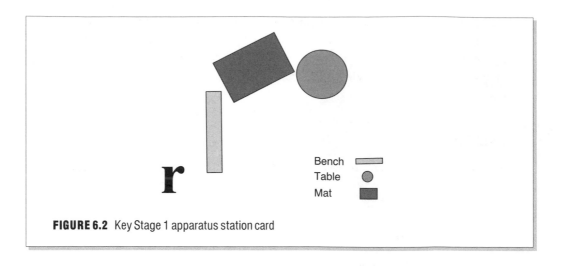

FIGURE 6.2 Key Stage 1 apparatus station card

- Encourage use of space around apparatus
- Encourage planning the route across the apparatus
- Set specific challenges for each apparatus formation.

Planning the layout of the room

- Ensure apparatus 'stations' allow sufficient travelling proximity between them (enough to accommodate 'rolling out', 'walking away' or 'jumping from' space).
- Allow up to 2m between apparatus and walls/windows.

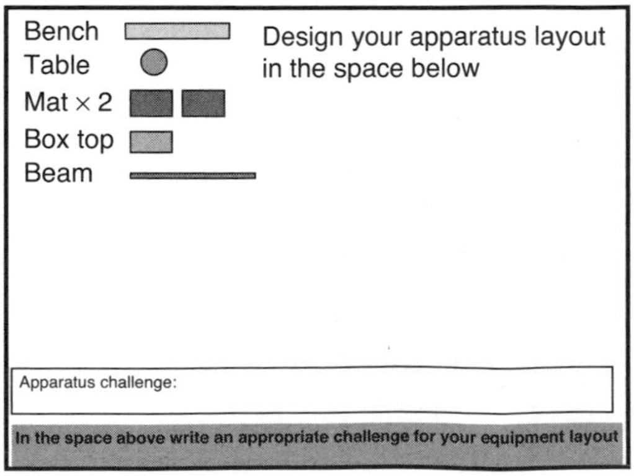

FIGURE 6.3 Key Stage 2 apparatus station card

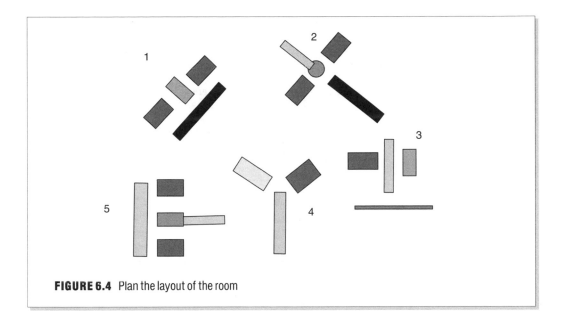

FIGURE 6.4 Plan the layout of the room

To begin with, pupils should be restricted to working at a single station. After sufficient time to explore the theme at that station there may be time to move to another station.

To evaluate and improve sequences of movement on floor and apparatus requires an

---

Teaching tip

Organise pupils into apparatus groups. Each group can assemble and dismantle the same apparatus station each week. Appoint a different group leader on a weekly basis to organise assembly and dismantling.

---

ability to appreciate quality in technique and composition. This will develop through regular opportunities to see and discuss high-quality gymnastic performance. Working from task cards (see example in Figure 6.5), viewing images, and watching video recordings and live performance in class will help to develop an appreciation of what is possible and raise pupils' expectations of performance. Not least, the opportunity to talk about gymnastics with their peers provides another opportunity to develop speaking and listening skills and extend their vocabulary.

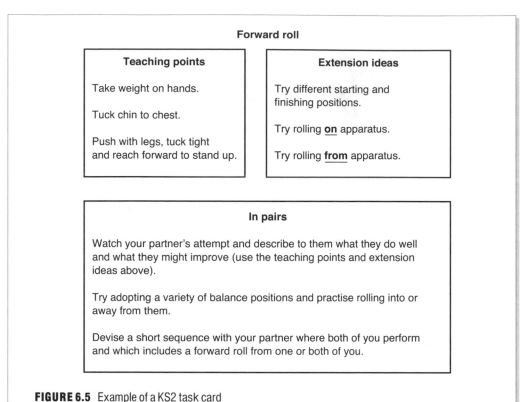

Forward roll

Teaching points

Take weight on hands.

Tuck chin to chest.

Push with legs, tuck tight and reach forward to stand up.

Extension ideas

Try different starting and finishing positions.

Try rolling **on** apparatus.

Try rolling **from** apparatus.

In pairs

Watch your partner's attempt and describe to them what they do well and what they might improve (use the teaching points and extension ideas above).

Try adopting a variety of balance positions and practise rolling into or away from them.

Devise a short sequence with your partner where both of you perform and which includes a forward roll from one or both of you.

FIGURE 6.5 Example of a KS2 task card

Swimming and water-based activities

Being able to swim is a prerequisite for a wide range of other water-based activity experiences such as sailing, canoeing, waterskiing and snorkelling. The pool environment offers such diverse potential that it can be used to encourage pupils to develop and extend their thinking skills in each of the five other activity areas. In water, pupils can try to outwit their opponents through playing games; they can strive to replicate movements as in gymnastics; they can race as in athletics; they can solve problems as in outdoor and adventurous activities; and they can choreograph expressive, rhythmical movement phrases as in dance. Swimming is both vital and versatile, so much so that the single attainment target for physical education remains that all pupils should be able to swim 25 metres unaided by the time they reach the end of Key Stage 2. Hardy (2000) suggests that the presence of the attainment target, rather than leading to an enhanced swimming experience for pupils, ironically can lead to a narrow curriculum focused exclusively on meeting the target. In so doing, he warns, pupils may not fully develop the basic skills and understanding of safety around water that the target was introduced to guarantee. Many would argue that swimming is a natural activity and that the earlier children are introduced to water, the sooner they will acquire the confidence and co-ordination required for efficient and effective propulsion. Despite not being compulsory at Key Stage 1, in order to equip pupils with the knowledge, skills and understanding required to meet the attainment target, many schools are choosing to introduce pupils to swimming as early as possible.

During Key Stage 2 pupils should be taught to:

a) pace themselves in floating and swimming challenges related to speed, distance
b) and personal survival
c) swim unaided for a sustained period of time over a distance of at least 25m
d) use recognised arm and leg actions, lying on their front and back
e) use a range of recognised strokes and personal survival skills (for example, front crawl, back crawl, breaststroke, sculling, floating and surface diving).

In order for pupils to demonstrate these competencies, Robertson (1994) argues that the swimming curriculum should address three core skill themes:

- Confidence building;

- Personal survival;

- Whole stroke techniques.

Confidence building is essential, and here are some suggestions for activities:

- Water entry and exit; travelling through water; bringing water to the face; submerging to collect items from the bottom.

- Changing shape in the water (including prone and supine positions); floating (using buoyancy aids as appropriate); regaining feet from prone and supine floating positions.

- Playing travelling games involving moving arms and legs to change speed and direction in the water.

Once pupils have developed water confidence, rapid progress can be made with developing new techniques.

Personal survival skills include pushing off; gliding; swimming under water; turning; rolling; treading water; feet and head first surface diving; entering and exiting the water without the use of steps. For whole-stroke techniques, practical experience of a range of propulsive techniques on the front, back and side, using a 'whole – part – whole' methodology, is an effective way of improving pupils' skills and their knowledge and understanding of how the strokes work.

Teaching tip

Create and laminate task/information cards about stroke development practices for pupils to use independently, in pairs, or in small groups.

Water confidence activities

■ 'What's my name?' Think of a name, take a breath, put your mouth/head in the water and say the name. Your partner has to guess/lip-read your name through the bubbles!

■ 'Jellyfish'. Divide the group into two. One half of the group spread out in the water each holding on to a buoyancy aid to practise floating. The rest of the group have to cross to the other side without touching one of the 'jellyfish'. Jellyfish can only reach out with their tentacles if they are floating. If you are touched, join the jellyfish.

Personal survival activities

After some initial practice at the specified techniques pupils may be ready to take on challenges like that posed in QCA Unit 16 (core task 3), which asks:

How long can you keep going around a personal survival obstacle course without touching the ground? Try to keep going for set lengths of time, *e.g. 5 minutes, 8 minutes, 12 minutes.* The course should involve:

■ swimming on the surface

■ swimming under water

■ carrying equipment

■ floating or sculling for a set period of time

■ retrieving equipment from the bottom of the pool.

A circuit of different challenges around the pool might take the form shown in Figure 6.6.

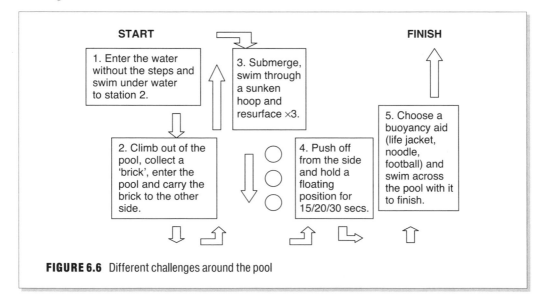

FIGURE 6.6 Different challenges around the pool

Whole stroke development activities

To avoid the monotony of simply swimming endless widths and lengths, keep pupils motivated by providing them with the opportunity to use their developing techniques in challenging tasks, and reflect on the outcomes of those tasks. Try using activities such as timed swims, distance swims, medley swims, team relay swims.

For each of these activities pupils should be encouraged to compete against the clock and keep a record of their personal best times. See the QCA website for further swimming challenges.

Evaluating and improving performance in swimming activities

Pupils rarely get the chance to view their swimming technique or to compare their technique with another. For this reason, it is advisable to establish a buddy system where one pupil swims while their partner observes their effort. It is now possible, through using digital technology, to show pupils video footage of their performance or compare still images of their technique with that of their peers or elite swimmers.

Through the effective use of demonstrations, video extracts and a buddy system, pupils will develop their knowledge and understanding to help develop their own and others' technique.

Teaching tip

Use a buddy system to encourage pupils to observe and talk to each other about their technique. Use technique cards to help the observer focus on specific features of the stroke, as shown in Figure 6.7.

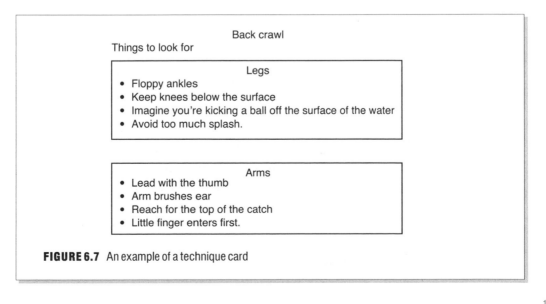

Back crawl

Things to look for

Legs
- Floppy ankles
- Keep knees below the surface
- Imagine you're kicking a ball off the surface of the water
- Avoid too much splash.

Arms
- Lead with the thumb
- Arm brushes ear
- Reach for the top of the catch
- Little finger enters first.

FIGURE 6.7 An example of a technique card

Athletic activities

Whether as observers or participants, by the time they enter Key Stage 2 pupils are likely to have gained some personal experience of an athletic event. Across the country, the raw material of track and field athletics is practised informally in the playground on a daily basis. As pupils challenge themselves, and one another, to run faster, throw further and jump higher they are engaging in a rudimentary form of athletics, at the heart of which lies a burning curiosity to find out what they are capable of and an intrinsic desire to compete. Primarily concerned with the pursuit and fulfilment of individual potential, rather than the measurement of success in specified technical events, the athletic experience in the primary school should be viewed as a means to an end, not an end in itself.

The National Curriculum advises that, at Key Stage 2, pupils should be taught to:

a) take part in and design challenges and competitions that call for precision, speed, power or stamina
b) use running, jumping and throwing skills both singly and in combination
c) pace themselves in these challenges and competitions.

Almond (1989) and O'Neill (1996) agree that the traditional teacher-centred approach to teaching athletics, which privileges 'events' and the learning of recognised techniques, represents a narrow and exclusive method. A broader and more inclusive approach, in which the child is at the centre of the process, they argue, is more likely to ensure that pupils remain motivated to learn, regardless of their athletic prowess. A pupil-centred approach demands that we rethink the roles of pupil as 'athletic performer' and teacher as 'event coach'. In pupil-centred athletics the content and presentation of lessons should be such that all pupils are encouraged to strive to improve, fulfil their potential and enjoy the athletic challenge. This is unlikely to be realised using the traditional model in which we may find pupils running against one another over set distances to establish a rank order. Through planning a progressive programme, in which pupils learn to gather information about their performance through measuring, recording and comparing, their focus is shifted from, 'Who is best?' to 'What is my best?' and 'How much better can I get?'

Track and field athletics represents only one form of athletic endeavour. Athletic events include all of those activities in which objective measurement, such as time, distance and weight, determines the winner. Thus rowing, cycling and weightlifting fall into the same broad sport category as pole vault, javelin and 100m sprint. In athletic events, participants strive to maximise their performance to finish ahead of their opponents, improving their chances through dedication to training in preparation for competition. It is usually through participating in activities linked to individual track and field events, however, that pupils get their first taste of the athletic experience.

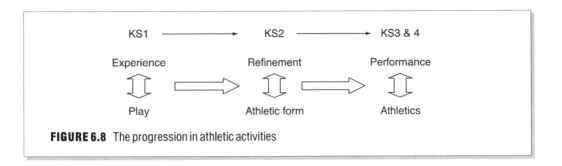

FIGURE 6.8 The progression in athletic activities

Through measuring, comparing and evaluating their efforts in the fundamental movement patterns of walking, running, jumping and throwing, pupils will be made aware of their physical capacity, begin to understand and develop a love of competition, and enjoy the sweetness of success. As O'Neill (1996) points out, through careful planning and structured teaching, competition and success become compatible for all pupils, not just the physically gifted. The challenge for all teachers is to set a range of differentiated tasks that serve to motivate all pupils to strive to improve. In our experience, most primary pupils will approach such tasks with vigour and enthusiasm, making the teaching of athletic activities a pleasure.

Pupils' earliest exposure to athletic challenge is through play. The core skills of athletic activities, running, jumping and throwing, are also integral to gymnastics, games and dance. Improvement in co-ordinating these actions will arise as a natural consequence of regular opportunities to practise. During Key Stage 2, these movements can be isolated, explored and refined. At Key Stage 3 and beyond, these movements are further developed according to the structures and rules of specific events (see Figure 6.8).

A pupil-centred athletics curriculum will centre around running, jumping and throwing in many different ways. Having practised these *within* other activities at Key Stage 1, at Key Stage 2 these actions need to be *isolated* to be *improved*. The following lists the types of activities that might be included in an athletics programme, under each of these headings:

Running

- Technique
- At different paces
- Over different distances
- Acceleration and deceleration
- Starting and finishing
- Around the bend
- Over obstacles

Technical tips

- Run on balls of feet
- Slight lean in the direction of travel
- High knee lift
- Vigorous forwards and backwards movement with the arms

SAFETY: Make sure pupils' shoes are secure and properly laced.

- In relays
- Tactics

Teaching tip

Show pupils images of runners and ask them to comment on their technique. This will highlight the key points and help them to improve their running.

Jumping

- Phases
    - Preparation
    - Take off
    - Flight
    - Landing
- For height
    - scissor technique
    - roll technique
- For distance (single jumps)
    - standing start (one- or two-footed take off)
    - running start
- For distance (combination jumps)
    - standing start
    - running start
- Assisted – using springboards or low platforms.

Technical tips

Standing broad jump – to show use of arms swinging backwards and then forwards at take off.

Scissor technique – stand sideways to the bar. Take-off foot is the one further from the bar. Kick lead leg upwards and over the bar. Take-off foot follows behind.

Roll technique – stand sideways to the bar. Take off foot is the one nearer to the bar. Swing leg up and over the bar, causing the body to turn to face the bar. Take-off leg follows.

SAFETY: Always land on your feet.

Throwing

- For accuracy
- For distance
- Using different techniques
    - Underarm
    - Push
    - Pull
    - Sling
    - Heave

Technical tips

Key points for all throws:

'Legs first, arms last'.
Transfer weight 'from back to front'.
Throwing is an explosive event so 'make it fast'.

> ## Teaching tip
>
> When planning to improve pupils' skills in athletics lessons, always include activities for at least two of the three core skills. Select a focus activity (e.g. running) and a secondary activity (e.g. throwing).

Pupils will enjoy practising the core athletic skills athletics through problem solving. Try the following:

Running

How far can you run? Pupils work in pairs to mark and measure how far they can run in 3 secs, 8 secs, 12 secs. Vary the task by changing the starting position – lying, sitting, kneeling, standing. Collect distances for each time and place the data in a graph when pupils return to the classroom. Repeat the exercise over different times, e.g. 1 min or 3 mins.

Jumping

Can you jump your own height? Pupils work in pairs to mark on the ground their body length. Using different jumping techniques, can they jump to equal or exceed their own height?

World record jumps How many jumps do you need to take to match the world record high jump, pole vault, long jump and triple jump? Measure and mark out all the distances on the field/playground and ask a partner to count your jumps.

Throwing

Which goes furthest? Using three different objects (large ball, quoit, small ball) conduct an investigation with a partner to find out which ball goes furthest. Each athlete throws each ball three times using each technique. Each athlete completes a table like the one shown in Table 6.11.

Whilst measuring and recording performance data provides opportunities to reflect on the magnitude of performance, it is equally important to encourage pupils to develop their observation skills and identify quality in performance. Pupils' knowledge of performance will accumulate through looking at live demonstrations, still images or diagrams and video of the core actions. Older pupils can even be encouraged to develop their own performance task cards as a guide for one another when watching their partner's performance. Figure 6.9 shows an example.

TABLE 6.11 Which goes furthest?

Object/technique	Sitting push			Kneeling push			Standing push		
Attempts	1st	2nd	3rd	1st	2nd	3rd	1st	2nd	3rd
Large ball									
Quoit									
Small ball									

Discuss your results with your partner.

Which was the furthest throw?

Which technique proved best for distance?

Which object travelled the shortest distance?

Can you explain your answers?

Teaching tip

Working in threes, pupils can switch between the roles of performer, judge and coach. The role of the judge is to ensure that the rules for the event are followed and to be fair and consistent in measuring and recording the outcome. The coach is responsible for helping the performer prepare for their turn, to write down the result and to observe and comment on the performance.

Outdoor and adventurous activities

The experience of moving in different, challenging and changing environments has, for many years, been acknowledged to contribute to pupils' personal, moral, social and emotional development. The outdoor and adventurous experience has been designed therefore to provide opportunities for pupils to develop physical, psychological, cognitive and emotional skills, such that they can draw upon these resources when faced with unforeseen challenges.

Martin (2000) helpfully draws the important distinction between *outdoor and adventurous* (O&A) activities and *outdoor pursuits*. Whereas managing learning in outdoor pursuits will normally require additional qualifications, reduced pupil–teacher ratios and take place away from the school site, he argues that O&A activities can be taught by the class teacher, using existing facilities on the school site and to the whole class at the same time (p. 187). O&A activities are process-oriented, and designed to engage pupils in developing the necessary thinking skills to solve problems, and to

Overarm throw

When your partner throws, check to see if they:	First attempt	Second attempt
• Stand sideways on to the target		
• Start with their opposite foot forwards (right arm thrower should have left leg forwards)		
• Take their throwing arm back behind their body but keep their hand above their shoulder		
• Lean slightly backwards using their other arm to balance		
• Turn their hips and chest towards the target		
• Move their weight forwards on to their front leg		
• Move their arm quickly		
• Keep both feet on the floor		
• Keep looking at the target		

FIGURE 6.9 An example of a performance task card

build trust, confidence and co-operation. The success of O&A activities thus relies heavily on the teacher's skilfulness in evoking a sense of adventure for their pupils. Pupils' tolerance of adventure, or their *adventure threshold*, will shift as they experience new situations. It remains vital, therefore, that teachers are sensitive to the range of adventure tolerance in any class and avoid setting challenges that will cause pupils' adventure threshold to be lowered rather than raised. Well-managed O&A activities will provide pupils with feelings of exhilaration, accomplishment and pride.

The National Curriculum advises that, at Key Stage 2, pupils should be taught to:

a) take part in outdoor activity challenges, including following trails, in familiar, unfamiliar and changing environments
b) use a range of orienteering and problem-solving skills
c) work with others to meet the challenges.

O&A activities in Key Stage 2 can therefore be broadly categorised into three areas, focusing on the development of:

1 Orientation skills

2 Communication/collaboration skills

3 Problem-solving skills.

Acquiring and developing skills in O&A activities

The skills identified in Table 6.12 could be introduced at any stage from Year 2 onwards. In addition to trying these activities during lesson time, pupils should be encouraged to practice these skills during active playtime and at home. The review questions identified at the foot of each table focus on evaluating and improving performance.

The skills identified below are best learned through application in a range of activities in different contexts. Try the suggestions shown in Tables 6.13 and 6.14.

TABLE 6.12 Outdoor and adventurous activities at KS2

Activities	Adaptations	Technical tips	Signs of success
Orientation Orientating a map Identifying features on a map Finding where you are Planning and walking on a short route along a trail	Simple/complex maps. Large/small landmarks. More/less distance between signposts on a trail. Familiar/unfamiliar terrain.	Hold map parallel to ground in front of chest. Move feet rather than the map to line up key features/landmarks.	Pupils talk to each other about how to orientate a map. Able to locate position on map. Able to navigate around a marked trail unaided.
Communication/ collaboration Giving instructions Listening to instructions Trusting your partner/ earning your partner's trust Being sensitive towards others	Simple/complex instructions. More/less 'risk'. More/less confident partners.	Think about what to say before speaking. Always be polite. Reassure partner with positive talk.	Groups start working quickly without argument. Pupils place trust in one another.
Problem solving Assessing risk Decision making Analysis of outcome and process Reviewing and target setting	Simple/complex problems. Provision of more/less verbal guidance.	Use planning time before acting. Listen to a range of views before deciding on course of action. Prioritise action.	'Blameless' post-activity discussion. Constructive thoughtful analysis.
Review questions	Can you explain how to set a map to one of your parents? Can you describe the qualities of a good team leader?		

TABLE 6.13 Orientation – finding your way

Activities	Adaptations	Technical tips	Signs of success
Treasure hunt In pairs or small groups, collect items from a list.	More/fewer items.	Encourage pupils to stay together and plan where to go to collect items before they start the hunt. Encourage the use of directional terms – right, left, ahead, behind.	Pupils co-operate in planning.
Follow a trail In pairs or small groups, pupils follow a picture trail collecting a letter at each location. Make as many words as possible with the letters collected.	More/fewer photos. Easier/harder to locate.	Use digital photos of landmarks around the school campus for the location of clues.	Pupils listen to each other's ideas and take it in turns to lead.
Orienteering Using a map to locate and visit a series of points on a permanent orienteering course.	Familiar/unfamiliar terrain. More or fewer control points. Work in small groups/pairs.	Decide on the order of points before setting off.	Collecting all control points. Speed of completion.
Review question	Can you identify any potential hazards on your journeys around the school?		
What next?	Work from simple maps to follow trails in unfamiliar locations.		

Since much of the learning that takes place through these O&A activities is associated with personal development rather than technical proficiency, the thinking, talking and reviewing that takes place after the event is an important part of the process. There are numerous ways in which activity reviews can be conducted. Since not all pupils will be confident to express themselves openly, it is good practice to vary the way in which pupils are asked to reflect and share their feelings about participation. The following suggestions are worth considering and can be conducted as a whole class or in smaller groups:

■ After any activity, pupils sit down with the teacher for a whole-class question and answer session on what they liked/disliked about the activity and how it made them feel.

■ Make a large circle with skipping ropes (sometimes referred to as a 'racoon circle'). All pupils start inside the circle. Pupils are encouraged to say something about the

TABLE 6.14 Communication/collaboration activity and problem solving

Activities	Adaptations	Technical tips	Signs of success
Alphabet soup Groups of six pupils create large letter shapes on the floor.	More/fewer pupils to accommodate.	Take a picture of the shape for pupils to review and improve their position.	Accurate letter shapes. Effective collaboration.
Stepping stones Groups of six pupils cross the hall using only hoops to stand in.	More/fewer hoops. Larger/smaller hoops. More/less time.	Make sure the gap between the hoops can be straddled.	Evidence of planning before setting off.
Jungle trek Groups of six pupils collaborate to travel over each of the obstacles on their jungle adventure.	More/fewer attempts. More/less time.	Obstacle course around the school hall to include: stepping stones, rope swing, climbing frame, sloping bench bridge.	Pupils can describe how they feel when they are successful as a group. Pupils can describe how they could improve their group performance.
Review questions	What did your group do really well? What could your group do to work together even more effectively? Did you break any of the rules? What should happen if rules are broken?		
What next?	Mix the groups. Take similar tasks outdoors. Take similar tasks to unfamiliar environments.		

experience in order to step outside the circle. The review is complete when the circle is empty.

■ The teacher writes down key words on a whiteboard which relate to the activity. Using their own mini whiteboards, pupils are encouraged to write down one of the key words which relates to how they did or how they felt during the activity. Pupils then search among the class for anyone else who has the same word. They sit together and explain why they chose that word.

Developing knowledge and understanding of fitness and health

During Key Stage 2 pupils should be taught:

a) how exercise affects the body in the short term

b) to warm up and prepare appropriately for different activities

c) why physical activity is good for their health and wellbeing

d) why wearing appropriate clothing and being hygienic is good for their health and safety.

The short-term effects of exercise

Lay out a line of markers at the side of the activity space to act as a guide to temperature, breathing rate or heart rate as follows:

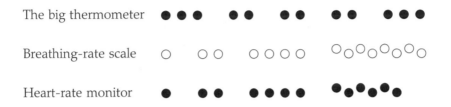

Ask pupils to position themselves on the scale at the start of an activity, in the middle, and at the end. This provides a good start to a conversation about the immediate impact of exercise.

Warming up

The warm up (and the cool down) are important features of any lesson and should be part of a seamless movement experience for the pupils. Introducing pupils at Key Stage 1 to the concept of getting ready for action, and for inaction at the end of the lesson, is vital to establish good habits for the future. At Key Stage 2 a typical warm up will combine the mobilisation of joints and pulse-raising activity in whole-body actions performed with control, often under the direct command of the teacher. This should be followed by some held stretched shapes, or stretching 'moments', in which pupils enjoy what should be the pleasant and comfortable sensation of stretching groups of muscles in combination. By Years 5 and 6 pupils should be able to independently identify warm-up routines for particular activities and be able to perform appropriate stretches for specific parts of the body – upper arm, front and back of upper leg, back of lower leg, chest and back.

Engaging pupils in conversations about the short-term effects of exercise will lead to discussions about why they should change for PE, the different types of clothing used in different activities and the importance of preparing the body prior to and following any kind of exertion. Encouraging pupils to examine the extent to which exercise is both a normal and pleasurable part of their daily lives will provide opportunity to reflect on their personal responsibility for maintaining their health.

PE provides a useful link to the Key Stage 2 science programme of study and offers good potential for making cross-curricular links. Furthermore, 'being healthy' and 'being happy' are core themes in any school's Personal Social and Health Education curriculum, as articulated in the recent 'Every Child Matters' policy initiative.

Chapter summary

This chapter has provided a glimpse of each of the activity areas making up the PE curriculum experience for pupils at Key Stage 2. We have sought to demonstrate how to build upon the work carried out in Key Stage 1 and develop pupils' knowledge, skills and understanding within the context of the National Curriculum. The four aspects of learning remain at the core of our thinking about how to structure and present learning experiences. Providing pupils with a coherent programme of accessible and age-appropriate experiences in which they can enjoy success is the key to nurturing a lifelong love of physical activity. Underpinning our approach is an emphasis on playful experiences that do not steer pupils into adapted forms of adult sporting activity too soon. Take your time and have fun with your pupils.

Questions for reflection

- Is the Key Stage 2 PE programme in your school pupil-centred or activity-centred?
- If you had to choose between athletic activities and outdoor and adventurous activities, which would you decide to leave out?
- Thinking about a PE lesson you have recently taught or observed in Key Stage 2, which of the four aspects of learning was most prominent? Which, if any, were absent?
- How well does your teaching of PE at Key Stage 2 meet the needs of all pupils?

Planning, teaching, assessment

What happens *before* the lesson? Planning and preparation

Chapter objectives

By the end of this chapter you should be able to:

■ Understand the principles and purposes associated with effective long-, medium- and short-term planning for physical education;

■ Develop knowledge of differentiating learning experiences in PE to accommodate a spectrum of pupils' needs;

■ Know how to organise pupils and resources for effective learning.

Planning the physical education journey

PLANNING CAN BE CONSIDERED as a process in which decisions are taken about how to reach a specified destination. If we think about being 'physically educated' as the destination, we can plan the journey accordingly:

■ Where do we want to go?

■ When do we want to arrive?

■ How will we get there?

■ How do we know when we have arrived?

Inevitably, however, the journey towards being physically educated will be long and complex, with no clear ending and no specified route. When planning a long and unpredictable journey such as this, it makes sense to break it up into manageable stages, where key milestones along the way can be marked and celebrated and used to measure progress by. During each stage of the journey, to avoid being knocked off course, potential hazards must be anticipated and avoided. By embracing the challenges and opportunities that such journeys inevitably bring, both leaders (teachers) and travellers (pupils) will emerge more knowledgeable, confident and skilled than when they embarked. Teachers charged with planning the physical education journey for their pupils have the additional challenge, however, of ensuring that every pupil's passage is smooth, continuous and progressive, despite moving from one key stage to the next and, in so doing, often moving schools. This inevitably means that colleagues will need to share with others information about the pathway they have been following and that pupils will need to be knowledgeable about their own progress on this journey. For this reason, teachers' planning needs to be both well thought through and clearly documented.

Whilst planning is one of the most significant factors affecting teacher effectiveness (Bailey, 2000), preparing detailed plans to support teaching and learning is often considered more of a chore than a pleasure. Where plans are in place, OFSTED (2005) reports that teachers appear to focus more on what activities will take place than on the learning outcomes associated with those activities. Whilst focusing on the detail of events at the micro level is commendable, and should contribute to high-quality outcomes, taking one's eye off the big picture can lead to a disjointed and ad hoc experience for the pupils. Thus it is important to recognise that all planning must be placed in context and that to plan for the entire physical education journey necessitates consideration of the process at a number of different levels. Raymond (1998) identifies these interdependent and mutually supportive layers in the planning process:

Whole school: how does PE contribute to the overall school aims and mission? Does the PE curriculum address and develop cross curricular themes? Is the PE curriculum appropriate and does it facilitate progression and continuity?

Key stage: What aspects of knowledge, skills and understanding are developed through which activity experiences at each key stage? How much time will be allocated to each activity area in each key stage?

Class: Which activity experiences will be used as the focus for each of the four aspects of learning? How will pupils' progress be monitored?

(Adapted from Raymond, 1998 p. 139)

For each layer to serve its purpose and usefully contribute to the achievement of the ultimate goal – the physically educated pupil – different questions need to be asked at each stage. Broad, strategic questions steer the thinking at the whole-school level whilst detailed operational questions govern what happens during lessons. Both the questions and the answers are to be found in the school's PE planning documentation which is usually organised hierarchically as follows:

- School PE policy – the big picture;

- Schemes of work – long-term plans;

- Units of work – medium-term plans;

- Lesson outlines – short-term plans.

The rationale for connecting the layers of planning in this way is to ensure that both teachers and their pupils are mindful of the fact that each activity within each lesson contributes in a small way to achieving the overall goal. The following section explains the layers in more detail.

The lexicon of planning in PE

School PE policy

This is a summary statement setting out the aims and objectives for PE in the school. This document describes the purpose, nature and management of PE in the school. It sets out the unique contribution of PE to the development of the whole child and draws connections between PE and other areas of the school curriculum. To be formally adopted by the school it should be agreed by all the staff and approved by the school governing body. All policy documents should be subject to review on a regular basis.

Scheme of work or the 'PE curriculum map'

This is the long-term plan for PE across the key stage or the school as a whole. This document provides an 'at a glance' illustration of the allocation of curriculum time to specific activity experiences across one or more key stages. It represents the school's interpretation of the National Curriculum requirements in its local context. The curriculum map is used to balance pupils' entitlement within the constraints of the school's access to facilities and resources. It is particularly helpful to colleagues if, in addition to naming the activity area and/or venue, the scheme indicates the central theme and key resources to use in developing the learning experience for pupils (i.e. published schemes which might be particularly helpful).

Unit of work

Each cell in the PE curriculum map represents a unit of work. This is the medium-term planning stage and provides further detail regarding what will take place over a half term period (usually between five and eight weeks). This is a very important level in the planning process in which the aims and objectives for whole-school PE are located within activity-based experiences. A well organised unit plan will make the planning of individual lessons much easier, will provide coherence and context to those lessons and should ensure good progression. Whilst each school tends to adopt a template for medium-term planning that suits their purpose, common features of the headings found on unit plans include: *learning objectives, expectations of the pupils, core* or *target tasks, outline content* (sometimes presented as a weekly itinerary), *resources, curriculum links, assessment opportunities.*

Lesson plan

This is the short-term plan which details the distribution of learning activities within the allocated lesson period. The format for lesson planning varies between teachers and schools but should include: *learning objectives, appropriately differentiated learning activities, class organisation and management, deployment of resources, the role of additional adults* and guidance on *assessment* (what to look for). Space should be provided at the end of the template for making notes, *evaluating* the lesson.

Learning objectives

Learning objectives (LOs) communicate what the teacher is trying to teach; what the pupils are expected to know, understand or be able to do (that they couldn't do before); how their achievement will be measured; and what is deemed to be good evidence that the intended outcome has been achieved. In short, LOs describe what the learner will know, feel or be able to do, under specified conditions and to a specified standard. To ensure balanced coverage, when planning for NCPE these should be categorised under the headings of the four aspects of learning.

Learning activities

These are the activities that are devised, selected and presented to help pupils achieve the learning objectives. A range of progressive learning activities should be planned in order to challenge all pupils appropriately. Teachers should be able to vary the presentation of the learning activities to appeal to different pupils' learning preferences.

Teaching points

These highlight important details in the learning activities which might relate to safety, technique or quality of movement. These can be presented in a number of different ways: orally, in print, through diagrams or images. Whilst there may be many teaching points for any particular learning activity, the teacher needs to be selective in the amount of information provided at any one time.

Initiating the planning process: three scenarios

The scenarios presented below provide a context for initiating the planning process at different stages. Consider each in turn and reflect on the nature of the questions posed at each stage. What would be your advice to Sophie, Alice and John?

Next year – thinking about the long term

Sophie has just been appointed as PE co-ordinator/Primary Link Teacher in her school, which is part of a large School Sport Partnership. She has been teaching for three years, is confident in her own teaching (particularly in games, athletics and swimming) and is very enthusiastic about her new role. Following her first meeting with the School Sport Co-ordinator, Sophie starts thinking about how PE at Key Stage 2 contributes to a pupil's physical education. What sorts of experiences do pupils need in order to become 'physically educated'?

Next term – thinking about the medium term

Alice has just been appointed to her first post as a newly qualified teacher in a large urban primary school. She is keen to get organised and wants to make a positive start but she is a little nervous about teaching PE in Key Stage 1 independently for the first time. The curriculum map for PE suggests that, for one of their two PE lessons in the autumn term, her pupils will be 'doing' gymnastics. When Alice asked to see the planning documentation for PE she was directed to a published scheme which had recently been adopted by the school. Whilst this provides broad guidance about themes and content that would be appropriate for her year group, Alice is still confused. How does she convert these ideas into a series of progressive lessons that are appropriate and challenging for all of the pupils in her class?

Next week – thinking about the short term

John is in his second year of teacher training and has just taught his first PE lesson (Year 3 games activities) on school placement. He is a very competent footballer and he thought his knowledge of the game and his own skills would see him through. Very early on in the lesson he realised that his broad outline plan was insufficient to ensure that all pupils had a useful learning experience. The pupils were enthusiastic at the start but because they didn't understand what he wanted them to do, some of them started misbehaving. It took longer than expected to organise the groups, the playing areas and the equipment. The demonstrations didn't work and his explanations were too complex. In the short time that the pupils were active they made no progress. His expectations about the pupils' ability to cope were unrealistic. After the lesson, feeling disappointed, he reflects on his plan and tries to identify what he needs to do to improve things for next week, when his university tutor will observe the lesson.

What these familiar scenarios reveal is that planning for progress in PE is a multi-layered, complex and challenging activity. When planning for the long, medium or short term, the issues that need to be considered may vary but what remains common is the need to think carefully about what you are seeking to achieve. Visualising the goal – an effective demonstration; a purposeful and safe lesson; a stimulating and inspiring unit of work; or a physically educated child – is an essential first step in the process of deciding how to get there.

Task 15 Planning for purpose

To resolve their problems, Sophie, Alice and John need answers to some key questions. Whilst there may be many different answers to the questions posed, it is important to ask the right questions. Some of the key questions to consider are suggested below. Can you identify any others?

Long-term planning

■ What should the pupils know, understand and be able to do in PE by the end of Key Stage 2?

■ What should they know, understand and be able to do at the end of Years 3, 4 and 5?

■ How much curriculum time should be devoted to PE to achieve these targets?

■ What activities will pupils need to experience to reach these targets?

Medium-term planning

■ What should the pupils know, understand and be able to do at the end of this gymnastics unit of work?

■ How much activity time will they have to reach this target?

■ What resources will be needed in order to get them there?

Short-term planning

■ What should the pupils know, understand and be able to do by the end of the next lesson?

■ How will the pupils be organised?

■ In what order will pupils attempt the tasks set?

■ How will their performance be assessed?

Thinking about planning – planning for pupils' thinking

Teaching is a professional thinking activity and what is actually done in the classroom is largely dependent upon the teacher's thought processes that have gone on before the lesson.

(Mawer, 1995, p. 54)

Mawer's (1995) attention to teachers' thinking is an important starting point when considering how to plan for effective learning experiences in physical education. The fact that physical education lessons are designed to engage pupils in active, practical experiences in direct contrast to the sedentary, non-practical 'classroom' lessons which occupy much of the school day, does not render the former 'thoughtless' and the latter 'thoughtful'. Often movements are controlled automatically and we only become aware of the thinking which controls movement when it gets in the way of doing it well. Helping pupils to refine their movement performance requires that teachers give due consideration to the thinking required to underpin effective performance, i.e. to teach effectively we have to understand the 'thinking' behind the 'doing'. This means that we need to understand the essence of an activity and the demands that each domain makes on pupils' thinking if we are to plan effectively for improvements in their understanding.

It is a common misconception that being able to do something well is a prerequisite to teaching it well. This reveals a basic confusion of knowledge of 'doing', with knowledge of 'teaching'. Knowledge of 'doing', what we call 'content knowledge', is acquired through personal practice and experience, and it can be extremely valuable to teachers, even initiating the desire to want to teach. In order to teach effectively, however, experienced practitioners continuously draw upon a wealth of other knowledge – knowledge of learners, of curricula, of pedagogy and of context. The synthesis of all of this knowledge – which Shulman (1987) refers to as *pedagogical content knowledge* – enables the teacher to transform personal, practical experience into powerful and effective learning experiences. This takes a great deal of careful thought and planning.

In addition to the accumulated personal and professional experience teachers bring to any teaching/learning episode in PE, the way in which teachers think about PE is, to a greater or lesser extent, determined by a number of factors:

- Statutory curriculum requirements (the National Curriculum);
- Local Authority policies and guidance;
- School aims/mission;
- School architecture;
- School development plan;
- School PE policy;
- Pupils', parents' and other teachers' (particularly headteachers' expectations).

Whilst each of these factors help to shape our perceptions, since its introduction in the early 1990s, the National Curriculum has become, by far, the most significant. The way in which the National Curriculum defines PE imposes frameworks for thinking about how activity experiences should be organised and presented to pupils. Not least, the selection and categorisation of movement experiences into six *activity areas* and the

TABLE 7.1 Linking NCPE activity areas to pupils' thinking

Activity area	Pupils learn to think about:
Dance activities	how to express and communicate ideas, emotions and concepts.
Gymnastic activities	how to replicate actions, agilities and sequences as accurately and precisely as possible.
Games activities	how to outwit the opposition.
Athletic activities	how to produce the best possible performance in relation to fastest, longest, highest, nearest.
Outdoor & Adventurous activities	how to solve problems and overcome challenges for a successful outcome.
Swimming	how to develop all of the above but in water-based contexts.

designation of four *aspects of knowledge, skills and understanding* (acquiring and developing skills; selecting and applying skills tactics and compositional ideas; evaluating and improving performance; and developing knowledge and understanding of fitness and health) provide an 'official' definition of how we should think about physical education and therefore how any aspect of physical education should be planned for, organised and delivered.

Table 7.1 illustrates how each activity area of the National Curriculum encourages pupils to think in different ways and reminds us that this should underpin the plans that we make.

The simple truth is that effective teaching rarely occurs by accident. Teachers have to think through a host of issues prior to delivering a practical learning experience to ensure that the challenges set are meaningful, purposeful, safe and appropriate and meet the expectations laid down in the National Curriculum.

Questions to answer

In the early stages of teaching, planning a coherent learning experience which adequately addresses all of these issues can be quite daunting. Some of the questions that these issues present would include: What are the pupils going to do? What will my role be? What do I want the pupils to learn? How will I share this with them? How do I get the level of challenge right? How will I keep everyone safe? How will I keep control of the pupils in the space? What equipment/resources will I need? When should I get the equipment out? How much space will each pupil/group need? What if there isn't enough equipment to go around? How do I get the apparatus out? How should I group the children? Who should work with whom? How much time should they have on each activity? How do I know when they are making progress? Who should I spend my time with? Who can help? What if the pupils know more about the activity than I do? Who should I get to demonstrate? How will I involve all of the pupils when there is such a wide range of ability?

Organising your thoughts

To help impose some kind of order on this cascade of questions, we suggest that thinking in categories can be helpful. Initially these might be as follows:

- Content-related questions – what will happen?
- Process-related questions – how will it be organised?
- Timing-related questions – when will it take place?
- People/resource-related questions – who will do what, with which equipment?

Task 16   Categorising all the questions

Categorise the series of questions into those related to *content*, *process*, *timing* or *people*. Then try adding other questions of your own.

Whilst it is very easy to become singularly focused on content-related issues, it is equally important to continually ask:

- Why am I asking the pupils to do this?
- In what way does this contribute to the overall aim?
- What will pupils learn as a result of this experience?

These questions serve to remind us that in physical education we deploy physical activity as an educational tool and that the central purpose in doing so is pupil, rather than activity, development. Whilst we cannot necessarily predict precisely what every pupil will learn in every situation, by identifying explicit learning objectives we do at least acknowledge a rational purpose behind the selection and ordering of lesson activities. Thus we now turn our attention to the identification and articulation of learning objectives.

Planning for pupils' learning

We know that pupils are learning when we see changes in what they can do, their attitudes, and the ways in which they think and behave. Regardless of the timeframe for which you are making plans (long, medium or short term) it is vital that you set out clear and challenging expectations for pupils which look beyond becoming competent performers in sporting activity and consider the development of the whole person. Casbon and Spackman (2005) suggest that it is sensible to start by looking at:

- What pupils have already learned, experienced and achieved;
- What they already know, understand and can do;
- What they need to learn next in order to improve, make progress and achieve more.

Given that it is unusual for there to be a wealth of existing data about pupils' progress in PE, it is important to seek out information in order to establish a *benchmark*. This can be done by:

- Talking to the pupils' previous class teacher to check what they have already experienced and achieved;
- Asking the pupils questions, to check their level of knowledge and understanding;
- Setting the pupils physical tasks to determine what they can do.

Once you have been able to identify your pupils' needs, the next step is to set out clear *expectations*. Using the national expectations set out in the PE National Curriculum, by the end of Key Stage 1 most pupils can be expected to achieve level 2, improving to level 4 by the end of Key Stage 2. (For further details on the levels of attainment, see Chapter 9.) The key to rendering these expectations meaningful and achievable is to communicate these clearly to the pupils. Sharing with your pupils the goals you have set for them can be a very powerful device in ensuring that they are met. To return to the travel analogy, when you know where you are going, you are better placed to identify the landmarks on the way. Giving pupils direction through setting clear targets, helps them to make connections between individual activities, lessons and groups of lessons and see a coherent path towards progress.

The planning 'gap'

For many teachers however, establishing benchmarks and setting expectations are often thought of as collaborative activities, discussed in working parties and subsequently agreed and adopted by the whole staff team. A more pressing individual planning issue is the selection, ordering and organisation of the *activities* which pupils will undertake – 'What are my pupils actually going to do in the lesson – tomorrow, next week and thereafter?' Whilst these are legitimate concerns, we need to remember that a preoccupation with devising discrete activity-focused lessons, and blocks of lessons, can militate against continuity and progression (OFSTED, 2005). Whilst many teachers have devoted a great deal of time and effort to thinking about and articulating, in PE policies and schemes of work, the ways in which pupils can and should benefit from a stimulating, challenging, relevant and connected physical education, the programme that is delivered to the pupils, in many cases, has continued relatively unchanged over many years. This is what we refer to as the planning 'gap'.

The planning 'gap' exists where broad, age-appropriate and inclusive goals are in place but are not effectively translated into practice. Whilst this may occur for any number of reasons, our concern here is to help teachers to recognise and close the gap.

Target learning tasks

One key strategy for making more explicit connections between the long-term policy aims and the short-term lesson experience is to adopt a system of progressive 'core' or 'target' learning tasks. According to the BAALPE (2005) DfES/QCA core tasks provide:

- Authentic contexts for performance in which pupils can use and demonstrate what they have learned;
- A complete piece of work for pupils to work on (like a 'best' work that might end up on a classroom display);
- A visual 'end product' to provide pupils with a clear and achievable goal;
- A vehicle for celebrating pupils' progress and achievement.

By assembling a 'staircase of tasks' to mark progress in knowledge, skills and understanding, the problem of connecting the PE policy goals with the individual units, and the learning activities undertaken within those units, is made more explicit and, in so doing, the planning 'gap' closes. If a staircase of tasks can be established in each area of activity, teachers can exercise choice in deciding which route to follow to achieve their goals.

Figure 7.1 shows a staircase leading to a physically educated pupil. Each riser represents a target/core task. The 'zoom view' shows a single riser consisting of a series of smaller steps – individual lessons.

Thus rather than adopting a *bottom-up* approach to planning the PE curriculum, we argue that working backwards from the main goal, or a *top-down* approach, is better suited to mapping progression towards the goal of the physically educated pupil. By sharpening our focus on pupils' development of knowledge, skills and understanding, and establishing landmarks, (in the form of end-of-school, end-of-key stage, end-of-year, end-of-unit targets) to monitor their progress by, we give direction and purpose to the PE experience. Within this structure, devising appropriately challenging and progressive target learning tasks takes on critical significance. A good starting point is to develop ideas through using the DfES/QCA core tasks. These can be embedded into the planning process as described or adapted to suit specific contexts.

When choosing or designing target learning tasks to help your pupils to achieve a particular intended outcome, keep the outcome clearly in mind and include activities that specifically address the intent of the outcome. It is particularly important to use

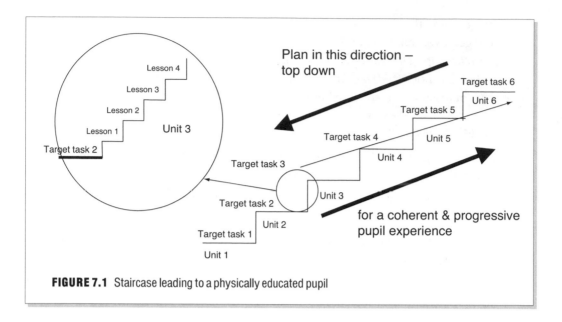

FIGURE 7.1 Staircase leading to a physically educated pupil

learning activities that are appropriate and inclusive, and that motivate the pupils. A *target learning task* should describe, in pupil-friendly language, a challenge that will enable pupils to show what they have learned over a series of lessons.

Example: DfES/QCA Unit 5 Gymnastics, Core Task 1

Choose two ways of travelling, e.g. walking backwards safely and a roll, and link these to make a short movement phrase which you can remember and perform on the floor. Make sure you know where you start and finish, and what shapes you will make to start and finish.

When presented to the pupils this might be adapted to:

We will be learning to make our own gymnastics sequence. Your sequence will include: a clear starting shape, two different ways of travelling and a clear finishing shape. Practise your sequence until you can link these movements smoothly and then show it to a partner.

We will be looking for:

- stillness at the start and at the end;
- clear movements and shapes;
- smooth links from one action to the next.

To accommodate the pupils' different levels of experience, variations to the level of challenge could be made as follows:

Level 1	Level 2	Level 3
1. Start in a Y shape.	1. Start in a Y shape.	1. Choose a starting shape.
2. Jump forwards three times.	2. Choose a travel.	2. Choose a travel.
3. Lie down.	3. Choose a turn.	3. Choose a turn.
4. Roll back to your starting position.	4. Choose a different travel.	4. Choose a different travel.
5. Lie on your back in a star shape.	5. Lie on your back in a star shape.	5. Choose a finishing shape.

Task 17 Target learning tasks

Can you think of further ways to challenge more able pupils?

In our experience, when pupils know what is expected of them and are successful in meeting the challenges set for them, their progress picks up momentum. As BAALPE (2005) points out, in response to high-quality, appropriately pitched lessons pupils:

- show their enthusiasm for taking part in activities;

- want to do activities again and get better;

- take part in activities during break times and after school;

- look happy and enjoy themselves in PE.

By now your head will be spinning with the sheer number of issues to take into consideration. We've reached the point therefore when we need to think about how to commit thoughts, ideas and solutions to paper.

Planning in writing

It's not so much the planning itself that many teachers find mundane, it's the process of committing your thoughts to paper that often proves to be less appealing! Bailey (2000) points out, however, that a clearly laid out lesson plan serves several purposes. It helps to:

1 remind the teacher of important teaching points;

2 identify gaps in knowledge and stimulate further research/development of additional resources;

3 warn of potential 'crisis' points in the lesson;

4 provide a record of what has taken place.

Whilst this is true for a teacher working alone, the written record becomes even more important where teachers work collaboratively and share their planning ideas. The articulation of thinking (Williams, 1996) that the preparation of a lesson plan demands, enables the teacher to address the immediate organisational issues of the lesson. However, we should continually remind ourselves that lessons, and the activities within them, form a small part of an interconnected web of experience. Figure 7.2 provides a schematic view of the different components of the 'planning web'.

In the next section we present example templates which can be adapted to suit individual school needs in order to illustrate what information should be captured at each layer of the planning process.

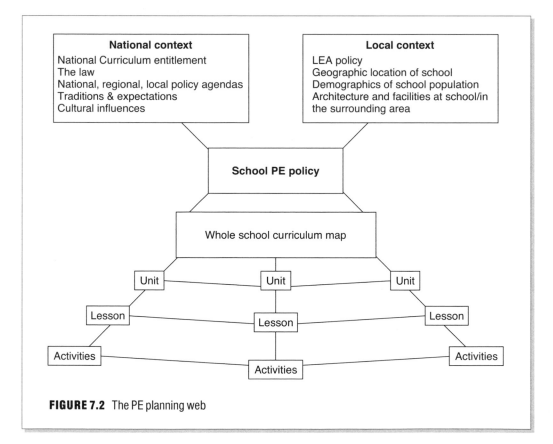

FIGURE 7.2 The PE planning web

Examples of PE planning templates

Example of a school PE policy: Ravensgate Primary School

Ravensgate Primary School Physical Education Policy

1. Rationale, aims and objectives

1.1 Physical education develops our pupils' knowledge, skills and understanding, so that they can perform with increasing competence and confidence in a range of physical activities. High-quality physical education promotes physical literacy amongst pupils, an understanding of the body in action and a greater awareness of self in the physical world. It involves the development, selection, application and review of skilful action and promotes positive attitudes towards a healthy lifestyle. We aim to enable pupils to make informed choices about physical activity throughout their lives.

1.2 Our objectives for PE are:

- to enable children to develop and explore physical skills with increasing control and co-ordination;
- to develop the way children perform skills and apply rules and conventions for different activities;
- to increase children's ability to use what they have learnt to improve the quality and control of their performance;
- to teach children to recognise and describe how their bodies feel during exercise;
- to develop the children's enjoyment of physical activity;
- to develop an understanding in children of how to succeed in a range of physical activities and how to evaluate their own success.

2. PE from 5 to 11

2.1 The Foundation Stage

We encourage the physical development of our children in the reception class as an integral part of their work. As the reception class is part of the Foundation Stage of the National Curriculum, we relate the physical development of the children to the objectives set out in the Early Learning Goals, which underpin the curriculum planning for children aged 3 to 5 years of age. We encourage the children to develop confidence and control of the way they move, and the way they handle tools and equipment. We give all children the opportunity to undertake activities that offer appropriate physical challenges, both indoors and outdoors, using a wide range of resources to support specific skills.

continued on next page

2.2 Key Stage 1
We have adapted the National Curriculum to the local circumstances of the school. At Key Stage 1, pupils develop their learning through experiencing dance, games, gymnastics and swimming.

2.3 Key Stage 2
At Key Stage 2, pupils develop their learning through experiences in athletics, dance, games, gymnastics, outdoor and adventurous activities and swimming.

3. Contribution of PE to other curriculum areas
PE contributes to pupils' learning across the curriculum in a number of ways.

3.1 In PE we encourage the development of speaking and listening skills by asking children to describe what they have done and to discuss how they might improve their performance.

3.2 Through the use of the internet, digital images and video, pupils are encouraged to develop and use ICT skills to assist their movement development.

3.3 Through learning about the benefits of exercise and healthy eating, fair play, collaboration, co-operation, respect and sensitivity towards others, we encourage pupils to make appropriate and informed decisions about how to conduct their lives.

4. Inclusion in PE
4.1 In PE we provide learning opportunities that enable all pupils to make progress. By setting appropriate learning challenges and responding to individual needs, we monitor each pupil's attainment and progress against national expectations.

5. Resources
5.1 There is a wide range of resources to support the teaching of PE across the school. PE equipment is located in the PE store, which is accessible to children with adult supervision. The hall contains a range of large apparatus, which pupils are taught to set up and put away safely as part of their work. Pupils will participate in outdoor activities, using areas around the school campus (playground, school field and adventure play area) and a range of other off-site facilities (swimming pool, country park and residential centre).

continued on facing page

6. Health and safety

6.1 The general teaching requirement for health and safety applies in this subject. We encourage the children to consider their own safety and the safety of others at all times. Pupils are required to change for PE into the school PE kit for each activity. Our teachers set a good example by wearing appropriate clothing when teaching PE. No jewellery is to be worn for any physical activity.

7. Extra-curricular activities

7.1 The school provides a range of PE-related activities for children at the end of the school day. These encourage children to further develop their skills in a range of the activity areas. Details of the current club activities are available on the school website. The school regularly participates in local and regional sports competitions. This is designed to be inclusive, foster an achievement culture and develop a sense of pride in belonging to our school.

8. Context

This policy statement relates to Ravensgate Primary School, Ravenborough. It was developed during a PE-focused staff training day on 10 July 2006. It was approved by the governing body on 12 September 2006. It will be reviewed in July 2007.

Example of a work/curriculum map for PE: Comberton Primary PE family

	Year 1 of Cycle						Year 2 of Cycle					
	Autumn A	Autumn B	Spring A	Spring B	Summer A	Summer B	Autumn A	Autumn B	Spring A	Spring B	Summer A	Summer B
Foundation Year 1	**Dance** 'On parade' (CAS)	**Dance** 'Dot, wiggle, dash' (CAS & TOP)	**Dance** 'Bob the Builder'	**Gym** 'Stretch & curl' (VS)	**Games** Kicking & striking (CAS & TOP)	**Games** Throwing & catching Sports day practice	**Dance** Penguin small (TOPS)	**Dance** Body talk (TOPS)	**Dance** Exploration (TOPS)	**Gym** Pathways (VS)	**Games** Kicking & striking (CAS & TOP)	**Games** Throwing & catching Sports day practice
	Games Rolling & receiving (CAS & TOP)	**Gym** Travel & stop (CAS)	**Gym** Jump & land (CAS & TOP)	**Games** Travelling with an object/ball (CAS & TOP)	**Games** Throwing & catching (CAS & TOP)	**Swimming** Water confidence & safety (QCA Unit 1)	**Games** Rolling & receiving (CAS & TOP)	**Gym** Travelling (VS)	**Gym** Taking weight on different body parts (VS)	**Games** Travelling with ball (CAS & TOP)	**Games** Throwing & catching (CAS & TOP)	**Swimming** Water confidence & safety (QCA Unit 1)
Year 2	**Dance** Action words (CAS) Dancing dice (TOP)	**Dance** Sadness & happiness Ugly Bug Ball (CAS)	**Dance** Weather forecast (TOP)	**Gym** Matching & mirroring (VS)	**Games** Rolling & throwing (CAS & TOP)	**Games** Throwing & catching Sports day practice	**Dance** Machines (TOP)	**Dance** Weather forecast (TOP)	**Dance** Shadows (TOP)	**Gym** Spinning turning twisting (VS Unit I)	**Games** Rolling & throwing (CAS & TOP)	**Games** Throwing & catching Sports day practice
	Games Throw/catch & strike (CAS & TOP)	**Gym** Body shape (CAS)	**Gym** Rocking & rolling (CAS & VS)	**Games** Foot control Dribble, kick receive (CAS & TOP)	**Swimming** Water confidence & safety	**Swimming** Water confidence & safety	**Games** Throw/catch & strike (CAS & TOP)	**Gym** Flight (VS Unit D)	**Gym** Wide/narrow curled (VS Unit G) (Body shape)	**Games** Foot control Dribble, kick receive (CAS & TOP)	**Swimming** Water confidence & safety	**Swimming** Water confidence & safety

Years												
Years 3 & 4	**Dance** Witches (CAS)	**Gym** Curling & stretching (CAS & VS Unit L)	**Dance** Water, rain (CAS)	**Gym** Pathway & level (CAS & VS Unit N)	**Games** Invasion: ball-handling skills (CAS Yr 3 and TOP)	**Athletics** Throwing, running, jumping (CAS)	**Dance** Vikings (CAS)	**Gym** Flight (CAS & VS Unit U)	**Dance** Trad. English dance (CAS) Dorset Ring dance (TOPS)	**Gym** Rotation (CAS) Rolling (VS Unit S)	**Games** Invasion: Ball-handling skills (CAS Yr 3 and TOP)	**Athletics** Refine running, jumping, throwing (CAS)
	Games S & F: throwing & catching (CAS Yr 3 and TOP)	**O & A** Outdoor & adventure (CAS)	**Games** Invasion: Ball on the ground (CAS Yr 4 and TOP)	**Games** Net/wall games: tennis (CAS Yr 4 and TOPS)	**Swimming** Activities & water safety (QCA Unit 1/2)	**Swimming** Games in the pool (QCA Unit 1/2)	**Games** S & F: throwing & catching (CAS Yr 3 and TOP)	**O & A** Outdoor & adventure (CAS)	**Games** Invasion: Ball on the ground (CAS Yr 4 and TOP)	**Games** Invasion games: Ball on the ground (CAS & TOP)	**Swimming** Activities & water safety (QCA Unit 1/2)	**Swimming** Games in the pool (QCA Unit 1/2)
Years 5 & 6	**Gym** Partner work (CAS & VS Unit X)	**Dance** African rhythm & beats (CAS)	**Gym** Balance (CAS & VS Unit P)	**Dance** Dance football (CAS)	**Games** S & F: bowling, batting Cricket (CAS Yr 5 and TOP)	**Athletics** Improve run, throw, jump. (CAS)	**Dance** Sun, sea & sand (CAS & TOP Shoreline)	**Gym** Symmetry & asymmetry (CAS & VS Unit M)	**Dance** Ancient Egyptian (CAS & TOP Power Circle)	**Games** Partnerwork Holes & obstacles (CAS & VS Unit Z)	**Games** S & F: Rounders/ Korfball (CAS Yr 5 and TOP)	**Athletics** Jumping & throwing Running sprint, pace & relay (CAS)
	Games Invasion Attack & def Rugby (CAS Yr 5 and TOP)	**O & A** Outdoor & adventure (CAS)	**Games** Invasion Attack & def Football (CAS Yr 6 and TOP)	**Games** Net/wall games: tennis (CAS Yr 6 and TOP)	**Swimming** Activities & water safety (QCA Unit 2)	**Swimming** Games in the pool (QCA Unit 2)	**Games** Invasion Attack & def Netball (CAS Yr 5 and TOP)	**O & A** Outdoor & adventure (CAS)	**Games** Invasion Attack & def Hockey (CAS Yr 6 and TOP)	**Games** Net games: tennis (CAS Yr 6 and TOP)	**Swimming** Activities & water safety (QCA Unit 2)	**Swimming** Games in the pool (QCA Unit 2)

Note: The abbreviations in brackets relate to published schemes being used across the Comberton family of schools to support the teaching. [Planning a two-year cycle is necessary where classes are composed of mixed year groups.]

Examples of units of work

The following examples show two different medium-term planning templates. The plans have been selected to show different year groups in different activity contexts.

Example 1

Weekly activities for: Subject: Classes: Years: **Half**

PE   Athletics   1 and 2   R, Y1, Y2   **Term:**   Summer A 2004

Learning objectives

- to be able to run confidently over different distances;
- to be able to throw, kick or roll and catch an appropriate object;
- to be able to jump in different ways.

Week	Outline	Details
Week 1: Focus: moving feet to position body appropriately	**Each week the children will warm up in a broadly similar pattern, jogging first and then stretching gently, with exercises to make sure that joints are properly warm. They will then rotate in groups to take part in various activities, some of which will be in teams.** a) potato race, putting out or retrieving beanbags; b) rolling and receiving balls down a line; c) standing long jump; d) longer distance, run in pairs, with rests.	Each week there will be markers, spots, cones, canes, a variety of balls, beanbags, hoops, skipping ropes and bats. Playground chalk will be needed.
Week 2: Focus: using the opposite hand to foot when throwing	Half group coaching on a) throwing activities – beanbags, tennis balls, foam balls, footballs; b) jumping over little cane hurdles in a row. The other half of the group will be improving fitness by doing scout's pace around the edge of the field.	

	Cross-curricular links: communication, language, science (human body and mechanics)
Week 3: Focus: swinging arms to enable a higher jump	Half group coaching on a) throwing/rolling/kicking and catching/retrieving using balls of different weights and sizes; b) jumping up to touch a weighted band suspended from a netball ring. The other half of the group will participate in a variety of short relay activities.
Week 4: Focus: transferring weight when kicking	Children to work in groups, taking it in turns to lead warm-up exercises for the others to follow. Ch to evaluate the exercises and suggest improvements. a) skipping with a rope static/swaying/turning; b) batting a ball along a course on the ground; c) kicking a ball against the kicking wall from markers; d) running and walking a longer distance.
Week 5: Focus: pointing hand in direction of target when throwing	Three groups to work on relay races of various kinds whilst one group performs an obstacle course which will include: walking along benches, going through hoops, in and out of cones, over and under canes, throwing beanbags into a basket and running back to the start. Ch to suggest ways of improving performance and try them out. Everyone to help clear up and talk about what they have enjoyed.
Week 6 Competition in groups using a carousel	Potato race* ■ Long run taking turns in pairs ■ Throwing a beanbag ■ Jumping over little canes or hurdles* ■ Kicking a ball at a target ■ Rolling a ball into a basket ■ Running to hoop, through and on to collect a bean bag, reverse* Children coached on * activities, and encouraged to work co-operatively, helping to coach one another by making helpful comments. Plenary: children to make suggestions about improving performance in different areas.

Example 2

Unit No: 3	Key Stage: 2	AREA OF ACTIVITY: O&AA	Title of Unit: Intro to O&AA	Year 5	Target Level(s): 3/4
		X-curricular links : Geography	Core task: QCA unit 20 task 1	Time: 6 x 50	Venue: Outside/Hall

Unit objectives		Assessment opportunities
Acquiring and developing skills/techniques/ideas	Selecting and applying skills/strategies/ideas	■ Performance of orienteering skills and basic compass work.
To practise and perform different trails and orienteering activities focusing on map orientation and basic compass work.	To solve simple group problems using basic navigation and communication skills.	■ Ability to communicate with others in pair and group tasks to solve problems.
Understanding health and fitness	Evaluating and improving performance	■ Evaluation of own and group performance.
Understand how preparation for O&AA may differ from other activities.	To discuss and evaluate the effectiveness of pair and group performance.	■ Performance of core task.

Structure	Lesson 1	Lesson 2	Lesson 3	Lesson 4	Lesson 5	Lesson 6
Intro	Introduce pupils to the O&AA unit. Explain that the focus is on working within the school environment to solve challenges in groups. Explain core task.	In the hall unless weather is nice. Do the numbers warm-up. Encourage non-friendship groups. End up with pairs.	Star orienteering. In pairs pupils are allocated a map of the school site and a control card. Allow some discussion of the map for familiarisation.	Point to point orienteering. In groups of 3. Each group is allocated one map with controls marked and a control card.	Introduce a compass and teach/review the 8 cardinal points. Play the compass game warm-up.	Introduce pupils to a compass. The red part of the compass always points North. Teach how to take a 'bearing'.

Develop 1	In 3s. Pupils have to find the 'photo place' in 10 photos of the school site. When they find the place there should be a control there so that they can record that they have been there.	'Beanbag' challenge. Each pair has 3 hoops and must move around the hall collecting beanbags. They must only step in their hoops and must carry beanbags with them. Discuss how pupils solved the problem.	Look at the key on the map to identify features. Pupils have to find the different controls marked on the maps (one control marked on each map) and return to the central point each time for a new map.	Allow pupils 5 minutes to plan their route. Ask different groups to go to different controls first so that they can all go at the same time. Perform core task.	Pupils follow a route between cones laid out in a grid square and record the letter code for each cone on their control card. North needs to be clearly marked. Try core task on different course.	Practise walking on a bearing. Start from a small marker, walk on a bearing for 30 paces, after 30 paces add 180 degrees to the bearing and walk 30 paces back. Where should you be?
Develop 2	When each group has seen and visited each photo place discuss the route pupils took to each photo. Was it the shortest? How did they identify each location?	Play number warm-up again. End up with 4 groups of 7. Two groups work while two groups evaluate. Aim is to make a square with the rope while blindfolded. Let all 4 groups have a go before sharing evaluations.	Discuss how to set a map, how to plan the shortest route, and the importance of recording the control information clearly.	Each group follow their own route finding the controls. They only return to the start after finding and recording all the identification letters/numbers on their control card.	Pairs design a route for another pair to follow. They can use the control signs from task one and rearrange them. Pairs complete each other's courses.	Repeat above but walk three sides of a triangle. Follow a short route marked on a map as compass bearings. Use key features to check accuracy.
Conc.	How did each group work together? Any communication or leadership issues?	Discuss communication and organisation within groups.	Discuss reasons for any mistakes. What helps teams to be successful?	Discuss how they decided which way to go. How did they find their way? How well did they work together?	How easy was it to: a) Design a course? b) Follow instructions? c) Meet the core task?	Discuss evaluate progress made against LOs. Set targets for improvement.
Key Vocab	Control marker, control card.	Safety, listening, co-operation.	Route, star orienteering, key, symbols.	Point to point orienteering, map orientation.	Cardinal points, compass.	Compass needle, bearings, pacing.

Swimming lesson plan

Pupils:	Yrs 5/6	Main theme:	Front crawl arm action	Equipment:	Float each, sinkable objects (10), sinking hoops, task cards
No.:	24 (HA:6, MA:10, LA:8)	Contrast:	Underwater search		
Time:	30 mins in water	Lesson:	5th of 10	Adult support:	TA to work with LA group.
Learning objectives:			a) to refine the performance of front crawl arm action b) to be able to describe and comment on a partner's front crawl arm action c) to understand the principles of safe practice when working under water.		

Time	Gp	Learning activity	Teaching points	Organisation
3m	LA MA HA	Introduction/warm up Enter pool 4 x width any stroke Enter pool 6 x width any stroke Enter pool 8 x width any stroke	i) Long body, face down ii) Reach for half width glide iii) Breathing to minimum.	In gps working in pairs, x completes and y follows.
2m	All	Group stretch Tricep stretch, pectoral stretch	i) Demonstrate position and describe what to do ii) Stay low in the water iii) Hold for 8s.	All in standing depth
		Main Theme		
3m	All	Front crawl – whole stroke Continuous swim for 3min	Think about arm action: 'big pull'	In pairs, work/rest Select demonstrators

12m	All	Demonstrations of action Gp watch several demonstrations using task cards for guidance Gp stand in shoulder depth and imitate action	i) Fingers enter first ii) Elbow high on recovery iii) Pull along centre line of body iv) Hand exit at hip.	Organise head-on and profile demonstrations (4 pupils) Still working in pairs T advise individually and encourage observer to describe swimmer's arm action. Reinforce TPs with observer.
	LA	Single arm pull ½ W + change arm (using kick board)	LA Can walk on bottom MA Use legs to kick HA No kick board	
	MA	Single arm pull ½ W + change arm (using kick board)		
	HA	Single arm pull ½ W + change arm (no kick board) Introduce whole stroke again as appropriate		
		Contrasting activity		
8m	LA	Collect objects thrown by partner (seen)	Attempt feet- and head-first surface dives.	Gps A + B use single channels. Gp C use deep water
	MA	Collect objects thrown by partner (unseen)		
	HA	Collect objects thrown by partner (unseen) but must swim through sunken hoop to search and collect		
2m	All	Scull on back, float and slowly complete 360°		

Assessment: a) ability to describe and imitate correct arm action in FC; b) ability to observe and communicate accurately with partner; c) demonstrating awareness of, and concern for, others.

Evaluation:

Structuring the learning experience

As the examples of medium-term and short-term planning templates demonstrate, giving due consideration to the order in which the activities selected to deliver the objectives are presented is of vital importance. Establishing a natural flow to the learning experience, whereby pupils are *introduced to, assimilate, consolidate, apply* and then *adapt* new knowledge and skills, will increase the likelihood of the objectives being successfully met.

Planning tip

Having drafted initial ideas for your medium-term plan, check for evidence of incremental progression *within* and *between* lessons. Look for *horizontal* and *vertical* progression:

Medium-term plan						
Phase	Week 1	Week 2	Week 3	Week 4	Week 5	Week 6
	Vertical progression Each activity builds on the previous activity, towards a meaningful conclusion.	**Horizontal progression** Each lesson builds on the previous lesson, towards a meaningful conclusion.				

Planning the phases of the lesson

Having experienced PE as a pupil, you will be familiar with the traditional approach to the structure of lessons. Table 7.2 illustrates what might be planned for in each phase and the way in which this structure can be used to focus on different aspects of learning.

Planning tip

Whilst the transitions between phases should ideally be seamless, careful planning of critical moments in the lesson – such as the organisation/reorganisation of groups, the distribution/retrieval of equipment and the provision of important information – can make all the difference.

TABLE 7.2 Phases of the lesson

Lesson structure	Plan to	NCPE aspect of learning
Introduction	Outline the objectives, the success criteria, the ways in which pupils will be assessed and the range of activities that will take place.	
Warm up	Prepare pupils physically and psychologically for the activities to follow. This should be consistent with the nature of the experience in the rest of the lesson. Warming up for gymnastics by playing a game of tag will not appropriately prepare pupils for what will follow.	Knowledge and understanding of fitness and health
Development	Introduce new knowledge and skills through relevant and challenging practical tasks.	Acquire and develop skills/Evaluate and improve performance.
Application	Provide opportunities for pupils to show what they can do, what they know and understand. This might be through showing a dance phrase, playing a small-sided game or solving a problem.	Select and apply skills, tactics and compositional ideas/Evaluate and improve performance.
Conclusion	Summarise what has been learned, celebrate success and look forward to the next lesson. Cooling down through low-intensity activity and stretching will help to calm pupils down for their return to the classroom.	Knowledge and understanding of fitness and health/Evaluate and improve performance.

Differentiation in planning

Just as all good teachers adjust the level of challenge in classroom activities according to the needs of their pupils, in PE teachers must ensure that pupils are challenged appropriately. Guiding principles on differentiation include the following:

1 assume that learners are different;

2 adjust the nature of tasks not just the quantity;

3 adopt multiple approaches to content, process and product;

4 focus on students to render learning engaging, relevant and interesting;

5 blend whole-class, group and individual instruction in a natural flow;

6 learn with pupils.

Using the STEP framework to differentiate

The acronym STEP (space, task, equipment, people) can be a useful reminder to help teachers differentiate activities to enable all pupils to achieve their personal targets. Table 7.3 is an example of applying STEP in gymnastics.

TABLE 7.3 Differentiation of a task, using STEP

Devise, practise and perform a sequence that includes a balance, a roll, a jump and a turn.

	Easier	Harder
Space	In own space	Sharing the space around the room
Task	Copying a set routine	Devise your own routine
Equipment	On the floor only	Using a mat and a bench
People	Working on own	Working alongside or with a partner/group

Task 18

Try applying the STEP principle to this core task:

In teams of four, find out ways of running:

- the fastest time as a relay team over a shared distance of 60m
- the longest distance as a relay team over times of 1 minute, *e.g. 1 minute 30 seconds, 2 minutes, 3 minutes.*

(DfES/QCA Unit 18 Athletic Activities, Core Task 2)

Chapter summary

In this chapter we have highlighted some of the key issues to take into consideration when planning for pupils' progression in PE. We have considered the context in which planning takes place and the key questions that need to be answered at different levels in the planning process. Above all we have stressed the importance of being committed to purposeful planning, namely, planning for pupils' learning. We have made the case for plotting pupils' progression through meaningful authentic target tasks, which provide purpose and direction to any PE programme.

Planning, like teaching, will improve with practice. In the early stages of teaching for learning, it is likely that you will remain heavily reliant on your written plans. As you gain more experience and grow in confidence, your repertoire of strategies for promoting high-quality learning will inevitably improve and consequently you will become less plan-dependent. Whilst experienced teachers still plan carefully, the focus of their planning changes. No longer preoccupied with content, organisation and class management issues, experienced practitioners can direct their energies elsewhere and use their plans to explore new ways of challenging pupils to reach new heights.

Questions for reflection

- Look at your school PE policy alongside some examples of your short- and medium-term plans for PE. Are these documents as well 'connected' as you would like them to be?

- Look at two examples of medium-term planning from different activity areas. To what extent do they reveal a focus on 'doing' activities compared with pupils' learning?

- How favourably does differentiation in PE compare to differentiation in other subjects?

- What changes would you need to make to your PE planning to address pupils' learning preferences more effectively?

What happens *during* the lesson? Teaching a lesson

Chapter objectives

By the end of this chapter you should be able to:

- Know the characteristics of effective teaching in PE;

- Appreciate the need to use a range of teaching strategies;

- Appreciate the need to use a range of teaching approaches;

- Understand that flexibility in teaching is vital to meet the demands of pupils.

Teaching to learn

THIS CHAPTER BEGINS with a question. What is meant by quality teaching in PE? Some might say that this is something that cannot be defined, whilst others will talk about teaching lessons where pupils are active for the majority of the time. Others relate it to enjoyment or the reproduction of skilled movements. When you watch a really good PE lesson, regardless of the activity or indeed age of the pupils, there is one aspect that sets it apart. That is the amount of *learning* that takes place because of that teaching. Quality teaching is simply teaching that leads to more pupil learning. The literature on teaching in PE is confusing, with words such as *good, effective* or *high quality*, and the search to pin this down has been going on for many years. Research findings have told us a lot about the ways in which teachers teach in PE and the effect these have on what and how much pupils learn in lessons. An interesting and comprehensive review of studies into teacher effectiveness in PE is given by Mawer (1995). Drawing upon such research from notaries (such as Metzler, 1990; Siedentop, 1991; Silverman, 1991), we offer what amounts to key characteristics of effective teachers in PE. A summary is provided in Table 8.1.

> ## Task 19 What is quality teaching in PE?
>
> What do you understand by 'quality teaching in PE'?
>
> Make a list of skills and qualities necessary to teach effectively in PE.

TABLE 8.1 Characteristics of effective teachers of PE

Characteristics of effective teachers	Descriptions
They plan work effectively.	Know what it is that they wish to accomplish and have clear instructional goals.
	Design effective class-management procedures.
	Provide realistic and attainable goals for pupils.
	Progress work in sequence.
They present new material well.	Explain new concepts with clarity.
	Have effective communication skills.
	Make use of modelling and demonstrations.
They organise and manage pupils and learning experiences.	Have management structures, routines and class rules.
	Make their expectations clear.
	Create business-like environments.
	Use resources effectively.
They are actively involved in teaching.	Have developed observation skills.
	Give feedback relating to learning objectives.
	Demonstrate skills. Explain clearly.
	Monitor pupil progress.
They provide supportive learning environments.	Individualise guidance.
	Are enthusiastic and positive.
	Plan lessons that involve pupils in decision-making.
	Provide greater time for pupils to learn.
They possess a repertoire of teaching styles.	Possess them and know when to use them for best effect.
They teach for understanding.	Use a variety of skills/strategies to develop discussion.
	Provide opportunities for pupils to apply their learning.
	Scaffold tasks appropriately.

eaching children is complex. You may regard teaching as an *art* and might agree that the endeavour involves an application of one's knowledge both educationally and ethically to the everyday reality of teaching (Schwab, 1969). Or you might agree it is about being reflective and modifying this knowledge according to the requirements of the practical situation in ways that are much more than being technical experts (Carr, 1989). Alternatively, you may agree that teaching PE is a *science* (Siedentop, 1991) and about having a set of skills that build up from basic to more advanced. Whilst there is obviously no correct answer, the stance taken in this book is a middle one. We acknowledge that effective teachers in PE demonstrate flexibility, intuition and creativity (in sympathy with the teaching as an art form notion) and they are also self-reflective and constantly reflect on the professional teaching (Hellison and Templin, 1991). We also believe that good teachers are disciplined and systematic in their approach and although they have inevitably developed personal styles, they have a thorough knowledge and a composite set of teaching skills (in sympathy with the teaching as a science). This would seem to encompass the best of both worlds. Our view is that:

Knowledge (of children's development and of the subject) + pedagogical skills = quality teaching!

As outlined in Chapter 1, the goals of PE are multifaceted and therefore for pupils to achieve these goals is no easy task. The skilled teacher of PE requires a sound toolkit of teaching skills because *how* we teach is just as important as *what* we teach. Although it is not possible to present all teaching skills here it is possible to identify some of the important ones, and this is the focus of the next section.

A toolkit of teaching strategies

First, consider Martin's story. Martin was a good classroom teacher. He had just completed his course in teacher training and passed it well. He was conscientious and had read the recommended books on his course and had observed several teachers 'doing a PE lesson', yet he himself had never taught a whole lesson. It was the second week into his teaching career when he was timetabled to teach Year 4 PE in the school hall. A little nervous but confident he could do it, this is how the lesson went – and went wrong.

He entered the hall behind the class, his mind on the maths lesson he was to teach later in the day. With his mind preoccupied he had forgotten to get himself changed. The class entered the hall to his rather feeble instruction, 'Find a space everyone'. Looking up he saw children running everywhere. Chaos reigned. Eventually gaining order he set them a task he had written down from his teacher training course. An observer watching the lesson would have concluded that the lesson was dull. He lacked sparkle. He taught in one style only. He did not question or challenge. Children were unclear about what to do. He told them nothing after the set tasks were completed. The time dragged on: twenty minutes seemed an eternity. His first PE lesson was a disaster.

Afterwards Martin was puzzled. The content of his lesson surely was OK, so what was wrong? He reflected some more and realised that it was in his delivery and teaching skills that the problems lay. Martin had not understood that the *how* of teaching is just as important as the *what* of teaching. He needed a toolkit of teaching tools.

Be a positive and enthusiastic role model

This is simple but immediately effective! Share your enthusiasm for PE with your class. Teaching is much more than instructing children how to perform a forward roll correctly or execute a short corner in hockey. Evidence to support being an enthusiastic role model exists in the literature (Rosenshine and Furst, 1973; Rolider *et al.*, 1984) and readers are referred to the descriptors of enthusiasm advanced by Behets (1991) whose list comprises vocal intention, articulation, word selection, encouragement, gestures, body movements and overall energy level.

Take the advice of Smith and Cestaro (1998) and lead by example. If your pupils see you living the active lifestyle you teach about and not just talking about it, no motivation is stronger to want to participate in and enjoy your PE lessons! Ensure you dress appropriately for every PE session and are always enthusiastic. Raise awareness of PE events on notice-boards around the school. Create a display in the hall. Make pupils aware of the role of nutrition and healthy eating. Bring PE and the promotion of health into your classroom. Class topics such as 'Ourselves' and 'My body' offer many possibilities for cross-curricular learning and show how health and PE pervade the curriculum. You might wish to offer to run an after-school club. Bring in experts to give instruction in activity areas where you feel less confident. Broaden the curriculum in your school by offering new activities such as baseball or pop-lacrosse. Organise trips to other facilities that offer physical activities, such as to a local climbing wall. Be interested and actively promote children to become involved in all sorts of physical activity outside school. This can range from skateboarding in the local area to structured classes in dance and martial arts. Children look to you for encouragement and reinforcement. Show this in what you say and how you say it, with words and with body language. Facial expressions are especially powerful communicators of enthusiasm, as are signals like thumbs up and hand-claps. Use lots of smiles. Unlike Martin, if you make your lessons interesting, varied and fun and you enjoy them, so will your pupils!

Giving explanations and instructions

Good teachers are also very good communicators. A recipe for disaster is to become the teacher who spends most of the lesson talking and rambles on, oblivious that the children are bored. Research has found that pupils spend much of their time waiting, listening to the teacher and being organised for activities instead of actually doing them (Siedentop and Tannehill, 2000). Children are normally extremely well motivated in PE and what they want above everything else is to *do* some! When giving explanations or instructions, make use of the KISS principle, which is 'Keep it short and simple'. The younger the child, the shorter the attention span, so it is imperative that the teacher captures the attention of the group at once. Make eye contact with the group. You could consider having a signal to signify that you have important things to communicate. Speak clearly and politely at just above a normal speaking voice. Establishing a regular routine is advised. Due thought must be given to the positioning of the group you are going to talk to. Explain to children *why* an activity or an aspect of it is important. Avoid over-elaborate explanations and remember to match the language and complexity of your instructions or explanations to the age and ability levels of your class. Play–teach–play is a useful technique, and one that is especially effective with pupils who just want to play a game. In this, pupils begin by playing games then practise relevant skills in context and then put these back into their games. In this way the connection between skills practice and playing games is solid because pupils see a direct relevance of the skills they are practising and their purpose in a game.

Giving instructions is the process of providing information, and generally instructions are delivered orally. For instructions to work well, pupils need to know what they have to do and how they should go about it. This requires decisions relating to the size and formation of a group, equipment to be used, starting and stopping and any relevant conditions to the activity. (The conditions, for example, might include changing player roles in a game or specifying the number of passes before shooting at goal.) Readers may find the three factors in successful explanations identified by Perrott (1982) as useful: *continuity* referring to the way the explanations connect across a lesson; *simplicity* – the match between language and the learner's ability and age; and *explicitness* which relates to assumptions that pupils understand more than they actually do. Check understanding by using a phrase such as, 'Does everyone understand? Are you sure?' These are sound guiding principles for both types of teacher–pupil interactions.

Observation

Barrett defined this skill as 'the ability to perceive accurately both the movement response of the learner and the environment in which the response took place' (1983, p. 22). To a novice teacher the task of trying to observe everything and everybody in a PE lesson is daunting. It is also impossible. We offer three pieces of advice. First, acquire the skill of scanning a group. This is similar to a lighthouse beam sweeping across the sea. It does not stop but continues from one side to the other.

With experience this skill is soon acquired and will be of great value in all environments where PE takes place. Second, focus in on one component. For example you watch a Year 5 pupil trying to serve a tennis ball. No easy skill for the pupil but you as the teacher are aware that things are obviously badly amiss. Linked to feedback (which we cover shortly), you are advised to concentrate your observations on the element that is most in need of rectifying. This might be the swing plane of the racket up to the point of impact with the ball. You would then provide the necessary feedback to the learner based upon your observations.

Observation is an important tool when the class is working on a variety of tasks within a lesson, such as when working on various pieces of apparatus in gymnastics. Good observation skills need to employed here but once again a focus can be most helpful. The teacher may have decided to focus on whether the class have answered the task set, how well it is being answered or may wish to observe an individual or group at work. A third technique in observation is to have a third person to observe with you. A colleague not involved in teaching a group can be an invaluable aid and if this person is briefed in advance and knows exactly what to look at, there are many benefits to be accrued.

In order to observe, you must be in the right place. Positioning is an important consideration and is directly linked to the purpose of the observations. To observe a pupil's technique it is necessary to be close enough to see it in detail, whereas in order to scan the whole group working in the hall, a position in the centre of the space is ineffectual. For this purpose, adopting a position on the periphery essentially with one's back to the wall is much better. Observation offers much benefit when the focus is on pupil behaviour or assessing how much time pupils spend on task. Observation schedules designed to measure 'time on task', or academic learning time (Berliner, 1979) or ALT-PE can be quite revealing. Somewhat alarming statistics reported in Mawer (1995) show that pupils spend only about 15% of their time engaged on tasks during lessons.

Observation is also closely linked to analysis. In fact it may be thought of as the first stage of analysis. If we take the common skill of rolling, what should the teachers need to look for when a child is performing it? Using a forward roll as an example, Task 20 requires you to identify what to look for in a proficient performance.

Task 20   What to look for when observing a forward roll

Observe a pupil perform a forward roll at least once. Then answer the following questions:

- What was the initial position?
- Can you describe the pupil's body shape at the start, during and at the end of the movement?
- Where were the pupil's hands?
- Did you notice what the head position was like?
- Was the final position balanced or not?
- Can you describe the roll's speed/direction?
- What was the level of proficiency – beginner, intermediate or advanced?

Demonstrations

Social learning theory (Bandura, 1977) proposes that we learn from copying the behaviour of significant others. This has immediate and powerful implications for teaching physical education: what you as the teacher do gives a reference for pupils and this is immediately evident when using demonstrations. As suggested by Bailey (2001), demonstrations rely upon the sharing of visual information, and PE has many visual features such as shape or form in dance which lend themselves more to seeing than to verbal explanations. This being said, the combination of demonstration followed by explanation is a highly effective teaching tool. Don't talk during the demonstration. Let pupils watch, then talk afterwards.

Demonstrations by pupils can be used to showcase pupil work, and celebrating work in gymnastics and dance is common in primary school assemblies. Demonstrations have powerful motivational qualities too by encouraging other pupils to imitate what they have just seen. Readers are referred to *Teaching Physical Education: A Guide for Mentors and Students* (Williams, 1996) for an accessible account of the purposes of demonstrations in PE. Children quite naturally learn from watching others. A 3 year old will watch an adult balancing on one leg and try to copy the movement. A 6 year old, watching others playing hopscotch in the playground, will quite naturally imitate the same movements. Although demonstrations are recognised as important aspects of presenting information, other evidence suggests that many motor tasks are presented to learners without a visual demonstration (Werner and Rink, 1989). The old adage of 'a picture paints a thousand words' is certainly true and remains so for pupils at all stages in their learning. Beginners are provided with a mental picture of the movement overall whilst more proficient performers benefit from specific points being highlighted, helping them both to remember and reproduce the movement (McCullagh, 1993).

Who demonstrates is an important consideration. The obvious choice is the teacher, provided that an accurate representation of the skill or movement can be given: 'Watch me while I demonstrate . . .'. Ideally demonstration is followed by an oral explanation that focuses attention on key elements. There are times when pupils should demonstrate, and the advice is to share this around the class so that not the same few children get to demonstrate all the time. There is some evidence (Darden, 1997) that learning will occur if a demonstration from a peer is less than perfect because children perceive the movement to be similar to their own and are motivated to try it. Pinpointing is a technique used after a demonstration where the teacher asks a pupil with good technique to demonstrate, allowing relevant points to be emphasised. In a Reception class where children are learning to jump for height, the following might be heard: 'Look everyone how Jodie bends her knees to land. They are really *squashy*. Let me see you all try this now'. The use of verbal cues such as 'squashy' helps pupils to attend to the critical features of a skill in a relevant way and has received much support in the literature (Housner and French, 1994; Roach and Burwitz, 1986). A number of such cues exist for many physical activities which get pupils to create a mental image associated with a component of a skill. With advanced performers this may take the form of mental rehearsal strategies where performers create images of themselves performing the skill or routine (such as in gymnastics), or with beginners using cue phrases. When helping children to achieve a streamlined body shape in swimming to push and glide, a phrase like 'See yourself sliding across the top of a polished table' is often helpful. There are many such phrases and you may want to compile a list for future reference. The use of charts, diagrams and increasingly DVDs are also effective ways to provide visual information accurately and are instructional and motivating (Melville, 1993). Digital and camcorders are highly effective, provided these are used in short episodes, and downloading videoclips from the internet will serve the same purpose. As with all demonstrations, careful thought should be given to viewing arrangements. Should the demonstration take place before, during or after the children have experienced the movement skill? Consider viewpoints so that all children see the demonstration from different angles, and if appropriate, being performed with both sides of the body (such as in throwing techniques or in gymnastics). The use of video and DVD enable the movement to be frozen or shown at a slow speed, which is particularly helpful in dynamic actions such as hitting with a bat or throwing.

Questioning

Questioning is a potent teaching strategy and one that is important to master. Questions in PE can be used for a number of purposes and findings from Brown and Edmundson (1984) show that these range from allowing pupils to express their feelings to encouraging thinking and understanding of ideas. Four of the main purposes of questions are given below, with examples:

Questions to focus attention

■ In Sarah's demonstration, what do you notice about her body shape in her forward roll?

■ Look at Karla's hands before she catches the ball? What are her hands doing?

■ Watch this short video clip of Tony's group playing our basketball game. Can you tell me why the place Mark is standing in to receive the pass from Sally is so good?

Questions to test knowledge

■ Who can tell me why it is important to warm up before we do any exercise?

■ How many points are in contact with the floor in a headstand?

■ In athletics, what was the little phrase we used to help get us into the right positions for throwing?

Questions to develop deeper understanding

■ Why do we use our arms to run fast? How does it help?

■ Remember we talked about centre of gravity? Can you tell me why the first balance you did was better than the second one?

Questions to encourage reflection

■ What have *you* learned from today's lesson?

■ Think about what I have just said about safety. Why is this so important in the swimming pool?

Questioning is such a powerful tool that it not advisable to leave it to chance or use questions in an ad hoc way in lessons. Planning is the key. It is always a good idea to make the precise questions to be used in a lesson explicit on a lesson plan and record at what phase of the lesson they can be put to best use. Questions that require pupils to observe and comment upon their own or another's performance might occur during the main part of a lesson, whereas those requiring pupils to reflect might appear at the end of the lesson. Brown and Wragg (1993) developed their 'IDEA' approach to planning for questioning and there is much merit in adopting this approach:

I – identify what key questions are needed in relation to lesson objectives.
D – decide on the level and timing of your questions.
E – use extensions and supplementary questions too.
A – analyse the answers you are likely to receive.

When questions are planned in advance and have a specific purpose, they invariably have clarity and precision. Consider the language you use to ask the questions, and relate this to the age and ability of your pupils. Brevity is best. Avoid jargon and make the question audible to the group. Make sure also that those receiving the question know that it is a question! One well-planned and precise question is much better than a stream of questions fired out by the teacher which do not allow the class time to respond or are not even perceived as questions.

In addition, the literature refers to different levels of questioning. Although there are endless questions to ask, the types of questions can be categorised to correspond with different levels of thinking (King, 1992; Thorpe, 1992). There is evidence (Galton *et al.*, 1980) showing that low-level questions in lessons require pupils merely to recall information (e.g., Who can remember what we did in last week's lesson?) or deal with basic organisational issues (e.g., Which group is collecting the balls today?) but that higher-order questioning can produce higher-order thinking in pupils (Schwager and Labate, 1993; Tishman and Perkins, 1995). Higher-order questions stimulate pupils to seek out information for themselves, engage in problem solving and encourage them to think deeply and critically. Examples of the kinds of higher-order questions that teachers might ask are shown in Table 8.2, mapped against the processes of analysis, synthesis and evaluation that Bloom (1956) equated with higher-order thinking in pupils.

TABLE 8.2 Higher-order questioning mapped against Bloom's taxonomy of higher-order thinking skills

	Foundation Stage	Key Stage 1	Key Stage 2
Analysis	Everyone watch my jump. (Teacher performs.) What did I do to jump up high in the air?	Watch how players in this group use space in this mini game. What do you notice?	Observe the DVD showing the front crawl arm action. Can you tell me three things about how it was performed?
Synthesis	How could you make your first shape and your second shape different?	Make up a partner game to improve dribbling a ball with a hockey stick. How will you go about this?	Can you as a group generate ideas to solve the problem-solving challenge set up for you?
Evaluation	Balance on one leg and hold it until I count to three. Which was the best way to do this for you?	I want this group to observe Group B's dance. Can you judge it against the three points we decided on earlier?	Can you come up with a way of marking technique for throwing the foam javelin?

Giving feedback

If you were asked to wear a blindfold and then kick a football to a goal a reasonable distance away, with no one to give you advice, you would probably not do very well. Hardly surprising, and yet this is not dissimilar to how many youngsters feel when they are performing movement skills in PE lessons. Although they can usually see what their movement has been like, what they also need is someone to tell them what exactly to look for in their performance and/or what they need to do now to improve it. This is why giving feedback is an important teaching skill because without it, systematic learning is not going to happen. So what is feedback?

Feedback is the information received about one's performance. This can take one of two common forms. *Intrinsic feedback* is what we receive through our senses naturally. In the example above you would receive information from sensors in your muscles and joints about the kick. So, for example, you would obtain new knowledge about your leg position prior to the kick, the feel on impact and, if you were not blindfolded, the flight of the ball in the air and where it landed relative to the target. *Extrinsic feedback*, also known as augmented or enhanced feedback, is provided by someone or something external to the situation. Normally this will be the teacher (hence its use as a teaching tool), but it can also be a displayed time, score of a judge or a video replay of the performance. There are two categories. *Knowledge of results* (KR) informs about the movement's success. You will hear phrases like, 'Goal! Great shot Sally' or simply, 'Missed' that give little information. *Knowledge of performance* (KP) is more effective and gives information on the movement itself. Phrases like, ' OK. Your shot went high. Try to keep your hands closer together in future', provide information on the goal but also important information on the *quality* of the movement.

The properties of external feedback make it a useful pedagogical tool because:

- It motivates pupils to continue to practise when improvement is slow.
- It provides specific information on how to perform the action effectively.
- It reinforces correct performance and decreases performance that is incorrect.
- It allows the teachers to assess how quickly a skill is being learned for individuals or a whole class.

The literature on teacher effectiveness (Boyce, 1991; Silverman *et al.*, 1992) and motor learning (Magill, 1994) are generally positive about teachers' use of extrinsic feedback in enhancing pupil learning. What we see as the next step is to embed this into practical teaching to make most use of it. Here are six suggestions as to how this might be accomplished:

1   Avoid general statements like 'Good' and increase your use of specific feedback statements. Whilst general phrases may have an effect on promoting a positive environment, especially with younger pupils (Sharpe, 1992), older children will

benefit from specific feedback such as 'Next time I want you to hold the balance slightly longer. Hold it and count to three'.

2   Get children to focus on a small number of points in any task you set them and give feedback in relation to these.

3   Keep what you say simple and match your language to the age and ability of the class (or individual pupils).

4   Use positive feedback on most occasions such as, 'Carrie, I like how you showed both curled shapes and the long stretched shapes on the apparatus' and avoid negative statements (Kniffen, 1988) like, 'That is not a proper throw Darren'.

5   Give feedback as soon as possible after the action is observed and decrease its use as learning progresses so as not to make pupils dependent on having it.

6   Make sure you give feedback to *all* pupils (Sharpe, 1992).

Extrinsic feedback is a valuable teaching tool chiefly because it lets your pupils know how they are performing by providing them with information about correct and incorrect aspects of their performance.

Teaching movement concepts and skills

The movement concepts and skills described in Chapter 2 operate as organising centres, give cohesion to the Foundation Stage and primary curricula in a sequential and progressive way. In this next section we present some specific examples of how to teach movement concepts and skills, using dance to illustrate.

In Chapter 2, a hierarchical model of movement skills based on the work of Gallahue (1982) was presented. We believe that this offers a good basis for teaching movement skills progressively from the Foundation Stage through to the end of Key Stage 2. Pre-school and primary age children need to acquire and develop fundamental movement skills in the categories of stability, locomotion and manipulation described in that chapter. This builds upon the rudimentary skills they have acquired in the first two to three years of life and enables them to apply these and learn specific sports skills in a progressive manner as Figure 2.2 showed. Teachers of children from 3 to 11 should concentrate their efforts on the first three elements of the model: *exploration, discovery* and *combinations*.

Exploration

Teachers should allow pupils time to get an idea of what the movement is all about. Proper technique is less important as pupils experiment with different ways of executing the movement in an almost unlimited range of possibilities. There is no 'best' response, only different ones. In teaching, seek to guide pupils to achieve success within their own limits and avoid presenting the correct model to novice learners.

TABLE 8.3 Movement concepts and skills in dance lessons

Movement concept	Specific concept	Activity
Body awareness	Body parts	*Skeleton dance* Isolate different body parts in turn. Explore how the arms move, then the legs, feet, fingers, the head.
	Shapes	*Letters* Make letters with the body (sitting, lying, kneeling and standing): solo (e.g. T, Y, A); with a partner (e.g. C, W, O) or threes (e.g. B, Q).
	Non-locomotor actions	*Turning!* Use the action words *spin, twist, spiral* to create a short dance motif. Make up other turning words. Combine turning with other actions.
	Supports	*Shape dance* Small groups create short motifs based on meeting and parting; forming diamonds and squares by contacting and supporting each other's bodies.
Space awareness	Location	*Statues* Class tiptoe into space. Freeze on a signal. Change travelling action. Play musical statues.
	Directions	*A foggy day* Imagine getting lost in a fog. Moving forward, backward and sideways. Add balance shapes and jumps.
	Levels	*Volcanoes* In one spot, move and show level changes to represent a volcano bubbling, spurting, showering. Extend into small group dance.
	Pathways	*Kites* Move around as if following a kite on a piece of string. Emphasise a variety of pathways, straight, curvy and zig-zag. Include level and speed changes.
	Extension	*Butterflies* Represent the lifecycle of a butterfly from caterpillar to emerging butterfly. Combine actions and levels. Begin in a curled shape and end with a stretched butterfly shape.

continued on facing page

TABLE 8.3 continued

Movement concept	Specific concept	Activity
Effort	Time	*Minibeasts* Moving like different insects. Slow like snails, fast like ants. Show a parade with groups moving like the different insects.
	Force	*Strong and light* Strong – stamping, stepping, clapping. Light – tiptoeing, floating. Move like an elephant. Float like a cloud.
	Flow	*Balloon dance* To accompany music, children use balloons to make a flowing dance.
Relationships	Body parts	*Dancing feet!* Stamp out rhythms with flat feet and heels. Tap dancing. Pointed toes and high knees (Irish dancing). Spinning on heels (Kathak). Steps in traditional folk dances.
	Objects	*In the box* Explore a large box. Skip around it. Jump into it, peep out. Travel in it. Leap out. Compose a short dance.
	People	*Follow my leader* Children march around behind the teacher. Vary actions. Change the leader, once confident.

After the teacher provides some guiding principles, the class engage in finding out for themselves. Teaching hopping in Foundation Stage, the teacher should encourage pupils to try hopping on different legs, to hop various distances and heights and explore what part the arms play in the movement. By using fun games and challenges, the child will learn some fundamentals of the movement in a broad sense.

Discovery

This second tier also involves skills being taught indirectly. The teacher sets the problem for pupils to solve. It differs from movement exploration because this latter method has a limited range of possibilities. The teacher restricts the possibilities of movement responses which allow for several solutions to be acceptable. Observing the movement responses of the pupils allows the teacher to prompt and guide and the pupils to assess and reassess their performance. In teaching in Key Stage 1, the teacher may pose the problem, 'What is the best way to throw a tennis ball for distance?' Through observation and a series of prompts, the teacher gradually moves the children to adopt several techniques that 'they have discovered for themselves'.

Combination

Normally this requires teaching indirectly and directly (this concept is expanded upon in the next section) and involves pupils in combining skills already acquired. Skills may be taught indirectly by continuing with the exploration and discovery methods previously described, and extending them by putting several of the skills together. In a gymnastics warm up in Key Stage 1, the teacher might say, 'I want you to run and then jump' or in Key Stage 2, 'Run, stop, roll sideways and continue running'. A more direct teaching approach requires a model of what the performance should look like, and this is presented to the class using strategies such as explanation and demonstration. Pupils then seek to replicate this model, based upon their individual capabilities. After a practice period, the teacher presents the model again and comments upon the observed responses from the class. An example of this might appear in an athletics lesson with Key Stage 2 pupils which is focused on jumping for distance. The class have already learned skills such as running, hopping, leaping and jumping, and the teacher sets the task: 'Combine any three skills to jump as far as you can'. Typical responses involve combinations such as hop, jump, jump; leap, hop, jump or hop, hop, leap. Such a scenario is ideally set up for the teacher to circulate amongst the class and provide individual feedback as pupils perform their movement combinations.

Direct and indirect teaching approaches

It seems there has always been a good deal of interest in what might be termed 'teaching approaches' in PE. What is clear from both professional and research literature is that a characteristic of an effective teacher is having a repertoire of instructional approaches and knowing when to use them to facilitate pupil learning and understanding (Mawer, 1995). Although different writers employ terms such as 'teaching style' or 'strategies', for the purposes of this book we prefer to use the broader term of 'teaching approaches' since it combines both these elements together. Mosston and Ashworth's landmark work, the Spectrum of Teaching Styles (1986) describes the extent to which decisions in lessons are taken by pupil or teacher. In the model, decisions made by teachers define their teaching behaviours and those made by learners define their learning behaviours. Both teachers and learners make decisions in each of the category sets defined within the spectrum. What varies is the involvement and the shift in decision-making, moving between direct and indirect teaching. At the extreme end of direct teaching is the 'command style' in which all decisions are made by the teacher. At the other end of indirect teaching, is the 'learner initiated style' where pupils may ask and answer their own questions regarding the work

TABLE 8.4 Characteristics of Mosston's Spectrum of Teaching Styles

Spectrum style	Teacher–Pupil characteristics	Learning intentions	PE tasks
Style A Command	Teacher makes decisions. No allowance for pupil individuality.	Motor skill acquisition.	Learning a dance motif by copying the teacher.
Style B Practice	Individuals work at own pace. Some individual feedback given.	Motor skill development.	Solo practice dribbling a ball around cones.
Style C Reciprocal	Pupils work in pairs. One performs, the other gives immediate feedback.	Working with others. Observation and analysis.	In twos, observe each other's swimming technique.
Style D Self-check	Pupils assess their own learning against set criteria.	Assessing their own performance. Making judgements.	Throwing in athletics. Success criteria are provided on a teaching card.
Style E Inclusion	Allows for individual practice. Assumes motivation and awareness of limits.	Maximising involvement. Helping others to succeed.	Using hurdles set at different heights and distances in athletics.
Style F Guided discovery	Pupils are involved in discovering a pre-determined learning target. A discovery process.	Discovery learning. Matching response to question or stimulus.	Pupils find the best way to cross climbing apparatus using hands and feet.
Style G Divergent	Problem-solving. Pupils are encouraged to find alternative solutions. Creative.	Independent thinking. Group work.	Devising a new co-operative game using a range of equipment.
Style H Individual	Teacher decides on area for study. Acts as adviser to pupils.	Planning. Increasing levels of understanding via performance.	Making individual decisions about a dance routine.
Style I Learner initiated	Learner takes initiative on content and process of learning. Teacher is adviser. Limited relevance to Primary PE.	Understanding through selection/application. Taking personal responsibility.	Discussion with teacher about a project on keeping healthy.
Style J Self-teach	Learner is fully independent. Very limited relevance to Primary PE.	Understanding and application.	Little application in schools below KS4.

context. Direct teaching, according to Mawer (1995) is one of the most popular modes of teaching around and continues to receive much support empirically. It involves telling or showing pupils what they have to do, supervising progress and evaluating it. It is the teacher who chooses the lesson content, communicates the task and designs content progression. Pupils play little part in any of the decisions concerning the lesson (p. 148–9). Teaching approaches that involve pupils much more in the decision-making process in their lessons are located at the opposite end of the spectrum and are allied to indirect teaching. Such approaches involve pupils in taking the initiative and creating or solving problems and encourage them to be more independent and self-reliant in their learning (ibid., p. 196). What follows is a broad interpretation of the spectrum styles, including both direct and indirect teaching, based on the work of Williams (1996) but with examples given relevant for the 3–11 age range.

However convenient, it would be wrong to assume that certain teaching styles might be associated with particular activity areas in PE, for example that games is better taught in a practice style, whereas dance benefits from instruction in an inclusion style. Findings from the BAALPE study (1989) confirm that teaching in different activity areas of NCPE (including games and gymnastics) was most effective when various styles were utilised. The spectrum was never envisaged as a straitjacket wherein teachers work in a constrained way. Effective teaching of PE is about using the spectrum's inherent mobility, and moving along it in both directions. Certain teachers may appear to be able to switch from one style to another instinctively, but this ad hoc approach is not desirable (Coates, 1997). The spectrum provides a way of analysing one's own teaching in a rational way, of identifying the effects of that teaching and assessing the competency of it.

Task 21 Identifying your personal teaching styles

Refer to your teaching plans for five PE lessons. Match them with the teaching styles in Mosston's spectrum to identify your predominant styles.

- What are your most common teaching styles?
- How successful do you think your lessons were when you used these styles?
- Could you have included other styles alongside these?
- Can you see any advantages in adding or substituting other teaching styles?

The importance of adopting variety in teaching PE is inherent in the documentation from the first National Curriculum in 1992. This confirmed that a single teaching approach would be insufficient as more was becoming expected of pupils in terms of thinking about their work and developing skills in communication, problem-solving and decision-making. The need to seriously consider *how* content is delivered to pupils and the need for flexibility in delivery to cater for pupil abilities and needs is evident in recent documentation:

> the curriculum itself cannot remain static. It must be responsive to changes in society and the economy, and changes in the nature of schooling itself. Teachers, individually and collectively, have to reappraise their teaching in response to the changing needs of their pupils and the impact of economic, social and cultural change. Education only flourishes if it successfully adapts to the demands and needs of the time.
>
> (DfEE, 1999, p. 13)

Chapter summary

Teaching physical education in the National Curriculum is complex. We began this chapter by describing the key characteristics of effective teaching and offered our own definition of quality teaching in PE. In order to achieve the multiple aims in the subject, highly developed pedagogical skills are required, a number of which have been outlined in the chapter. A variety of teaching approaches are also required, as discussed with reference to Mosston's spectrum (1986). There is no single way of teaching. Deciding on what teaching tools or approaches to use varies from class to class and will also vary according to the age of the pupils. In any PE lesson the teacher is involved in adjusting and reviewing tasks according to the needs and responses from pupils. Being able to use a teaching approach that is matched to the learning intentions of a lesson allows teachers to set high standards of achievement and facilitate pupils' learning and thinking effectively.

Questions for reflection

- After reading this chapter, has your idea of what makes quality teaching in PE changed? Would you define it any differently?

- What additions would you make to the toolkit of teaching skills offered in this chapter?

- Think of a lesson you have taught or observed recently. How was feedback used in the lesson? How effective was this?

- With reference to Mosston's spectrum, what are your predominant teaching styles? Do these change according to the activity areas you are teaching? Does it matter what age range you teach?

Web link and further reading

www.peprimary.co.uk

Graham, G., Holt-Hale, S. and Parker, M. (1993) *Children Moving: A Reflective Approach to Teaching Physical Education.* London: Mayfield Publishing.
Movement concepts and movement skills are thoroughly addressed throughout this useful book.

Macfadyen, T. (2000) The effective use of teaching styles. In R. Bailey and T. Macfadyen (eds) *Teaching Physical Education 5–11.* London: Continuum.
Chapter 4 is a detailed discussion on styles and strategies and points out the advantages and disadvantages of teaching styles in Mosston's spectrum.

Mawer, M. (1995) *The Effective Teaching of Physical Education.* London: Longman.
Three chapters in this excellent book are especially relevant. Chapter 8 discusses what is meant by a teaching style and a strategy. Chapters 9 and 10 deal with direct and indirect teaching–learning strategies.

Williams, A. (1996) *Teaching Physical Education: A Guide for Mentors and Students.* London: David Fulton Publishers.
Chapter 4 and Chapter 5 are really good reading on teaching styles and strategies.

What happens *during* and *after* the lesson? Assessment, recording and reporting

---

Chapter objectives

By the end of this chapter you should be able to:

■ Understand the principles and purposes associated with effective assessment of pupils' achievement and progress in PE;

■ Be able to develop templates for recording and reporting judgements in PE that are fit for purpose;

■ Devise a process whereby you may reliably and consistently judge evidence of pupils' attainment in PE and use this to construct a coherent report.

What is assessment in PE?

THIS CHAPTER SEEKS to demystify the whole area of monitoring and assessing children's achievement in PE. It gives straightforward advice on what to look for across the 3–11 continuum. Emphasis is placed on observation of movement with reference to OCM (Tacklesport, 2003), and strategies to develop observational skills of assessment in fundamental motor activities are provided. Integration of technologies to assist assessment is suggested. Finally, examples of reporting to parents are given from each of the age phases.

What is certain is that everybody involved in education – teachers, pupils, parents and administrators – have a view on what assessment is, its role, and its purposes. What is also certain is that there will be a range of views expressed about its importance. Whilst the views of these different parties will certainly vary, all would probably agree on one thing at least: whether we like it or not, assessment is a central feature of teaching and learning practice and therefore a permanent feature of the school day. It is here to stay.

For the purposes of this chapter, the term 'assessment' refers to all those activities undertaken by teachers, teachers' assistants and pupils, specifically to provide information about the teaching and learning process. We believe that this broad definition articulates the essential principles and purposes of assessment, namely that it is necessary to enable us to access reliable and valid information about our teaching *and* pupils' learning. There is little consensus however regarding the type of information that we need to access to effect improvements in teaching and learning in PE. Equally contentious is the method(s) we should employ to capture that information. These important topics are the subject of the first section of this chapter. Thereafter, subsequent sections will address the recording and the reporting of assessment judgements.

Perceptions of assessment

The results of a brief word-association exercise conducted recently with physical education teacher trainees revealed that the term assessment is synonymous with 'nerve-racking', 'tests', 'exams', 'coursework', 'stress' and 'failure'! Whilst we recognise that this quick straw poll is hardly robust scientific research, it does reveal a broadly negative perception of assessment and points to assessment being the source of considerable anxiety. In an increasingly standards-focused (some might say 'obsessed') education system, teachers, pupils and parents are, at some point, likely to experience some degree of assessment anxiety. Further probing, however, reveals that this anxiety stems not from the assessment process itself but from the social consequences arising from the treatment of the information it yields. The current trend in education for creating rank order lists or league tables of performance based on assessment data reflects a simplistic and reductive approach to data analysis. In a social and cultural context in which success is traditionally associated with rewards and failure brings with it sanctions, one might legitimately argue that the pressure to avoid being labelled as 'failing', renders traditional assessment conditions highly stressful. Consequently, a pupil's performance may not necessarily be representative of their true capability. Given that it is difficult to predict who is likely to be affected in this way and by how much, it would seem that some forms of assessment will be, at best, unreliable or, at worst, futile. This basic flaw in the assessment process has been recognised for a long time and has been the impetus behind a great deal of research investigating assessment practices in schools.

Regardless of the perceptions of any assessment process, one of the unavoidable features of assessment activity is the exercise of judgement. To arrive at a judgement that accurately describes a pupil's current level of knowledge, skill or understanding involves making comparison. Piotrowski (2000) suggests that these comparisons can be made in relation to:

- Criteria or learning objectives, known as criterion-referenced judgements;

- The performance of others, known as norm-referenced judgements;

- The pupil's previous achievements, known as ipsative judgements.

Whilst each form of comparison can be useful at different times, deciding which should be used on which occasion can be a source of tension. McMillan (2000) suggests that this is just one of several tensions that teachers need to discuss during the development of assessment policy. Other sources of tension include the purpose, timing, type, focus and the scope of assessment (see Table 9.1).

TABLE 9.1

Assessment tensions	Debate
Purpose	Assessment for learning v assessment for auditing
Type	Traditional v alternative; authentic v contrived
Timing	Formative v summative
Focus	Added value v absolute standards
Scope	National tests v local tests

Having engaged with these debates, teachers should be in a better position to determine what kind of activities they need pupils to participate in to collate the evidence necessary for consistent and accurate evaluation of achievement.

Assessment practice in PE

Given that assessment is a complex process, it is not surprising that assessment in PE is frequently reported as one of the areas of professional responsibility in which practitioners feel most vulnerable. QCA (2005, p. 15) report that 'assessment and recording remain problematic in Key Stages 1 and 2'. In many schools, systematic assessment procedures for PE are either not in place or they are highly complex. Either way this is not conducive to teachers making accurate judgements about the standard and quality of their pupils' work. This is compounded by the fact that the vast majority of teachers in primary schools feel that they do not have the subject knowledge required to make valid judgements. Consequently, the use of assessment to inform planning in PE is a considerable weakness. One of the key reasons why this has remained the case for over a decade with relatively little progress evident (see DES, 1992; OFSTED, 1998; QCA, 2005) is that teachers' attention has been focused elsewhere, principally on raising standards of pupils' performance in core subject standard assessment tests (SATs). Given that the overall judgement about a school's effectiveness does not weight performance in PE particularly heavily, there has been little impetus to address this issue. However, times are changing and our attention is shifting. With a growing body of evidence suggesting that high-quality PE can effect whole school change and contribute to the raising standards agenda across the curriculum (QCA, 2005), increasingly schools are recognising that a commitment to good assessment practice across all subjects can improve pupils' motivation and engagement with learning. Not least, growing public concern about the health of children in the UK and the subsequent changes in legislation, has extended schools' accountability in these areas. These subtle shifts have had the effect of causing assessment in PE to move up the order of priorities.

As Piotrowski (2000) illustrates, it is quite possible to teach pupils without engaging in any assessment. If we were to adopt a laissez-faire approach to the organisation and management of learning, we might choose to provide pupils with opportunities to acquire new knowledge, skills and understanding without ever attempting to track their progress or determine their success. In this mode of instruction, pupils may be learning but without tracking their progress we would never know. Equally, without embedding any monitoring process into our teaching we would not know the extent to which our selected methods were working. This is not good teaching. One of the distinguishing characteristics of a good teacher is their capacity to use assessment to promote learning and improve their own teaching. To confirm this view the literature is replete with lists of the specific purposes of assessment (see Hopper *et al.*, 2000; Piotrowski, 2000; McMillan, 2000; Casbon and Spackman, 2005), arguing that, amongst other things, assessment enables teachers to:

- establish what pupils already know, understand and can do;
- identify pupils' specific needs;
- give pupils feedback about their progress;
- set appropriate targets for pupils;
- motivate pupils to continue to improve;
- level pupils' achievement;
- evaluate teaching;
- improve curriculum planning (in the short, medium and long term);
- gather information for distribution (to parents, colleagues, inspectors, governors);
- assure the quality and fitness for purpose of the programme.

What this list reveals is that good assessment practice relies on collating a range of information from a number of sources. PE has a tradition of collecting quantitative data (e.g. personal bests, school records, fitness scores). Sometimes this information can be particularly useful and serve to motivate pupils. For more complex actions, where changes in the outcomes of performance may be less obvious, shifting the focus

TABLE 9.2. Examples of quantitative and qualitative assessment data

Quantitative data	Qualitative data
■ Claire can do 100 skips in 3 mins.	■ Imogen can describe how to throw for distance.
■ 18/28 children completed the task.	■ Pupils are showing more creativity in their dance compositions.
■ 65% of pupils obtained level 2 at the end of Key Stage 1.	■ Since introducing pupil referees in games lessons, pupils seem to play more fairly.
■ 20 pupils asked about attending gym club after school.	■ Using task cards in swimming has improved pupils' knowledge of how to do front crawl well.
■ Class 3B are now able to stay active for 20 mins which represents an improvement of 5 mins.	■ After doing problem solving activities in O&AA, pupils' planning skills have improved.
■ Since introducing sport education in PE, Yr 6 attendance has improved by 12%.	

to qualitative indicators of performance can be equally revealing. Table 9.2 distinguishes between these different forms of assessment information.

Whilst some of these improvements may not have been originally planned for, a vigilant and reflective teacher will be sensitive to these changes, and adapt their practice to suit the needs of their learners accordingly.

In order to be able to answer the question, 'What have the children learned in PE today?' with any degree of confidence, we need to develop a range of tools that will provide us with information about how our pupils are progressing. Despite a wealth of activity and learning taking place in any lesson, compared with other subject areas, PE has traditionally been a relatively 'data-poor' environment. This is not due to a lack of learning but an absence of effective strategies for capturing what learning has taken place. The process of making judgements in PE is hampered by the nature of the activity. Maude (2001) sums up the difficulties well,

> Movement is not easy to observe analytically because it leaves no trace, as writing and painting do. Movement is transitory and in most children's experience is not repeatable.
>
> (Maude, 2001, p. 79)

Whilst this point is well made, it should not be taken as cause for abandoning any efforts to collect information about pupils' performance in PE. On the contrary, it should be the catalyst to urge us to explore other possibilities. To make reliable judgements about a pupil's physical competence, from observation alone, requires that teachers hone their observation skills and develop their knowledge of performance expectations. This takes a great deal of time, effort and practice and will inevitably lead to some errors, particularly where the teacher is trying to assess the whole class at the same time. The number and impact of such errors however, can be minimised by employing a range of other strategies, no different to those already used in classroom contexts. Raymond (1998) suggests the following strategies:

- Talking to pupils, individually or in groups as they are working or reflecting on their work;

- Listening carefully to what they say as they discuss tasks or evaluate their own or others' work;

- Observing children throughout the process and during the performance of their work;

- Looking at videos of the children planning/composing and performing their work;

- Analysing written work in children's personal diaries, the class log book, or written notes, diagrams and records of their work;

- Reflecting on relevant information contained in the children's profiles and records.

(p. 176)

Jefferies *et al.* (1997) suggest that there are many ways to assess a pupil's knowledge of the key parts of an action or skill, aside from actually demonstrating them to a teacher or peer. Allowing pupils to communicate their knowledge about an action / skill in non-physical ways is a more inclusive approach to gathering information about learning. For the pupil who understands the principles and practise of a skill but cannot yet perform that skill, cognitive assessment techniques provide a means through which their learning can be acknowledged and rewarded. Thus whilst direct observation will always lie at the heart of good assessment practice in PE, this should be supported by a framework of other assessment methods to enable practitioners to justify their judgements.

Observation in PE in the digital age

Meaningful assessment in the Foundation Stage and during the primary years should be benchmarked against the ages and stages of fundamental movement ability and motor skill development (Piotrowski, 2000). Developing a thorough understanding of the stages of progression for certain key motor skills (running, dodging, balancing, stopping, twisting, bending, stretching, pulling, jumping, climbing, catching, throwing, kicking, dribbling and striking with an implement) is beyond the reach of many generalist practitioners. However, the recent assimilation of new technologies into teaching has facilitated the development of new resources to support practitioners' knowledge of motor development *in situ*. One such resource is the CD-ROM '*Observing Children Moving*' Tacklesport/PEAUK (2003) which has been developed with three core principles in mind. These are that:

1 Movement observation involves *seeing, knowing, understanding and analysing.*

2 The more that is known about what is seen, the more informed the response can be.

3 The outcome of effective observation can be to raise standards for children in movement education and physical education.

This resource represents a landmark in guiding practitioners' observation and assessment of movement. The integration of video footage alongside guidance for the observation and assessment of twelve selected movement capabilities (run, gallop, strike, write, climb, roll, block-build, throw, jump, catch, kick and moulding clay) for the first time provides practitioners with the opportunity to see what early and later motor patterns look like. These can then be used with confidence as a benchmark against which observations and assessments of pupils can be made. Furthermore, working through this sort of material with colleagues will promote professional dialogue and will assist teachers in moderating the judgements of their pupils' performance. Designed primarily as a resource for practitioners working with pupils in the 3–7 age range, the more recent '*Observing and Analysing Learners' Movement*' Tacklesport/ PEAUK (2006) has been targeted at those working with pupils in the 7–14 age group. The trend towards integrating technology into everyday teaching in the primary school is likely to lead to a growth in both the demand for, and the availability of, such resources.

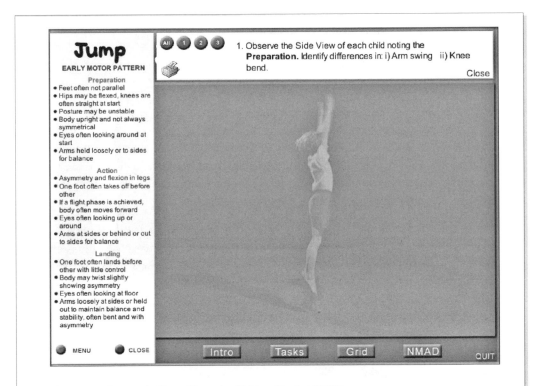

FIGURE 9.1 Screen shot from *Observing Children Moving* (2003)

Source: Tacklesport (2003): *Observing Children Moving.* Worcester: Tacklesport Consultancy Limited/ PEA UK

The guiding principles of assessment

We have considered the principles, purpose and the practicalities of assessment in PE. The guiding principles that have emerged can be summarised as follows:

- Build in regular assessment opportunities.

- Assess pupils in different ways.

- Reduce the number of pupils being assessed at any one time.

- Practise the skill of observing pupils in motion.

- Moderate assessment judgements with colleagues.

Task 22 Reflecting on the guiding principles of assessment

Consider the guiding principles in turn. Try to list ways in which you could embed each one into your current practice.

Planning for assessment – assessment for learning

Thus far, our analysis of the assessment process has demonstrated that assessment and planning are separate yet inextricably linked activities. The explicit planning of assessment opportunities to facilitate pupils' learning is known as assessment for learning (AfL). The Assessment Reform Group (2002) defines assessment for learning as:

> The process of seeking and interpreting evidence for use by learners and their teachers to decide where the learners are in their learning, where they need to go and how best to get there.

According to Leitch *et al.* (2005), AfL is a way of planning activities in lessons so that both the teacher and the pupils know what they are learning and how well they are learning it (p. 6). The deployment of pupil-centred learning processes, such as effective feedback, clear learning intentions, quality questioning, dynamic group work and self- and peer-assessment has led to suggestions that AfL contributes to raising standards and improving pupils' self-esteem. In AfL classrooms, teachers

- involve pupils in decision-making;
- convey a sense of progress;
- place less emphasis on grades;
- make learning goals explicit;
- develop pupils' self- and peer-assessment skills;
- promote learning goal orientation rather than performance.

(Leitch *et al.*, 2005)

Applying the principles of AfL to the PE 'classroom', Casbon and Spackman (2005) show that AfL leads to:

- Improvement – in performance, skills or ability to think;
- Progress – by enabling pupils to work in more demanding and complex situations;
- Achievement – by enabling pupils to achieve high-quality outcomes;
- Confidence – by increasing pupils' belief that they can perform well in PE;
- Positive attitudes – by increasing pupils' motivation, self-esteem and independence.

These outcomes are achieved through the cyclical process of planning, teaching and assessing, and reviewing for improvement.

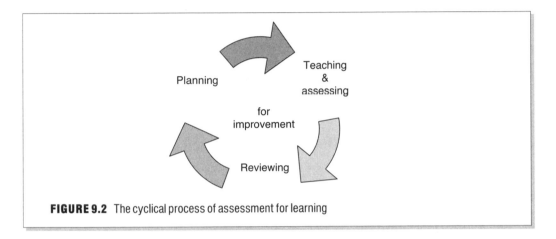

FIGURE 9.2 The cyclical process of assessment for learning

It is important not to confuse this process with the more commonplace plan–teach–review cycle that operates at the macro level and may help steer the annual review of the curriculum map for PE or the content of units of work. The assessment for learning cycle functions at the micro level, in which the teacher works with their pupils through a continuous process of teaching and assessing in pursuit of specified goals. Embedding this continuous process into our everyday practice provides opportunities to adjust the teaching approaches employed and the tasks set in order to make steady progress towards agreed targets. The key differences between the plan–teach–review cycle and the assessment for learning cycle is that the former takes place at the end of a programme and is conducted by teachers for pupils whilst the latter is a continuous process which involves the teacher and pupil working collaboratively to develop a learning conversation.

Developing the learning conversation with pupils involves:

- Explaining or agreeing the learning objectives for lessons or activities;
- Asking questions that prompt pupils to show their knowledge, understanding and skills;

- Sharing and explaining observations, analysis and interpretations;

- Supporting pupils in self-assessment, helping them to become aware of how they learn best and what they are learning;

- Supporting pupils in peer assessment encouraging them not to draw comparisons between each other;

- Making judgements about how well pupils are doing and what needs to be improved.

(Casbon and Spackman, 2005 p. 4)

Feedback

Just as teachers need to gather and interpret information to assess whether their teaching is effective, pupils need to have access to a constant stream of information providing feedback about how they are progressing. In the early years, teachers will need to help pupils tune in to what information is available and what it means in order for them to make sense of what is going on around them. As pupils gather experience, teachers can begin to increase the expectations on pupils to begin to gather and use this information for themselves.

Using questioning to enhance feedback

Questioning is an important process in the learning conversation. The right questions, asked at the right time, of the right pupils, can elicit responses that help to reveal how far pupils have progressed in their learning. Questions are used for a number of different purposes:

- As a prompt, e.g. What should we remember to do in this situation?

- As a challenge, e.g. Do you think you can do it more quickly?

- To develop thinking, e.g. What are your options from this position?

- To check knowledge, e.g. Can you explain why this happens?

What pupils do or say in response to this sort of questioning can be used as evidence of learning. The assessment of the quality of these responses, when evaluated against expectations, will act as a reference point for determining the next steps to continue to make progress. Prior to the introduction of the curriculum guidance for the Foundation Stage and the National Curriculum, teachers and other practitioners were left to their own devices to determine what was worth assessing in the physical domain. Often this resulted in devising long lists of age-appropriate physical tasks, which, in theory at least, would be used to judge whether or not pupils were making acceptable progress in their physical competence. As we have already identified, however, the process of becoming physically educated involves more than simply learning physical skills. A physically educated child develops knowledge and understanding that can

Task 23 Teaching strategy assessment

Reflect on the strategies you use to maintain the flow of feedback in PE, and complete the table. Tick the column that corresponds to the frequency of use in your teaching.

Strategy			Always	Sometimes	Rarely
Sharing the learning objective with pupils					
Sharing the criteria for success in a task					
Providing examples of good performance	Live demonstrations				
	Using video / DVD / internet				
Giving ample opportunity for repeated practice	Providing extra time				
	Providing extra information that can be accessed independently	Task cards			
		Image cards			
		Teaching points and/or questions			
Reminding pupils of the learning objective as the lesson progresses					
Suggesting improvements rather than giving complete solutions					
Asking questions about what pupils are doing and how they are making progress					
Using plenary time to pause, look back and look ahead	During lessons				
	At the end of lessons				
Discussing assessment information	With the class				
	With groups of pupils				
	With individual pupils				
Agreeing targets for progress	With the class				
	With groups of pupils				
	With individual pupils				
Now set yourself the target of increasing the number of 'always' ticks.					

(Adapted from BAALPE, 2005 p. 18)

be applied and adapted to suit new situations. The tools for assessing the development of these characteristics therefore need to be more sophisticated than lists of discrete skills.

During the Foundation Stage, assessment judgements made in relation to the physical development area of learning are made in relation to pupils' progress towards meeting the Early Learning Goals. These are that children can:

- Move with confidence, imagination and safety;

- Move with control and co-ordination;

- Show awareness of space, of themselves and of others;

- Recognise the importance of keeping healthy and those things which contribute to this;

- Recognise the changes that happen to their bodies when they are active;

- Use a range of small and large equipment;

- Travel around, under, over and through balancing and climbing equipment;

- Handle tools, construction objects and malleable materials safely and with increasing control.

Teachers and other practitioners should make the assessments as they go along, observing the children in their usual 'classroom' activities against a nine-point scale as shown in Table 9.3.

The National Curriculum sets out in a single attainment target the knowledge, skills and understanding that children should have achieved at the end of Key Stages 1 and 2. Whilst the programme of study offers opportunities for pupils to study a range of activity areas, it is progress in the four aspects of learning (acquiring and developing skills; selecting and applying skills, tactics and compositional ideas; evaluating and improving performance; and knowledge and understanding of fitness and health) that are the focus of the levels of attainment. Eight levels of attainment are prescribed, with the expectation that by age 7 most pupils will meet the criteria for level 2 and by age 11 most pupils will meet the criteria for level 4.

In Table 9.4, the level statements are shown in a grid format to help distinguish between the aspects of learning. The highlighted words and phrases are designed to focus the assessor's attention on the key characteristics sought at each level.

In Table 9.5, the grids provide examples of what to look for within the different activity areas. Some of the cells have been left blank for you to complete.

TABLE 9.3 Assessment of physical development in the Foundation Stage

Physical development in the Foundation Stage nine-point scale	Exemplification – What will you see pupils doing?
1 Moves spontaneously, showing some control and co-ordination.	Sean hears a plane flying overhead and looks up to watch it. He puts out his arms and moves around, making engine noises.
	The children move around the room to music, stopping immediately when the music stops and trying to hold their position until the music starts again.
2 Moves with confidence in a variety of ways, showing some awareness of space.	A favourite tape is playing outside. The children move enthusiastically, using their arms and legs and shaking their heads in time to the music.
	Jacob spends a long time pouring water from a jug into containers of different sizes, sometimes accurately and sometimes spilling it over the sides.
3 Usually shows appropriate control in large- and small-scale movements.	While watching the geese in the park, Olivia tries to imitate them by standing on one leg, sometimes overbalancing.
	Sohal uses his wheelchair with accuracy, avoiding bumping into doorframes and taking great care in the outdoor area.
4 Moves with confidence, imagination and in safety. Travels around, under, over and through balancing and climbing equipment. Shows awareness of space, of self and others.	A large group of children are 'Going on a Bear Hunt' and carry out the actions of the story outdoors, interpreting the different ways of moving and carefully avoiding bumping into each other.
	A group of children take the large blocks outside so that they have enough space to build a tower and can see how far away the bricks land when it falls, without the possibility of hurting anyone.
5 Demonstrates fine motor control and co-ordination.	A group of children are playing 'Snakes and Ladders'. They shake the dice carefully and roll them on to the floor in a controlled way. They pick up the counters and move them skilfully up and down the board.
	Gareth carefully fits the straw into the small hole in his juice carton.
	Faiza uses the mouse confidently while watching the screen to draw a tree on the computer.

continued on next page

TABLE 9.3 continued

Physical development in the Foundation Stage nine-point scale	Exemplification – What will you see pupils doing?
6 Uses small and large equipment, showing a range of basic skills.	*A group of children turn the role-play area into a cave, using rugs, large pieces of material and tables. They secure the covers to the table legs with string, which they cut and tie carefully.*
	Alex, who has hemiplegia, balances a koosh ball on a bat and walks forward, weaving between cones.
	Marshall swings all the way across the monkey bars, pretending to be a chimpanzee in a rainforest.
7 Handles tools, objects, construction and malleable materials safely and with basic control.	*Alistair and Ann are using the woodwork bench to make a wooden frame for their painting. When they have measured and cut the wood, they decide wood glue would be better than nails to join the sides.*
	Ryan, a child with language delay, points to the 'no' symbol when asked if Angie should take the sharp knife, which they had used with assistance, over to the sink.
8 Recognises the importance of keeping healthy and those things which contribute to this. Recognises the changes that happen to her/his body when s/he is active.	*After running outside in the playground, Blandine says to the practitioner, 'I'm hot 'cos I've been running – please can I have a drink?'*
	Aneek, having used the toilet, moves out of the area, stops and checks himself and signs in BSL to the practitioner, 'oops forgot wash hands go back clean' and goes back to wash them.
	After playing 'What's the time Mr. Wolf?' the children notice that their hearts are beating faster. They talk with the practitioner about other times this has happened, and why.
9 Repeats, links and adapts simple movements, sometimes commenting on her/his work. Demonstrates co-ordination and control in large and small movements and in using a range of tools and equipment.	*Iain invents ways of getting along a bench. He alternates between swinging his legs from side to side, and pulling himself along on his stomach, and repeats the sequence of movements.*
	During a physical activity session, Pandora moves confidently around the room, hopping, skipping and jumping. When told to find a space, she balances on two body parts (one hand and one leg). She is able to repeat the process using different body parts to balance on.

http://www.qca.org.uk/downloads/5828.handbook.web.2.pdf)

TABLE 9.4 Levels statements in PE: a guide to levels 1–5

	Level 1	Level 2	Level 3	Level 4	Level 5
Acquire and develop	*Copy, repeat* and explore simple skills and actions with *basic control* and co-ordination	Explore simple skills and *copy, remember,* repeat and explore simple actions with *control* and co-ordination	Use *skills,* actions and ideas *appropriately*	*Link skills,* techniques and ideas showing *precision, control and fluency*	*Combine skills,* techniques and ideas consistently showing precision, control and fluency
Select and apply	Start to link skills and actions together	*Vary* skills, actions and ideas and link these in ways that suit the activities	*Select* skills, actions and ideas and apply them with *co-ordination and control*	*Apply skills,* techniques and ideas accurately and *appropriately*	*Select and apply* their skills, techniques and ideas *accurately and appropriately*
	Start to link skills and actions to suit the activities	*Begin to show understanding* of simple tactics and basic compositional ideas	Show understanding of tactics and composition by starting to vary how they respond	*Perform showing an understanding* of tactics and composition	Performance *draws on what* they know about *strategy, tactics and composition*
Evaluate and improve	*Describe* their own and others' *actions*	*Talk about differences* between their own and others' performance	*Can see how their work is similar to and different from* others' work	*Compare and comment on* skills, techniques and ideas used in their own and others' work	*Analyse and comment on* skills and techniques and how these are applied in their own and others' work
	Comment on their own and others' work	*Suggest improvements* to their own and others' performance	*Use this understanding to* improve their own performance	*Use this understanding to* improve their own performance	*Modify and refine skills and* techniques to improve their performance
Fitness and health	*Talk about* how to exercise safely	*Describe* how their bodies feel during different activities	*Give reasons* why warming up before an activity is important	*Explain and apply basic* safety principles in preparing for exercise	Warm up and cool down in ways that suit the activity and *explain how the body* reacts during different types of exercise
	Talk about how their bodies feel during exercise	*Understand* how to exercise safely	*Give reasons* why physical activity is good for their health	*Describe the effects of* exercise on their bodies and *how this is valuable to their* fitness and health	*Explain why regular safe* exercise *is good* for their fitness and health

(Cambridgeshire County Council and Peterborough School Sport Partnership)

TABLE 9.5 Activity-specific level descriptions

To achieve a level 1 through gymnastic activities you must be able to:		What will you see pupils doing?	What will you hear pupils saying?
A&D	Copy, repeat and explore simple gymnastic skills & actions showing basic control and co-ordination.	Copying what the teacher does, what their classmates are doing, what they have seen on video/DVD and practising in their own space.	Watch what I can do!
S&A	Link your gymnastic skills together in ways which suit different gymnastic situations.	Practising simple patterns/sequences on the floor and on apparatus.	My sequence starts on the floor, takes me over the bench and finishes in a hoop.
E&I	Describe and comment on your own and pupils' work in gymnastics.	Sitting quietly while their classmates show their work. Being prepared to describe what they saw.	I saw Alfie making a star shape in the air when he jumped.
H&F	Talk about how to exercise safely in gymnastics and how your body feels during gymnastics activity.	Looking around them to check that the space is clear before they start.	We have to be careful not to trip when we are carrying apparatus. Gymnastics makes me feel hot.

To achieve a level 2 through dance activities you must be able to:		What will you see pupils doing?	What will you hear pupils saying?
A&D	Explore simple dance skills. Copy, remember, and repeat dance actions showing basic control and co-ordination.	Practising a pattern over and over again.	Look at my pattern. Oh, that went wrong. Watch, I'll do it again.
S&A	Vary your dance skills, actions and ideas. Link your dance skills in ways that suit different dance performances.	Changing the timing, pace, direction or level of the dance when working with a partner.	I've changed my dance to fit with the music.
E&I	Talk about the differences between your own and others' dances and suggest improvements.	Sitting quietly while their classmates show their work. Describing which movements they liked and explaining what they liked about them	I liked the way Annika jerked her arms. It made me think of a machine.
H&F	Show how to work safely in dance and describe how your body feels during different dance activities.	Offering responses when asked questions about how dance makes them feel	Remembering my dance makes me feel good. Dance is good exercise and keeps you fit

To achieve a level 3 through games activities you must be able to:	What will you see pupils doing?	What will you hear pupils saying?
A&D	Select and use your games skills, actions and ideas appropriately.	
S&A	Select games skills, actions and ideas and apply them with co-ordination and control. Show that you understand tactics in games by varying how you respond in different game situations.	
E&I	See how your work in games is similar to and different from other pupils' work. Use this comparison to improve your performance in games.	
H&F	Give reasons for the importance of warming up in games and explain why games playing can be good for your health.	

To achieve a level 4 through athletic activities you must be able to:	What will you see pupils doing?	What will you hear pupils saying?
A&D	Link your athletic skills & techniques together & use them accurately and appropriately in different athletic disciplines. Perform your athletics skills precisely, showing control and fluency.	Using a run up and large final stride to throw a tennis ball for maximum distance. Using the same techniques to throw a foam javelin.	
S&A	Use your athletic skills and techniques accurately and appropriately. Demonstrate an ability to apply tactical thinking in your athletic performance.		I've learned to pace myself so that I can run around the school field without stopping.
E&I	Compare and comment on athletic skills, techniques and ideas used in your own and other students' work. Use your comments to improve athletic performance.	Compare sprint times from different start positions (sitting, lying, kneeling, facing backwards) and discuss reasons for the differences.	

To achieve a level 4 through athletic activities you must be able to:

	What will you see pupils doing?	What will you hear pupils saying?
H&F	Explain and use basic safety rules in preparing for athletics. Describe what effect athletics has on your body. Know and describe how athletics is valuable to your fitness and health.	We must stretch carefully before sprinting to avoid pulling a muscle. Sprinting is an explosive activity and needs strong leg muscles. Training for sprinting will make my legs stronger.

To achieve a level 5 through outdoor & adventurous (O&A) activities you must be able to:

	What will you see pupils doing?	What will you hear pupils saying?
A&D	Combine your knowledge of skills, techniques and ideas for working in O&A contexts, consistently showing precision, control and fluency.	
S&A	Select O&A skills, techniques and ideas appropriately according to the context and apply these accurately. Show that you can apply strategic thinking in your responses.	We need to have a plan. Has anyone got any ideas? I think we could . . . What do you think?
E&I	Analyse your O&A skills and techniques and comment on how these are applied in your and others' work. Modify and refine your skills to improve your performance.	Taking turns to comment and listening to each other when reviewing how successful they were on a group task.
H&F	Warm up and cool down appropriately for O&A activities and explain how your body reacts during these types of activity. Explain why regular safe exercise is good for your fitness and health.	Organising a 'warm up' and 'cool down' routine for orienteering.

Recording assessment judgements

In the absence of any statutory requirement to maintain records of pupils' achievements in PE, teachers have been free to develop recording systems that suit their own requirements. Prior to adopting a system for recording attainment, it is worth reflecting on its role and purpose. In consultation with trainee teachers and colleagues in school, when asked, 'What do you need your assessment profile to provide?' a number of common features emerge. These are that an assessment profile must be:

- Simple, clear and easy to use;
- Informative and meaningful to a range of audiences;
- Related to, and helpful in developing, planning;
- Helpful in levelling pupils' achievement;
- Helpful in constructing reports.

We should therefore abandon recording systems that do not satisfy each of these criteria.

Task 24 Evaluating the usefulness of recording templates

Using the five given criteria as a guide, evaluate the fitness for purpose of the following recording templates.

Template 1

PE assessment for Unit					
Class		Yr(s)			
Learning objectives					
1. Acquiring and developing skills: 2. Selecting and applying skills: 3. Evaluating and improving performance: 4. Knowledge and understanding of fitness and health:					
Name		LO1	LO2	LO3	LO4

Symbols should be inserted as follows

w   means that the pupil is working towards the learning objective

✓   means that the learning objective has been achieved

ex   means that the pupil has exceeded expectations

Assessment carried out on   **by**

Review of Template 1

Criteria	Rating	Comments
Simple, clear and easy to use	✓✓✓✓	This template represents a traditional track-record for PE. On it, the teacher is able to note the extent to which each pupil meets each key objective. For a class of 28 pupils this could involve the teacher making 112 separate judgements for each unit of PE taught! There is no space for making additional notes which might provide evidence of what the pupil was seen doing or heard saying to warrant the judgement made and therefore it will be of limited value for levelling pupils' performance or informing subsequent reports.
Informative and meaningful to a range of audiences	✓✓	
Related to, and helpful in developing, planning	✓✓	
Helpful in levelling pupils' achievement	✓	
Helpful in constructing reports	✓	

Now try a similar excercise with the following two templates.

Template 2

CLASS		Unit Topic
Pitched at Level 2		**Games Unit 2, Year 1**
Acquiring and developing skills		1. Perform a range of rolling, throwing, striking, kicking, catching and gathering skills, with control.
		2. Show a good awareness of others in running, chasing and avoiding games, making simple decisions about when and where to run.
Selecting and applying skills, tactics and compositional ideas		1. Choose and use tactics to suit different situations.
		2. React to situations in a way that helps their partners and makes it difficult for their opponents.
		3. Know how to score and keep the rules of the games.
Evaluating and improving performance		1. Watch and describe performances accurately.
		2. Recognise what is successful.
		3. Copy actions and ideas, and use the information they collect to improve their skills.
Knowledge and understanding of fitness and health		1. Understand and describe changes to their heart rate when playing different games.
		2. Begin to anticipate what they will feel like after playing games.

Opportunities for assessment		
	Children who do not meet the criteria	**Children who exceed the criteria**
Date:		
Date:		
Date:		
Date:		

Northamptonshire County Council (2005)

Template 3

Physical Education Assessment Framework for Gymnastics

Class/Year group: Date:

LEVEL 4 EXPECTATIONS

	Level descriptors	Examples
A&D	Link your gymnastic skills and techniques together and use them accurately and appropriately on the floor and apparatus. Perform your gymnastic skills precisely, showing control and fluency.	*Put together in sequence combinations of agilities and actions introducing changes in direction and level to add variety. Aim for stillness in held balances and smooth links between actions.*
S&A	Show an understanding of the use of speed, level and direction in creating and performing gymnastic sequences.	
E&I	Compare and comment on gymnastic skills, techniques and ideas used in your own and others students' work. Use your comments to improve gymnastic performance.	
F&H	Explain and use basic safety rules in preparing for gymnastics. Describe what effect gymnastics has on your body. Know and describe how gymnastics is valuable to your fitness and health.	*Pupils explain why exercise helps them to take a more active role, keeps them fit and makes them feel good.*

Children not reaching level 4	Children exceeding level 4	Specific comments

Source: Adapted from Cambridgeshire County Council (2000) 'Assessment Framework'

Recording pupil voices in PE

One of the features absent from any of these recording templates is the opportunity for pupils to contribute to the assessment process. Giving voice to pupils has the potential to transform teacher–pupil relationships from passive or oppositional to more active and collaborative (Leitch *et al.*, 2005, p. 3). Consulting pupils can be a valuable additional source of information for use in judging progress in the development of knowledge and understanding, recognising added value in learning and targeting future action. Maude (2001) provides good examples of the use of both pictorial and written reflective devices.

In addition to written and pictorial records, the increasingly widespread availability of technology in schools opens up a number of possibilities for developing a system of profiling pupils' progress in PE through a range of materials (see Table 9.6).

By initiating a physical development tracking system in the Foundation Stage, which could evolve into a profiling system for Key Stages 1 and 2, the problems of transition and sharing of information between key stages disappear. It will not be long before such a profile can be stored and maintained solely through electronic means, facilitating easy access and transfer to interested parties. By sharing with pupils the responsibility for maintaining and updating an individual pupil's profile, the assessment and recording process can take on new significance and is likely to have a significant impact on pupils' motivation to learn (Rudduck *et al.*, 2003).

TABLE 9.6 Methods of profiling pupils' progress

Type of record	Maintained by
Personal profile – likes, dislikes, learning preferences, strengths, weaknesses	Pupil
Teacher assessments – including NCPE levels achieved	Teacher, teacher assistant, coach
Self-assessments	Pupil
Peer assessments	Peers
Video recordings	Teacher and pupil/parent
Digital photographs	Teacher and pupil/parent
Personal best performances	Pupil
Personal training programme	Pupil
Extra-curricular participation/representation	Pupil
Significant achievements/awards in PE	Teacher and pupil

Reporting

Teachers are obliged to formally report on a pupil's progress at least once each year. Whilst the standard of reporting has improved markedly since the days when 'Making satisfactory progress, keep up the good effort' was deemed acceptable, many teachers confess to being unclear about what makes a good summary report for PE. We suggest that good report writing involves compiling a descriptive summary statement that communicates clearly to its intended audience (usually parents) four key themes:

1 The opportunities that have been provided in PE.

2 What has been learned/achieved in relation to the aspects of learning (with supporting evidence).

3 An indication of the current level of attainment and an appropriate end of key stage target.

4 What the next steps need to be to continue to make progress.

Whilst it may be tempting to fill the space provided with a detailed outline of curriculum coverage to meet point 1, this should be a short standardised opening sentence or two, e.g.

> This year Class 2PB have enjoyed learning through dance, gymnastics, games and swimming activities. We developed dances to the theme of 'Monsters'; in gymnastics we have developed partner sequences; and in games we have learned about, made up and played our own small-sided net and striking and fielding games.

The bulk of the report should focus on points 2, 3 and 4. The recording template and individual pupil profile should yield statements easily. These and the level descriptors should be the principal guides to constructing positive statements. It is not necessary to comment on how each pupil has progressed in each activity area but referring to at least two different activity experiences will give readers a broader picture of progress made, e.g.

> Majid has shown increasing control and co-ordination in gymnastics and dance activities. He is able to remember short sequences, and links the movements together smoothly. He now needs to practise holding inverted balances for longer and incorporating these into his sequences.
>
> Majid has learnt about tactics in striking and fielding games and now thinks about where he would like to put the ball before he bats. When he is fielding, he needs to watch the batter carefully to anticipate where he needs to move to.
>
> He is always keen to answer questions and makes good suggestions after observing other pupils play. He now needs to listen carefully to other pupils' suggestions about his own work and use their observations to improve his performance.

Majid knows that it is important to warm up and cool down before and after activity. He needs to remember to always put this into practice.

Majid has achieved level 2 standard of attainment which is in line with expectations.

Chapter summary

McMillan (2000) summarises the assessment, recording and reporting process well when he concludes that:

- Good assessment enhances instruction.
- Good assessment is valid, i.e. it tests what it sets out to test.
- Good assessment is fair and ethical.
- Good assessments use multiple methods.
- Good assessment is efficient and feasible.
- Good assessment appropriately incorporates technology.

When we remember that assessment is an integral part of the teaching and learning process, it becomes less of an additional chore. If we remain flexible and open to trying novel approaches, it can even become fun! Assessment should occur naturally and not impede the spontaneity and flow of good teaching and learning. Above all keep things in perspective and remember that if you assess *some* of your teaching; record *some* of your assessments; and report *some* of these records, you will still make a big difference.

Questions for reflection

- Think about the processes through which you currently conduct assessment in your PE teaching. Are you satisfied that your processes result in consistent, reliable and valid judgements?
- How much influence over the assessment process do your current recording templates have? If these were adjusted, what difference would it make?
- Look back at some recent PE reports. Do pupils/parents know what the pupils need to do to improve?

Web links and further reading

http://www.ncaction.org.uk/subjects/pe/judgemnt.htm

http://www.nc.uk.net/nc/contents/PE–ATT.html

www.observinglearnersmoving.co.uk

www.observingchildrenmoving.co.uk/

Jefferies, S., Jefferies, T. and Mustain, W. Why assess in PE?. *PE Central*, 16 April 1997. Available online: http://www.pecentral.org/assessment/assessmentresearch.html (accessed June 2006).

McMillan, J. H. (2000). Fundamental assessment principles for teachers and school administrators. *Practical Assessment, Research and Evaluation* 7(8). Available online: http://PAREonline.net/getvn.asp?v=7&n=8 (accessed July 2006).

10

Physical education in the future

THESE ARE EXCITING TIMES for physical education. The PESSCL strategy is already having an enormous impact on the delivery of PE and sport in many primary schools. School Sport Partnerships are altering the structure and functions of how schools work collaboratively with external organisations. Workforce reforms and the Extended Schools initiative also appear to be influencing the teaching of PE in primary schools. The National Curriculum is now well established and provides a comprehensive framework for teaching PE in Key Stages 1 and 2, fully supported by the QCA Schemes of Work in this and other curriculum subjects. Physical Development as one of the six Early Learning Goals in the Foundation Stage clearly maps coverage for children between 3 and 5 years and establishes this age phase as a crucial stage in children's overall development and learning. Things are not standing still. More recently, the agenda in 'Every Child Matters' lends support to the physical wellness of all children, and the new Early Years Foundation Stage curriculum promises in September 2008 a curriculum that celebrates holistic development from birth and seeks to unite the excellent guidance on pedagogy and practice in 'Birth to Three Matters', the Foundation Stage curriculum and the National Standards for Under 8s Daycare and Childminding to establish a 'coherent development and learning framework for all young children from birth to the age of five' (DfES, 2007). Its messages (amongst others) about offering appropriate physical challenges, providing space and time both indoors and outdoors, and the importance of building a language of movement accord well with the messages given in the preceding pages of this text.

In this book we have examined physical education and articulated the principles around what quality PE from 3 to 11 is all about. We have offered a new definition of this for readers:

> Physical education, as part of the whole education process is a field of endeavour that is concerned with lifelong physical, intellectual, social and emotional learning that accrues through experiencing physical activities in a variety of contexts.

We have mapped out the boundaries of curriculum PE and argued the unique contribution that PE has to make to the education and lives of *all* pupils. Underpinning this, is the belief in the whole-child concept, and in our view of what abilities and characteristics a physically educated learner might possess. Knowledge here is the core business of the physical education community. We strongly urge a return to these core principles. Capel (2000) reminds us that PE teachers need to recognise the values on which their priorities are based and urges the profession to be clear about what they are attempting to achieve. This is indeed a call to clarify what is at the very kernel of the profession.

How might this best be achieved? We have already urged a return to principles. Once this is clarified and agreed upon, a second way is to focus attention on the methods of delivery of those principles that are most appropriate to the age and ability of pupils – the pedagogy. This is what Almond referred to as the 'missing ingredient' (1997, p. 17) and as Laker explains 'the pedagogy of educational practice dictates how the subject is taught, the values that are promoted and the attitudes and knowledge that are instilled in young people' (2000, p. 113). In order for this to be achievable, however, several other questions are raised. For instance, what structures are needed to support such programmes? What thinking is required for professionals to implement it? For every child to matter, there is a real need for the workforce to take stock and reflect critically on philosophies and practices. Careful consideration must be given to the goals, the expectations and attitudes of all professionals tasked with promoting this unique area of development and learning. We need to widen the lens away from traditional ideas of the curriculum to one that reflects a changing world and a changing educational climate.

Contemporary issues identified reflect the changing face of curriculum PE and school sport. Physical education must reflect modern society and a society that is constantly changing. Alongside many programmes of high quality revealed in local and national Ofsted inspections, there have been findings over the last ten years that show the profession is at a crossroads and where changes in thinking are required (Graham and Stueck, 1992; Locke, 1992; O'Sullivan et al., 1994; Penney and Evans, 1999; Penney and Chandler, 2000). What will be the nature of such change? We know that for many, change is no easy process. Issues like the perceptions of new teachers into the profession, the role of ITE in equipping future teachers with appropriate knowledge and skills to deliver the PE in schools of the future need to be tackled. There are pragmatic constraints like budget cuts and reduced facilities that have direct resource implications on the practical delivery of the subject. There are changes to be made to alter feelings of deprofessionalism and marginalisation amongst colleagues and countering competency models of instruction that are more concerned with class management than deep learning, to name but a few.

True change comes from within and is about not being distracted or diverted by external factors. Fullan (1991) commented that 'simple changes may be easier to carry out but they may not make much of a difference. Complex changes promise to accomplish more . . . but they also demand more effort, and failure takes a greater toll' (1991, p. 71). (Once again it demands that teachers reflect upon their own practices, beliefs and values.) Critical reflection has a long history in educational practice. It has been associated with professional identity (Beynon *et al.*, 2004) and is linked to quality. As Leeson, comments, 'unless we engage in this process [of reflection], the work we do has the potential to be ill informed and possibly dangerous because we may perpetuate practice that is no longer relevant, simply because that is the way it has always been done and no one has questioned whether it is still appropriate' (2004, p. 146). The measure of success of any changes in PE made will be the changes that bring improvements to the learning experiences for every pupil.

If these are the challenges of change, what of solutions? We offer the following ideas of our vision of the future:

- Continued professional development acknowledged as a lifelong process of learning.
- Involvement in professional (PE) organisations.
- School–university partnerships for research and teaching.
- Individual critical reflective practice.
- Work with other agencies (such as sports coaching organisations and health).
- Moving the now trite phrase of 'joined-up thinking' forward.
- Mentor programmes for Newly Qualified Teachers.
- PE tackling issues of social justice and inclusion in society directly.
- Clarification of the relationship between health and physical activity and PE.
- A position statement of the role of sport education in primary schools.
- A holistic approach to teaching children in PE.
- Rethinking how activity areas in PE can be structured, possibly shifting away from discrete areas to themes.
- Promotion of learning that moves pupils forward to model of self responsibility.
- An agreed pedagogy that is consistent and involves teacher and pupils in planning, delivery and evaluation of lessons.

There is almost universal concern about the future, and in education (and specifically physical education) this is also the case. What will happen next year, in the next five to ten years? As authors of this book we reject the notion of an inevitability for PE in the future, and one in which practitioners have little control. We support the idea that the profession can adapt and adjust to external drivers and forces and we champion the idea that the practitioners, researchers and university teachers should steer those changes and inform the policy makers.

On reading our book, we hope that we have been able to inform *your* understanding on the nature and scope of PE in schools and provide knowledge that informs your skills on how PE can be delivered effectively to children aged 3 to 11. We also hope that, not only have we answered questions but that this text has prompted you to reflect on your own experiences of teaching PE and to raise some more questions of your own. Most of all, we hope that, whether your teaching is in the Foundation Stage, in Key Stage 1 or in Key Stage 2, you are as excited about teaching this unique subject as we are, and are eager to talk with colleagues and try out some of the ideas we offer on practical teaching so that the learning experiences in PE of each one of your pupils will be purposeful, rewarding and memorable. The future starts now!

References

Chapter 1

Alderson, J. and Crutchley, D. (1990) Physical education and the National Curriculum. In N. Armstrong (ed.) *New Directions in Physical Education* vol. 1. London: Human Kinetics.

Almond, L. (1997) The context of physical education. In L. Almond (ed.) *Physical Education in Schools*. London: Kogan Page.

Almond, L. (2000) Physical education and primary schools. In R.P. Bailey and T.M. Macfayden (eds) *Teaching Physical Education 5–11*. London: Continuum.

Arnold, P.J. (1979) *Meaning in Movement, Sport and Physical Education*. London: Heinemann.

Arnold, P.J. (1997) *Sport, Ethics and Education*. London: Cassell.

Bell, T. and Penney, D. (2004) Developing thinking and problem-solving skills in the context of national curriculum for physical education in England. In J. Wright, D. Macdonald and L. Burrows (eds) *Critical Inquiry and Problem-solving in Physical Education*. London: Routledge.

Birtwistle, G. and Brodie, D. (1991) Children's attitudes towards physical education. *Health Education Research* 6, pp. 465–78.

Boreham, C.A, Twisk, J., Savage, M.J., Cran, G.W. and Strain, J.J. (1997) Physical activity, sports participation and risk factors in adolescents. *Medicine and Science in Sports and Exercise* 29, pp. 788–93.

Bruner, J. (1972) *The Relevance of Education*. London: Allen and Unwin.

Capel, S. (2000) Re-reflecting on priorities for physical education: now and in the twenty-first century. In S. Capel and S. Piotrowski (eds) *Issues in Physical Education*. London: RoutledgeFalmer.

Carr, D. (1997) Physical education and value diversity: a response to Andrew Reid. *European Physical Education Review* 4(1), pp. 75–91.

Coalter, F. (2001) *Realising the Potential: the Case for Cultural Services: Sport*. London: Local Government Association.

Department for Culture, Media and Sport (DCMS) (1999) *Sport and Arts: Policy Action Team 10 Report*. London: DCMS.

Department for Education and Science (1991) *Physical Education for Ages 5–16*. London: HMSO.

Department for Education and Science (1992) *Physical Education in the National Curriculum*. London: HMSO.

Department for Education and Employment and the Qualifications and Curriculum Authority (DfEE/QCA) (1999). *The National Curriculum for Physical Education*. London: HMSO.

Department for Education (1995) *Physical Education in the National Curriculum*. London: HMSO.

Department of National Heritage (1995) *Sport: Raising the Game*. London: DNH.

Dewey, J. (1916) *Democracy and Education: an Introduction to the Philosophy of Education*. New York: Free Press.

Dishman, R. (1995) Physical activity and public health: mental health. *Quest* 47, pp. 362–85.

Doherty, J. (2003) Extending learning in physical education. A framework for promoting thinking skills across the Key Stages. *British Journal of Teaching Physical Education*, Autumn, vol. 34, no 3.

Fox, K.R. (1988) The self-esteem complex and youth fitness. *Quest* 47, pp. 362–85.

Freedman, D., Kettel Kahn, L., Dietz, W., Srinivasan, S. and Berenson, G. (2001) Relationship of childhood obesity to coronary heart disease risk factors in adulthood: the Bogalusa Heart study. *Pediatrics* 108, pp. 712–18.

Green, K. (2000) Exploring the everyday 'philosophies' of physical teachers from a sociological perspective. *Sport, Education and Society* 5, pp. 109–29.

Hardman, K. and Marshall, J.J. (2001) *World-wide Survey of the State and Status of School Physical Education: the Final Report to the International Olympic Committee.* Manchester: University of Manchester.

Kirk, D. (1993) Curriculum work in physical education: beyond the objectives approach? *Journal of Teaching in Physical Education* 12(3), pp. 244–65.

Kirk, D. (1997) Schooling bodies for new times: the reform of school physical education in high modernity. In J-M. Fernandez-Balboa (ed.) *Critical Aspects in Human Movement: Rethinking the Profession in the Postmodern Era.* Albany: SUNY Press.

Kirk, D. and Tinning, R. (1990) *Physical Education, Curriculum and Culture: Critical Issues in Contemporary Crisis.* London: Falmer Press.

Klesius, S.E. (1971) Physical education in the seventies: Where do you stand? *Journal of Health, Physical Education and Recreation* 42, pp. 46–7.

Laker, A. (2000) *Beyond the Boundaries of Physical Education. Educating Young People for Citizenship and Social Responsibility.* London: RoutledgeFalmer.

McIntosh, P. (1976) The curriculum of physical education – an historical perspective. In J. Kane (ed.), *Curriculum Development in Physical Education.* London: Crosby Lockwood Staples.

Mangan, J.A. (1981) *Athleticism in the Victorian and Edwardian Public School.* Cambridge: Cambridge University Press.

Manners, H.K. and Carroll, M.E. (1995) *A Framework for Physical Education in the Early Years.* London: Falmer Press.

Ministry of Education (1952) *Moving and Growing.* London: HMSO.

Ministry of Education (1953) *Planning the Programme.* London: HMSO.

Murdoch, E. (1997) The background to, and developments from, the National Curriculum for PE. In S. Capel (ed.), *Learning to Teach Physical Education in the Secondary School: a Companion to School Experience.* London: Routledge.

Murdock, E. (1986) *Sport in Schools – a Desk Study for DES/DoE.* London: Sports Council.

National Association for Sport and Physical Education (1990) *Definition of the Physically Educated Person: Outcomes of Quality Physical Education Programs.* Reston, VA: NASPE.

National Association of Head Teachers (1999) The results of the survey of PE in schools. Press release, 4 March, NAHT.

National Curriculum Council (1992) *Physical Education: Non-statutory Guidance.* York: NCC.

Office for Standards in Education (Ofsted) (1995) *Physical Education and Sport in Schools – a Survey of Good Practice.* London: HMSO.

Parry, J. (1988) The PE curriculum from 5–16. In P. Wiegand and M. Rayner (eds) *Curriculum Progress.* Brighton: Falmer Press.

Parry, J. (1998) Reid on knowledge and justification in Physical Education. *European Physical Education Review* 4(1) pp. 70–4.

Penney, D. (1998) Positioning and defining physical education, sport and health in the curriculum. *European Physical Education Review* 4(2), pp. 117–26.

Penney, D. and Evans, J. (1999) *Politics, Policy and Practice in Physical Education.* London: Routledge.

Peters, R.S. (1963) *The Study of Education.* London: Woburn Press.

Physical Education Association of the United Kingdom (1998) Mission statement. *British Journal of Physical Education* 29 (2), pp. 4–7.

Qualifications and Curriculum Authority (1999) *Early Learning Goals.* London: QCA.

Reid, A. (1997) Value pluralism and physical education. *European Physical Education Review* 3(1), pp. 6–20.

Sallis, J., McKenzie, T., Alcaraz, J., Kolody, B., Faucette, N. and Hovell, M. (1997) The effects of a 2 year physical education programme (SPARK) on physical activity and fitness of elementary school children. *American Journal of Public Health* 87, pp. 1328–1334.

Shephard, R.J. (1997) Curricular physical activity and academic performance. *Pediatric Exercise Science* 9, pp. 113–26.

Sugden, D. and Talbot, M. (1998) *Physical Education for Children with Special Needs in Mainstream Education.* Leeds: Carnegie National Sports Development Centre.

Svoboda, B. (1994) *Sport and Physical Activity as a Socialisation Environment: Scientific Review Part 1,* p. 15, Strasbourg, Council of Europe.

Talbot, M. (1999) The case for physical education. Paper presented at the World Summit on Physical Education, Berlin.

Van Dalen, D.B. and Bennett, B.L. (1971) *A World History of Physical Education: Cultural, Philosophical, Comparative.* Englewood Cliffs, NJ: Prentice-Hall, Inc.

Whitehead, M. (2000) Aims as an issue in physical education. In S. Capel and S. Piotrowski (eds) *Issues in Physical Education.* London: RoutledgeFalmer.

Williams, A. (1989) The place of physical education in primary education. In A. Williams (ed.) *Issues in Physical Education for the Primary Years.* London: Routledge.

Chapter 2

Adams, J.A. (1971) A closed-loop theory of motor learning. *Journal of Motor Behaviour* 3, pp. 111–50.

Arnold, P.J. (1988) *Education, Movement and the Curriculum.* London: Falmer Press.

Bailey. R. (2000) Movement development and the primary school child. In R. Bailey and T. Macfadyen, *Teaching Physical Education 5–11.* London: Continuum.

Bailey, R. (2001) *Teaching Physical Education: A Handbook for Primary and Secondary Teachers.* London: Kogan Page.

Bucher, C.A. (1979) *Physical Education for Children: Movement Foundations and Experiences.* Basingstoke: Macmillan.

Buschner, C.A. (1994) *Teaching Children Movement Concepts and Skills.* Champaign, IL: Human Kinetics.

Department for Education and Science (1972) *Movement: Physical Education in the Primary Years.* London: HMSO.

Doherty, J.W. and Bailey, R. (2003). *Supporting Physical Development and Physical Education in the Early Years.* Buckingham: Open University Press.

Field, T.M. (1990) *Infancy.* Cambridge, MA: Harvard University Press.

Gallahue, D.L. (1982) *Developmental Movement Experiences for Children.* New York: Wiley.

Gallahue, D.L. (1993) *Developmental Physical Education for Today's Children.* Madison, WI: Brown and Benchmark.

Gallahue, D.L. and Ozmun, J.C. (1998) *Understanding Motor Development: Infants, Children, Adolescents, Adults.* Boston, MA: WCB/McGraw-Hill.

Graham, G., Holt-Hale, S. and Parker, M. (1993) *Children Moving: A Reflective Approach to Teaching Physical Education.* London: Mayfield Publishing Company.

Haywood, K.M. and Getchell, N. (1993) *Life Span Motor Development.* (Third edition). Champaign, IL: Human Kinetics.

Hirst, P.H. (1974) *Knowledge and the Curriculum.* Routledge and Kegan Paul.

Hopper, B., Grey, J. and Maude P. (2000) *Teaching Physical Education in the Primary School.* London: RoutledgeFalmer.

Kirchner, G. (1992) *Physical Education for Elementary School Children.* Dubuque, IA: Brown.

McMorris, T. (2004) *Acquisition and Performance of Sports Skills.* Chichester: John Wiley and Sons Ltd.

Maude, P. (1996) How do I do this better? From movement development into early years physical education. In D. Whitebread (ed.) *Teaching and Learning in the Early Years.* London: RoutledgeFalmer.

Melograno, V. (1979) *Designing Curriculum and Learning: a Physical Coeducation Approach.* Dubuque, IA: Brown.

Nichols, B. (1986) *Moving and Learning: the Elementary School Experience.* St Louis: CV Mosby.

Reid, A. (1998) The value of education. *Journal of Philosophy of Education* 32: 33, pp. 319–31.

Schmidt, R.A. (1975) A schema theory of discrete motor skill learning. *Psychological Review* 82, pp. 225–60.

Schmidt, R.A. and Wrisberg, C.A. (2000) *Motor learning and Performance.* Champaign, IL: Human Kinetics.

Thelen, E. and Smith, L.B. (1994) *A Dynamic Systems Approach to the Development of Cognition and Action.* Cambridge, MA: MIT Press.

Thomas, J., Lee, A. and Thomas, K. (1988) *Physical Education for Children: Concepts and Practices.* Champaign, IL: Human Kinetics.

Welford, A.T. (1968) *Fundamentals of Skill.* London: Methuen.

Wickstrom, R.L. (1983) *Fundamental Motor Patterns.* Philadelphia: Lea & Febiger.

Wright, H. and Sugden, D. (1999) *Physical Education for All.* London: David Fulton.

Chapter 3

Armour, K. (2006) On being accountable: A challenge to physical education teachers and PE-CPD providers. *New P.E. and Sports Dimension* 2.

Armour, K. and Yelling, M. (2004) Professional development and professional learning: Bridging the gap for experienced physical education teachers. *European Physical Education Review* 10(1), pp. 71–94.

Balyi, I. (2001) *Sport System Building and Long-term Athlete Development in British Columbia.* Canada: SportsMed BC.

Balyi, I. and Hamilton, A. (2000) Key to success: long term athlete development, *Sport Coach* 23 (1), pp. 10–32.

Cote, J. and Hay, J. (2002) Children's involvement in sport: a developmental analysis. In J. M. Silva and D. Stevens (eds) *Psychological Foundations of Sport.* Boston, MA: Allyn and Bacon.

Evans, J., Davies, B.and Wright, J. (2003) (eds) *Body Knowledge and Control: Studies in the Sociology of Education and Physical Culture.* London: Routledge.

Fernandez-Balboa, J.M. (1993) Sociocultural characteristics of the hidden curriculum in Physical Education. *Quest* 45, pp. 230–54.

MacPhail, A., Kirk, D. and Kinchin, G. (2005) Sport education in Key Stage 2 games. In D. Penney, G. Clarke, M. Quill and G. Kinchin (eds) *Sport Education in Physical Education.* London: Routledge.

Morley, D. and Bailey, R. (2006) *Meeting the Needs of your Most Able Pupils: Physical Education and Sport*. London: David Fulton.

Penney, D. (2002) Equality, equity and inclusion in physical education and school sport. In A. Laker (ed.) *The Sociology of Sport and Physical Education: an Introductory Reader*. London: RoutledgeFalmer.

Public Service Agreement (2002) Department for Culture, Media and Sport, available at: http://www.hm-treasury.gov.uk/Spending_Review/spend_sr02/psacms.cfm

Renzulli, J.S. (1998) *A Rising Tide Lifts All Ships: Developing the Gifts and Talents of all Students*, available at http://www.gifted.uconn.edu/sem/semart03.html (accessed August 2006).

Siedentop, D. (1994) *Sport Education: Quality PE through Positive Sport Experiences*. Champaign, IL: Human Kinetics.

Talbot, M. (1993) Gendered physical education: Equality and sexism. In J. Evans (ed.) *Equality, Education and Physical Education*. London: Falmer.

Whitehead, M. (2006) Physical Literacy and Physical Education Conceptual Mapping http://www.physical-literacy.org.uk/conceptualmapping2006.php (accessed August 2006).

Chapter 4

ACCAC (1996) *Desirable Outcomes for Children's Learning before Compulsory School Age*. Cardiff: ACCAC.

Anning, A. (1991) *The First Years at School*. Milton Keynes: Open University Press.

Armstrong, N. (1998) Young people's physical activity patterns as assessed by heart rate monitoring. *Journal of Sports Sciences* vol. 61, supplement 1, pp. 9–16.

Armstrong, N. and Welsman, J. (1997) *Young People and Physical Activity*. Oxford: Oxford University Press.

Central Statistical Office (1994) *Social Trends*. London: HMSO.

Cooper, M. (1972) *Observational Studies in the Nursery School*. Durham: University of Durham.

Department for Education and Employment (2000) *Curriculum Guidance for the Foundation Stage*. London: DfEE/QCA.

Department for Education and Skills (2002) *Birth to Three Matters*. London: DfES Publications.

Department of Environment, Transport and the Regions (2000) *Policy, Planning and Design for Walking and Cycling*. LT1/04, DTER.

Doherty, J. (2004) Tackling childhood obesity. *Nursery World* April.

Dudek, M. (2000) *Kindergarten Architecture: Space for the Imagination*. London: Spon Press.

Early Childhood Education Forum (1998) *Quality in Diversity in Early Learning: a Framework for Early Childhood Practitioners*. London: NCB.

Garrick, R. (2004) *Playing Outdoors in the Early Years*. London: Continuum.

Hutt, C. (1972) *Males and Females*. London: Penguin.

Hutt, S.J., Tyler, S., Hutt, C. and Christopherson, P. (1989) *Play, Exploration and Learning: a Natural History of the Preschool*. London: Routledge.

Isaacs, S. (1954) *The Educational Value of the Nursery School*. London: BAECE.

Lavin, J. (2003) Physical development into physical education: Is it fair play? In H. Cooper and C. Sixsmith (eds) *Teaching Across the Early Years 3–7*. London: RoutledgeFalmer.

Maude, P. (2001) *Physical Children, Active Teaching*. Buckingham: Open University Press.

Miller, L., Cable, C. and Devereux, J. (2005) *Developing Early Years Practice*. London: David Fulton.

Mutrie, N. and Parfitt, G. (1998) Physical activity and its link with mental, social and moral health in young people. In S. Biddle, J. Sallis and N. Cavill (eds) *Young and Active? Young People and Health-enhancing Physical Activity – Evidence and Implications.* London: Health Education Authority.

National Children's Bureau (2002) *More than Swings and Roundabouts: Planning for Outdoor Play.* London: Children's Play Council/NCB.

Ouvry, M. (2005) *Exercising Muscles and Minds: Outdoor Play and the Early Years Curriculum.* London: NCB.

Play Safety Forum (2002) Managing risk in play provision. www.ncb.org.uk.

Pollatschek, J. and O'Hagen, F. (1989) An investigation of the psycho-physical influences of a quality daily physical education program. *Health Education Research 9.*

Qualifications and Curriculum Authority (1999) *Early Learning Goals.* London: QCA.

Reilly, J.J. and Dorosty, A.R. (1996) Epidemic of obesity in UK children. *Lancet* 354, pp. 1874–5.

Sallis, J.F. and Owen, N. (1999) *Physical Activity and Behavioural Medicine.* Thousand Oaks, CA: Sage.

Siraj-Blatchford, I., Sylva, K., Muttock, S., Gilden, R. and Bell, D. (2002) *Researching Effective Pedagogy in the Early Years.* Research Report No. 356. London: DfES.

Sylva, K., Roy, D. and Painter, M. (1980) *Childwatching at Playgroup and Nursery School.* Oxford: Blackwell.

Tansley, A.E. (1967) *Reading and Remedial Reading.* London: Routledge and Kegan Paul.

Thomas, G. and Thompson, G. (2004) *A Child's Place: Why Environment Matters to Children.* London: Green Alliance.

Wetton, P. (1988) *Physical Education in the Nursery and Infant School.* London: Croom Helm.

Whitaker, R.C., Pepe, M.S., Wright, J.A., Seidel, K.D. and Dietz, W.H. (1998) Early adiposity rebound and the risk of adult obesity. *Pediatrics* 101, pp. 5–15.

Chapter 5

Bunker, D., Hardy, C., Smith, B. and Almond, L. (1994) (eds) *Primary Physical Education – Implementing the National Curriculum.* Cambridge: Cambridge University Press.

Douglas, M. (1999) *Hodder Primary PE: Dance.* London: Hodder and Stoughton.

Fisher, R. and Alldridge, D. (1994) *Active PE .* London: Stanley Thornes.

Hardy, C. (1994) Swimming. In D. Bunker, C. Hardy, B. Smith and L. Almond (eds) *Primary Physical Education: Implementing the National Curriculum.* Cambridge: Cambridge University Press.

Hardy, C. (2000) Teaching swimming. In R. Bailey and T. MacFadyen (eds) *Teaching Physical Education 5–11.* London: Continuum.

Hopper, B., Grey, J. and Maude, P. (2000) *Teaching Physical Education in the Primary School.* London: RoutledgeFalmer.

Reynolds, T. (2000) Teaching gymnastics. In R. Bailey and T. MacFadyen (eds) *Teaching Physical Education 5–11.* London: Continuum.

Smith, B. (1994) Gymnastic activities. In D. Bunker, C. Hardy, B. Smith and L. Almond. *Primary Physical Education: Implementing the National Curriculum.* Cambridge: Cambridge University Press.

Chapter 6

Almond, L. (1989) (ed.) *The Place of Physical Education in School.* London: Kogan Page.

Bunker, D. and Thorpe, R. (1982) A model for the teaching of games in the secondary schools. *Bulletin of Physical Education* 10, pp. 10–16.

Davies, A. (2000) Teaching dance. In R. Bailey and T. Macfayden (eds) *Teaching Physical Education 5–11*. London: Continuum.

Douglas, M. (1999) *Hodder Primary PE: Dance*. London: Hodder & Stoughton.

Hardy, C. (2000) The school experience as a working laboratory. *British Journal of Teaching Physical Education* vol. 31, no. 3.

Martin, B. (2000) Teaching outdoor and adventurous activities. In R. Bailey and T. MacFadyen (eds) *Teaching Physical Education 5–11*. London: Continuum.

O'Neill, J. (1996) *Athletic Activities for Juniors*. London: A & C Black.

Robertson, E. (1994) *Physical Education: A Practical Guide*. London: John Murray.

Chapter 7

Bailey, R.P. (2000) *Teaching Physical Education: A Handbook for Primary and Secondary Teachers*. London: Kogan Page.

Casbon, C. and Spackman, L. (2005) *Assessment for Learning in Physical Education*. Leeds: Coachwise/BAALPE.

Mawer, M. (1995) *The Effective Teaching of Physical Education*. London: Longman.

Ofsted (1994) *Primary Matters: a Discussion on Teaching and Learning in Primary Schools*. London: Office for Standards in Education.

Ofsted (2005) *Annual Report of Her Majesty's Chief Inspector of Schools*.

Raymond, C. (1998) *Coordinating Physical Education across the Primary School*. London: Falmer Press.

Shulman, L. S. (1987) Knowledge and teaching: foundations of the new reform. *Harvard Educational Review* 57, pp. 1–22.

Williams, A. (1996) *Primary School Physical Education: a Guide for Mentors and Students*. London: Falmer Press.

Chapter 8

Bailey, R. (2001) *Teaching Physical Education: A Handbook for Primary and Secondary School Teachers*. London: Kogan Page.

Bandura, A. (1977) *Social Learning Theory*. Englewood Cliffs, NJ: Prentice Hall.

Barrett, K. (1983) A hypothetical model of observing as a teaching skill. *Journal of Teaching in Physical Education*. 3, 1, pp. 22–31.

Behets, D. (1991) Teacher enthusiasm and effective teaching in physical education. *Physical Education Review* Spring, pp. 50–5.

Berliner, D. (1979) *Tempus educare*. In P. Peterson and H.Walberg (eds) *Research on Teaching: Concepts, Findings and Implications*. Berkeley, CA: McCutchan.

Bloom, B. (1956) *Taxonomy of Educational Objectives*. New York: Longmans.

Boyce, A. (1991) The effects of an instructional strategy with two schedules of augmented feedback upon skill acquisition of a selected shooting task. *Journal of Teaching in Physical Education* 11, pp. 47–58.

British Association of Advisers and Lecturers in Physical Education (BAALPE) (1989) *Teaching and Learning Strategies in Physical Education*. Leeds: White Line Press.

Brown, G.A. and Edmundson, R. (1984) Asking questions. In E. C. Wragg (ed.) *Classroom Teaching Skills*. London: Croom Helm.

Brown, G. and Wragg, E.C. (1993) *Questioning*. London: Routledge.

Carr, W. (1989) (ed.) *Quality in Teaching: Arguments for a Reflective Profession.* London: Falmer Press.

Coates, B. (1997) Refining your style. *Sportsteacher* Spring, pp. 18–19.

Darden, G. (1997) Demonstrating motor skills: rethinking that expert demonstration. *Journal of Physical Education, Recreation and Dance* 68(6), pp. 31–5.

DfEE (1999) *The National Curriculum for England and Wales.* London: QCA.

Gallahue, D. (1982) *Understanding Motor Development in Children.* New York: John Wiley.

Galton, M., Simon, B. and Croll, P. (1980) *Inside the Primary Classroom.* London: Routledge and Kegan Paul.

Hellison, D. and Templin, T. (1991) *A Reflective Approach to Teaching Physical Education.* Champaign, IL: Human Kinetics.

Housner, L.D. and French, K.E. (1994) (eds) Expertise in learning, performance, and instruction in sport and physical activity. *Quest* 46, p. 2.

King, A. (1992) Facilitating elaborative learning through guided student generated questioning. *Educational Psychologist* 27(1), pp. 11–126.

Kniffen, M. (1988) Instructional skills for student teachers. *Strategies* 1, pp. 5–10.

McCullagh, P. (1993) Modeling: earning, developmental and social psychological considerations. In R.N. Singer, M. Murphy and K.L. Tennant (eds) *Handbook of Research on Sports Psychology* pp. 106–26. New York: Macmillan.

Magill, R.A. (1994) The influence of augmented feedback during skill learning depends on characteristics of the skill and the learner. *Quest* 46, pp. 314–27.

Mawer, M. (1995) *The Effective Teaching of Physical Education.* London: Longman.

Melville, S. (1993) Videotaping: an assist for large classes. *Strategies* 6(4), pp. 26–8.

Metzler, M. (1990) *Instructional Supervision in Physical Education.* Champaign, IL: Human Kinetics.

Mosston, M. and Ashworth, S. (1986) *Teaching Physical Education.* Columbus, OH: Merrill.

Perrott, E. (1982) *Effective Teaching: a Practical Guide to Improving your Teaching.* London: Longman.

Roach, N.K. and Burwitz, L. (1986) Observational learning in motor skill acquisition: the effect of verbal directing cues. In J. Watkins, T. Reilly and L. Burwitz (eds) *Sports Science: Proceedings of the VII Commonwealth and International Conference on Sport, Physical Education, Dance, Recreation and Health.* London: E and F Spon.

Rolider, A., Siedentop, D. and Van Houten, R. (1984) Effects of enthusiasm training on subsequent teacher enthusiastic behavior. *Journal of Teaching in Physical Education* 3, pp. 47–59.

Rosenshine, B. and Furst, N. (1973) The use of direct observation to study teaching. In R. Travers (ed.) *Second Handbook of Research on Teaching* pp. 122–83. Chicago: Rand McNally.

Schwab, J.J. (1969) The practical: a language for curriculum. *School Review* 78, pp. 1–23.

Schwager, S. and Labate, C. (1993) Teaching for critical thinking in physical education. *Journal of Teaching in Physical Education* 64(5), pp. 24–6.

Sharpe, B. (1992) *Acquiring Skill in Sport.* Eastbourne: Sports Dynamics.

Siedentop, D. (1991) *Developing Teaching Skills in Physical Education.* Palo Alto, CA: Mayfield.

Siedentop, D. and Tannehill, D. (2000) *Developing Teaching Skills in Physical Education.* Palo Alto, CA: Mayfield.

Silverman, S. (1991) Research on teaching in physical education. *Research Quarterly for Exercise and Sport* 62(4), pp. 352–64.

Silverman, S., Tyson, L.A and Krampitz, J. (1992) Teacher feedback and achievement in physical education: interaction with student and practice. *Teaching and Teacher Education* 8 pp. 333–44.

Smith, T. and Cestaro, N.G. (1998) *Student-centred Physical Education.* Champaign, IL: Human Kinetics.

Thorpe, J. (1992) *Methods of Inquiry Programme.* Toronto: Ryeron Polytechnic Institute.

Tishman, S. and Perkins, D. (1995) Critical thinking and physical education. *Journal of Physical Education, Recreation and Dance*, August, pp. 24–30.

Werner, P. and Rink, J. (1989) Case studies of teacher effectiveness in physical education. *Journal of Teaching in Physical Education* 4, pp. 280–97.

Williams, A. (1996) *Teaching Physical Education: a Guide for Mentors and Students*. London: David Fulton.

Chapter 9

Assessment Reform Group (2002) *Testing, Motivation and Learning*. Cambridge: University of Cambridge, Faculty of Education.

Black, P. and William, D. (1998) Inside the black box: Raising standards through classroom assessment. *Phi Delta Kappan* 80(2), 139–48.

Caston, C. and Spackman, L. (2005) *Assessment for Learning in Physical Education*. Leeds: Coachwise/ BAALPE.

Department for Education and Science (1992) *Physical Education in the National Curriculum*. London: DES.

Hopper, B., Grey, J. and Maude, T. (2000) *Teaching Physical Education in the Primary School*. London: Falmer.

Jefferies, S., Jefferies, T. and Mustain, W. (1997) Why assess in PE? *PE Central*, 16 Apr. Available at http://www.pecentral.org/assessment/assessmentresearch.html (accessed June 2006).

Leitch, R., Lundy, L., Clough, P., Galanouli, D. and Gardener, J. (2005) *Consulting Pupils on the Assessment of their Learning (CPAL)*, available at http://www.tlrp. org/dspace/retrieve/1335/ CPAL+TLRP+Conference+paper+26Oct05.doc (accessed July 2006).

McMillan, J. H. (2000). Fundamental assessment principles for teachers and school administrators. *Practical Assessment, Research and Evaluation* 7(8). Available at http://PAREonline.net/ getvn.asp?v=7andn=8 (accessed July 2006).

Maude, P. (2001) *Physical Children, Active Teaching: Investigating Physical Literacy*. Buckingham: Open University Press.

Ofsted (1998) *Teaching Physical Education in the Primary School: the Initial Training of Teachers*. London: Office for Standards in Education.

Piotrowski, S. (2000) Assessment, recording and reporting. In R. Bailey and T. Macfayden (eds) *Teaching Physical Education 5–11*. London: Continuum.

Qualifications and Curriculum Authority (2005) *Physical Education 2004–5. Annual Report on Curriculum and Assessment*. London: QCA.

Raymond, C. (1998) *Coordinating Physical Education across the Primary School*. London: Falmer.

Rudduck, J., Arnot, D., Fielding, M., McIntyre, D. and Flutter J. (2003) *Consulting Pupils about Teaching and Learning*. Final report to the ESRC Teaching and Learning Research Programme.

Tacklesport/PEA UK (2003) *Observing Children Moving*. Worcester: Tacklesport.

Tacklesport/PEA UK (2006) *Observing and Analysing Learners' Movement*. Worcester: Tacklesport.

Chapter 10

Almond, L. (1997) The context of physical education. In L. Almond (ed.) *Physical Education in Schools*. London: Kogan Page.

Arnold, P.J. (1997) *Sport, Ethics and Education*. London: Cassell.

Beynon, J., Ilieva, R. and Dichupa, M. (2004) Re-credentialing experiences of immigrant teachers: negotiating institutional structures, professional identities and pedagogy. *Teachers and Teaching: Theory and Practice* vol. 10, no. 4. pp. 429–44.

Capel, S. (2000) Re-reflecting on priorities for physical education: now and in the twenty-first century. In S. Capel and S. Piotrowski (eds) *Issues in Physical Education.* London: RoutledgeFalmer.

Department for Education and Skills (2007) *The Early Years Foundation Stage: Every Child Matters, Change for Children.* Nottingham: DfES.

Fullan, M. (1991) *The New Meaning of Educational Change.* London: Cassell.

Graham, K. and Stueck, P. (1992) (eds) Critical crossroads: decisions for middle and high school physical education. *Journal of Physical Education, Recreation and Dance* 63(2).

Laker, A. (2000) *Beyond the Boundaries of Physical Education: Educating Young People for Citizenship and Social Responsibility.* London: RoutledgeFalmer.

Leeson, C. (2004) In praise of reflective practice. In J. Willan, R. Parker-Rees and J. Savage (eds) *Early Childhood Studies.* Exeter: Learning Matters.

Locke, L. (1992) Changing secondary school physical education. *Quest* 44, pp. 361–72.

O'Sullivan, M., Siedentop, D. and Tannehill, D. (1994) Breaking out: codependency of high school physical education. *Journal of Teaching in Physical Education* 13, pp. 421–28.

Penney, D. and Evans, J. (1999) *Politics, Policy and Practice in Physical Education.* London: Routledge.

Penney, D. and Chandler, T. (2000) Physical education: what future(s)? *Sport, Education and Society* 5(1), pp. 71–87.

Index